MW01014676

FINANCIAL MANAGEMENT
FOR LIBRARIES

ALA Neal-Schuman purchases fund advocacy, awareness, and accreditation programs for library professionals worldwide.

FINANCIAL MANAGEMENT
    for libraries

WILLIAM W. SANNWALD

CHICAGO / 2018

WILLIAM W. SANNWALD was assistant to the city manager and manager of library design and development for San Diego from 1997 to 2004, and served as the city librarian of the San Diego Public Library from 1979 to 1997. He is now a full-time faculty member in the business school at San Diego State University, where he teaches senior and MBA classes in management. Sannwald has been selected five times by students as the most influential professor and in 2018 his faculty colleagues selected him for a teaching excellence award. He also works as a library building and administrative consultant. He is the author of numerous books and articles on library architecture and management and has presented papers at national and international conferences. A past president of the Library Administration and Management Association (LAMA), Sannwald was twice a jury member of the joint American Library Association/American Institute of Architecture awards. He is the recipient of the San Diego AIA chapter's highest honor, the Irving Gill Award, for his contributions to library architecture.

© 2018 by the American Library Association

Extensive effort has gone into ensuring the reliability of the information in this book; however, the publisher makes no warranty, express or implied, with respect to the material contained herein.

ISBNs
978-0-8389-1560-8 (paper)
978-0-8389-1677-3 (PDF)
978-0-8389-1676-6 (ePub)
978-0-8389-1678-0 (Kindle)

Library of Congress Cataloging in Publication Control Number: 2017052250

Cover design by Alejandra Diaz. Images © Adobe Stock, Inc. Book design and composition by Kimberly Thornton in the Freight Text and Vista typefaces.

♾ This paper meets the requirements of ANSI/NISO Z39.48–1992 (Permanence of Paper).

Printed in the United States of America

22 21 20 19 18   5 4 3 2 1

Contents

1 Introduction to Budgeting and Strategic Planning   1

2 Accounting Concepts   13

3 Library Budget Development Process and Participants

4 Library Performance Measures and Operating Ratios   59

5 Budgeting and Forecasting   79

6   Revenue Sources   107

7   Capital Budgets   123

8   Budget Approval and Control   139

9 Budgetary Categories, Comparisons, Forms, and the Balanced Scorecard   175

Tables, Figures, and Exhibits

Tables

Figure

Exhibits

Preface

THIS BOOK HAD ITS GENESIS IN ONE OF THE REGIONAL WORKSHOPS
that I conducted for the Library Leadership and Management Association
(LLAMA). When LLAMA offered regional workshops throughout the United
States, I led one- or two-day sessions in planning library buildings, including new
construction, facility improvements, and remodeling and renovations; management; marketing; and budgeting. These regional workshops were great because
of the many wonderful people I met and worked with throughout the country.
When I submitted the manuscript for the sixth edition of my *Checklist of Library
Building Considerations*, Rachel Chance, an acquisitions editor for ALA, asked me
to write a book about library finance based on these LLAMA budgeting workshops. Researching and writing this book was a delight, and I hope that it is a
contribution to the profession.

There are many people to thank for their contributions to this book. I would
like to start with the three libraries I used as case studies to illustrate the finance
and budgeting techniques described in the book.

The San Diego State University (SDSU) library was a natural choice because I
have been teaching part time and full time in the university's business school for
thirty years. Two people at the library, Dean Gale Etschmaier, and Sallee Spearman, the director of budget and fiscal operations, graciously provided information about the university's budget planning. I was especially interested in the
interrelationship of individual universities in the California State University System and the chancellor's office, which has budget oversight. Individual universities in the system have a great deal of budgetary freedom in some situations and
considerable centralized control in others. Through the budget process, Dean
Etschmaier has been able to align the work and goals of the library with those
of the campus, by bringing together library stakeholders such as academics, stu-

dent services, and business services to create the university's budget. Both Dean Etschmaier and Ms. Spearman helped me understand the complex nature of juggling all the stakeholders when creating a final university budget. Dean Etchmaier reports to the SDSU provost.

Stephanie Sarnoff, the executive director of the Schaumburg (Illinois) Township District Library (STDL), shared the library's extensive financial records, many of which are exhibited in this book to illustrate budget concepts. The STDL was selected because the library has its own taxing authority, which is not common for most public libraries, which are usually part of a larger governmental organization. The library's financial and operating records are very transparent. I thank Ms. Sarnoff for generously giving me access to her financial information and answering my many questions. After Ms. Sarnoff retired, Monica Harris, her successor as executive director, proved to be a great resource by providing permission to reproduce many of the library's financial statements. The executive director reports to an administrative board.

The third library is the Chula Vista (California) Public Library (CVPL). I met with Betty Waznis, the library's director, to discuss the concept for the book a couple of weeks after I was assigned to write it. The CVPL is a department of the City of Chula Vista, a fast-growing medium-sized city very close to the Mexican border in southern San Diego County. The library has a lower level of financial support than Schaumburg, but has extensive community support and provides an excellent level of service to residents. The library is part of the city administration. Ms. Waznis reports to the city manager.

A few other people provided information that I have included in the book. Eva Poole, the director of the Virginia Beach Public Library (VBPL), provided material about her award-winning joint-use community college-public library building. Gordon Carrier, the design architect for the VBPL, sent me budget information about the project. Alexia Hudson-Ward, the director of the Oberlin College Library, provided material regarding the budget process in a private college library. My longtime LLAMA colleague, Larry T. Nix, enlightened me about how community funding of public libraries got started and spread in the USA.

I would like to thank some colleagues in the Fowler College of Business Administration at SDSU. Professor Janie Chang of the Charles W. Lamden School of Accountancy provided materials and advice that helped me better understand accounting. Professor Mehdi Salehizadeh, chair of the finance department, answered many questions about financial concepts and techniques. My management department chair, Lawrence Rhyne, supported my work on the book.

A special thanks to ALA's Rachel Chance, who acted as a muse for this book.

I would appreciate any comments or suggestions readers might have concerning financial management for libraries and please e-mail them to me. This book is a living concept, and I will keep your ideas for inclusion in future work.

William W. Sannwald
Sannwald@gmail.com

1

Introduction to Budgeting and Strategic Planning

Learning Objectives of This Chapter Are to:

- ☐ Understand what a budget is

- ☐ Understand the advantages to the organization of having a budget

- ☐ Illustrate how the library's budget is the outcome of its strategic planning process

- ☐ Explain the purposes of strategic planning

- ☐ List the types of budgets that may be used in libraries

- ☐ Review the way that budgets are developed

- ☐ Determine the accounting and financial tools required to prepare and analyze budgets

- ☐ Discuss the participants and procedures involved in the budget development process

THIS BOOK IS WRITTEN FOR AT LEAST TWO AUDIENCES. THE FIRST group comprises students in library and information science programs who must acquire the information, skills, and abilities required to become functioning professionals in a rapidly changing environment. They will be entering a world where information is the key to success, and will serve as gatekeepers and disseminators of information. To maximize their information skills, they must be proficient in allocating and controlling scarce resources and the budgetary and financial skills required to determine priorities about where to allocate resources.

The second audience consists of practitioners working in the information industry who need a reference to guide them in preparing and/or implementing budgets.

Budgeting and finance are keys to implementing a successful library program. Unfortunately, most librarians don't have a strong background in budgeting and finance, and when required to prepare or revise a budget and/or financing plan are faced with challenges that seem formidable. This book is designed to give readers the opportunity to learn the basics of budgeting.

For simplicity, the term *library* will be used in this book to describe all types of information centers. Most libraries are part of larger organizations, such as universities, schools, or governmental agencies. Three libraries, the San Diego State University (SDSU) Library, the Chula Vista Public Library (CVPL), and the Schaumburg Township District Library (STDL) will be used as case studies to illustrate budgetary practices and concepts. All three libraries are of a size and have a magnitude and scope to which most readers of this book can relate.

This chapter defines budgeting and examines its relationship to strategic planning, and introduces the major sections of the book.

What Is a Budget?

A budget is a plan driven by the vision, mission, goals, and objectives of the library. The Oxford American Dictionary defines a budget as "the amount of money needed or available for a specific item" (Mean 2003, 61).

Noreen, Brewer, and Garrison's *Managerial Accounting* expands the definition to define a budget as a "quantitative plan for acquiring and using resources over a specified time period" (2008, 6) and points out that budgets are used for two distinct purposes: planning and control. Planning involves developing goals and preparing various budgets to achieve those goals, whereas control involves the steps taken by management to increase the likelihood that all parts of the organization work together to achieve the goals set down at the planning period.

Noreen, Brewer, and Garrison (2008, 298) list the benefits of budgeting:

1. Budgets communicate management's plans throughout the organization.
2. Budgets force managers to think about and plan for the future. Absent the

need to prepare budgets, many managers would spend all their time dealing with daily emergencies.

3. The budgeting process provides a means of allocating resources to those parts of the library where they can be used most effectively.
4. The budgeting process can uncover potential bottlenecks before they occur.
5. Budgets coordinate the activities of the entire organization by integrating the plans of the various units and parts. Budgeting helps to ensure that everyone in the organization is pulling in the same direction.
6. Budgets define goals and objectives that can serve as benchmarks for evaluating subsequent performance.
7. Budgets represent what a library wants to do and to be, and how to achieve these goals. Budgets are the end product of the library's strategic planning process.

Budgeting and the Library's Strategic Planning Process

Strategic planning is what must take place before budgets are created. It is a process that involves describing the library's destination, assessing barriers that stand in its way, and selecting strategies for moving forward. This planning process will allow the library to develop a budget that meets its vision, mission, goals, and objectives. The main goal of strategic planning is to allocate resources in a way that provides organizations with a competitive advantage and this is accomplished through the budget process (Aguinis 2013, 60–65).

The author has taught a variety of MBA and upper-division undergraduate courses at the San Diego State University's Fowler College of Business, including strategic planning, performance management, general management, and organizational behavior. He has also completed strategic plans as a director and consultant at a number of libraries as well as in industry. Approximately twenty different management texts were used in the various courses and activities, and their definitions of vision, mission, goals, and objectives were not consistent.

Strategic planning has a hierarchy of goals starting at top of general goals down to specific objectives. The hierarchy includes vision, mission, and objectives and specific strategies.

An organization's vision statement is a goal that is "massively inspiring, overreaching and long term. It evokes a destination that is driven by passion" (Lipton 1996, 83–92). It is a statement of future aspirations. Some authors believe that a mission statement should be written before the vision statement is completed because the organization must know its identity and purpose is before it can provide a description of what it wants to become in the future. Others think the mission statement should come first. A good vision statement should have the following characteristics (Aguinis 2013, 71–72):

1. It should be brief so that all library employees can remember it.
2. It must be verifiable, a realistic depiction of what the library hopes to become.
3. It should be bounded by a time line—good vision statements specify a schedule for the fulfillment of the library's aspirations. Usually a mission statement should have a time horizon of ten to fifteen years.
4. It should be current and updated when the library's environment experiences major changes.
5. It should not be a laundry list of aspirations, but rather focus on those aspects of the library's performance that are vital to its success.
6. It should be written in a clear and straightforward manner, so all the library's stakeholders understand it.
7. It should be inspiring and encourage staff to be optimistic about the library's direction.
8. It should be a "stretch"—a challenging but doable dream.

Following are some library visions:

- *Dartmouth College Library*: "Inspiring ideas for personal transformation and global impact" (Dartmouth 2015).
- *San Diego State University Library*: "The Library and Information Access aspires to be a flexible and experimental organization that encourages innovation and collaboration to meet the evolving information, curricular, and research needs of SDSU. We will provide responsive and innovative public services and public spaces to the university and the community, foster information literacy, and create an intellectually stimulating environment through cultural events" (SDSU Library 2016).
- *The Chula Vista Public Library*: "A nucleus of learning, culture, and recreation, a catalyst for innovation business and growth, and a vital and robust community partner" (Waznis 2015).

A mission statement differs from a vision statement in that it encompasses both the purpose of the library and the basis of its competitive advantage. It provides information on the organization's purpose and scope., A good mission statements usually addresses

1. Why the organization exists
2. The primary markets or customer groups to be served
3. The unique benefits and advantages of products and/or services offered by the library
4. The technology to be used in production or delivery of the products and/or services (Dess et al. 2016, 26)

Following are three library mission statements:

- *Dartmouth College Library*: "The Dartmouth College Library fosters intellectual growth and advances the mission of Dartmouth College and affiliated communities by supporting excellence and innovation in education and research, managing, and delivering information, and partnering to develop and disseminate new scholarship" (Dartmouth 2015).

- *San Diego State University Library:* "The Library and Information Access supports the information, curricular, and research needs of the university's diverse community through the widest possible range of resources. We are committed to information literacy, lifelong learning, and creative endeavors in a welcoming environment."

- *The Chula Vista Public Library:* The library does not have a specific mission, but this statement from its planning document exemplifies what its mission may be: "Chula Vistans see their library not as a building full of books, but as a true community hub for whole-life enrichment. A central mission for the Library for more than a century has been educational support for all ages. The community believes strongly in the value and relevance of the Library's role in lifelong learning, and sees an opportunity for CVPL to evolve to support new directions in education. As educational institutions adapt to more collaborative and experiential modes of learning, the Library will focus on providing the resources, technology, and space where students can come together to continue learning outside of the classroom."

Strategic objectives are a set of organizational goals that are used to operationalize the mission statement, and that are specific and cover a well-defined time frame. To be meaningful strategic objectives should be SMART:

1. *Specific.* This provides a clear message as to what must be accomplished.
2. *Measurable.* There must be at least one indicator (or yardstick) that measures progress against fulfilling the objective.
3. *Achievable.* It must be an achievable target given the library's capabilities and opportunities in the environment. It must be challenging but doable.
4. *Results based.* Accomplishments must be consistent with the library's vision and mission.
5. *Time Sensitive.* There must be a time frame for achieving the objective (Colquitt, LePine, and Wesson 2017, 175).

Although SMART is a good mnemonic for the required characteristics for strategic objectives, it omits the very important "difficult," which is often the key to the library successfully meeting its objectives.

The SDSU Library has five major objectives in its strategic plan. Each objective has several initiatives or strategies for reaching that goal (SDSU 2016):

1. *Collections Goal:* Build a collection of information resources necessary for our user communities to excel in research, student success, and community engagement.
2. *Communications Goal:* Become a center of engagement for students, faculty,

staff, alumni, and the public through events, activities, and communication designed to bring diverse participants together.

3. *Spaces and Learning Environments Goal:* Create and continuously develop an aesthetically inviting, flexible, dynamic, and diverse environment that inspires creativity and contemplation, encourages collaboration and research, and stimulates the creation of content.

4. *Teaching and Learning Goal:* Advance teaching and learning through integration of library content and tools into the curriculum, delivery of information literacy instruction, and design of optimal learning environments for 21st century student success.

5. *Access to Information Goal:* Connect SDSU community of users with diverse needs to information resources.

Each objective identified by the SDSU Library has a number of initiatives (strategies) that provide specificity in what it hopes to achieve by accomplishing the goal. For example, Initiative 3 under the Collections Goal is to:

Construct a sustainably funded collection, which is aligned by subject and format with SDSU current curricular and research needs.

- *Objective 1:* Find cost saving measures through consortial agreements.
- *Objective 2:* Pursue and/or increase additional funding such as endowments, grants, research foundation grants and on campus funding measures by 25 percent over the next 3 Academic years to support Library collections 2014/2015–2018/2019.

The SDSU Library's budget will enable the library to operationalize the choices made during its strategic planning process.

Strategic Planning serves the following purposes (Aguinis 2013, 65):

1. It allows the library to define its identity and the reason that it exists.
2. It allows the library to plan for the future because it clarifies where the library wants to be and what it will take to reach its destination.
3. It allows the library to analyze its environment and anticipate environmental changes in its economic, political/legal, technological, demographic, and sociocultural environments.
4. It provides focus and enables the library budget to allocate scarce resources to the programs and services of most importance to the library.
5. It creates a common purpose for the library if all staff and the library's stakeholders agree on a common set of goals.
6. It provides visibility for the library to its stakeholders.
7. It is a daily guide to library staff on what is most important in accomplishing the library's goals.

Strategic planning should precede the budget development process whether the budget is for the next fiscal year or for a longer-range period of time. Budgets are simply a plan and the first step in the budget planning process is to determine the library's vision, mission, and objectives. Budgets are often considered the definitive policy document because an adopted budget represents the financial plan used by a library to achieve its goals and objectives

Types of Budgets That May Be Used in Libraries

Not all budgets are the same, and libraries may employ a number of budgets to meet unique circumstances. Some major types of budgets include:

1. Organization-wide operating budgets for the total library. These are usually tied to the library's fiscal year.
2. Long-range planning budgets. These budgets may extend out from three to five years. When the author worked as a marketing manager for Xerox University Microfilms (now ProQuest), he was responsible for preparing an operating plan or budget for the dissertation and out-of-print book program in the fall of each year, and a five-year long-range plan in the spring. Each planning document drove the other.
3. Budgets for an individual program or unit, a special activity or program within the library.
4. Capital budgets for the acquisition of buildings or major equipment.
5. Cash flow budgets that show how cash resources will be acquired and used during the budget calendar.
6. Budget windfalls and downturns showing unexpected revenues and expenses during the budgetary period.
7. Revenue budgets based on fees and development activities.

Budgetary Approaches

A number of budgetary techniques may be used in preparing a budget, and some may be combined to produce the library's final budget.

1. *Line-item budgets* are a series of "lines," each of which represents a different item of expenditure or revenue. One line may be for professional salaries and another line may be for books and materials.
2. *Incremental budgets,* also known as traditional budgets, develop out of a previous budget. Each period's budget begins by using the last period as a reference point. Only incremental changes in the budget request are reviewed.
3. *Formula budgets* use predetermined standards for allocation of resources. Budget criteria are established and then applied. This type of budget is focused on input rather than activities. For example, x number of staff are required for every 5,000 people that the library serves.

4. *Program budgets* allocate funds to groups of activities (i.e., programs) that are needed to achieve a specific objective.
5. *Performance budgets* focus primarily on what library staff members do or what functions they perform in providing library services. Tasks rather than programs are highlighted such as cataloging the library's books.
6. *Planning programming budgeting systems* (PPBS) concentrate on long-term objectives and purposes with alternative means to achieve them. The PPBS approach combines aspects of program and performance budgets.
7. *Zero-based budgets* (ZBB) require libraries to justify their budget requests in detail from scratch, regardless of previous appropriations. It is the direct opposite of an incremental budget.

Budgetary Tools

Budgets and finance have a language all their own. A working knowledge of accounting and finance is required in order to develop, monitor, and adapt budgets. Accounting is "the process of identifying, measuring, and communicating economic information various users" (Norton and Porter 2013, 11).

Financial Management is the subject of management that focuses on generating financial information that can be used to improve decision-making. Decisions are oriented toward achieving the various goals of the organization while maintaining a satisfactory financial situation. It encompasses the broad areas of accounting and management (Finkler, Smith, Calabrese, and Purtell 2017, 2).

Both accounting and financial management techniques will be included in a subsequent chapter as well as many different financial statements, work sheets, checklists, and examples.

Financing Libraries

Most libraries are part of a larger institution. For example, the library may be part of a university, town, corporation, nonprofit organization, school, and so forth. This usually means that the library is part of a larger budgetary process that determines budgetary timing and format. In some cases, the institution provides the library with a budgetary amount and allows the library to develop its budget with varying degrees of supervision. SDSU's library receives an operating budgetary amount from the office of academic affairs (part of the office of the provost), while the CVPL receives a budgetary allocation from the city manager's office.

Libraries have widened their resources employing innovative and aggressive development programs and partnerships with other organizations. Chapter 6 will review the revenue side of the budget equation.

Budgetary Controls

The budgetary process includes a planning and control cycle that involves all the library's activities from planning through directing and motivating, controlling, and then back to planning again. Things do not always go as planned and it is necessary to have a process in place to evaluate the budgetary process and adapt it to changing realities and environments faced by all library.

Cash Flow, Forecasting, and Tools for Determining the Size of the Budget

Cash flow is the measure of the amount of cash received or disbursed over a given time period, as opposed to revenues or expenses which frequently are recognized at a time other than when the actual cash receipt or payment occurs (Finkler, Smith, Calabrese, and Purtell 2017, 591). Because most libraries are part of a larger organization, cash is usually available to meet expenses for salaries, rents, books, and so forth.

Forecasting

Forecasting is an estimate of revenues and expenses during the selected budgetary period. It is a "guess" but usually based on historical data as well as informed estimates based on experience.

Determining the size of the library budget may be based on one or a combination of four techniques:

1. What does the library need? This budgetary amount is determined after a careful examination of the library requirements to meet the needs of its stakeholders. This is the preferred method and it is consistent with the library's strategic planning process.
2. What are the budgets of "similar" libraries? Often a library will compare its operations to such a library and examples of this will be given. This is referred to as *benchmarking*.
3. What are the standards for libraries for budgetary items? Quantitative standards for a library such as "number of books per student" have disappeared and been replaced by performance standards. However, some libraries have standards that are still in place.
4. What can the library afford, or what has it been allocated by its parent institution? This is usually the deciding factor or "dealmaker" for establishing the size of the library budget.

Budget Planning Team and Budget Preparation Process

The budget planning team will vary from library to library, and the library's parent institution usually is involved in budget decisions. Library control over budget priorities and allocations will range from complete control to having considerable direction from the parent institution over what is to be funded. A review of how a budget planning team may function will be featured in chapter 3.

Budget Presentation

The library typically creates a package of budget documents for review by the policy-making body for the library. Library staff will make a presentation to the organization's policy-making committee (university, city manager and/or council, etc.) in order to get the budget approved. Almost always there is a verbal presentation to explain the budget documents and answer questions.

EXERCISES

1. Explain why the library's planning process is critical to creating a budget.
2. Select a library that you are interested in and describe its formal planning process. How does the library's planning relate to the library's budget preparation?
3. For the library you have selected, list the steps required for formal budget approval.
4. Determine who in the library is directly responsible for overseeing the budget.
5. For the library you selected, list comparable libraries.

References

Aguinis, Herman. 2013. *Performance Management.* 3rd ed. Boston: Pearson Education Limited.

Colquitt, Jason A., Jeffrey A. LePine, and Michael J. Wesson. 2017. *Organizational Behavior: Improving Performance and Commitment in the Workplace.* 5th ed.: New York, McGraw Hill Education.

Dartmouth College Library. 2015. "Library Mission and Goals." www.dartmouth.edu/~library/home/about/mission.html.

Dess, Gregory G., Gerry McNamara, and Alan B. Eisner. 2016. *Strategic Management: Text and Cases.* 7th ed. New York: McGraw Hill Education.

Finkler, Steven A., Daniel L. Smith, Thad D. Calabrese, and Roberty M. Purtell. 2017. *Financial Management for Public, Health, and Not-for-Profit Organizations.* Thousand Oaks, CA: Sage.

Lipton, M. 1996. "Demystifying the Development of an Organizational Vision." *Sloan Management Review* 37 (4): 83–92.

Mean, Erin, ed. 2003. *Oxford American Dictionary and Thesaurus.* Oxford: Oxford University Press.

Noreen, Eric W., Peter Brewer, and Ray H. Garrison. 2008. *Managerial Accounting.* Boston: McGraw-Hill Irwin.

Norton, Curtis L., and Gary A. Porter. 2013. *Financial Accounting: The Impact on Decision Makers.* 8th ed. Mason, OH: South-Western/Cengage Learning.

San Diego State University Library. 2016. "SDSU Library." http://library.sdsu.edu/about-us.

Waznis, Betty. 2015. "Strategic Vision Progress Report, July 2015." Chula Vista, CA: Chula Vista Public Library.

2

Accounting Concepts

Learning Objectives of This Chapter Are to:

☐ Understand the history of accounting and the difference between financial and managerial accounting.

☐ Describe the difference between financial and managerial accounting.

☐ Identify the types of financial reports that may be used by libraries, including balance sheets, income statements, and others required or desired by the library.

☐ Understand the role of the Governmental Accounting Standards Board (GASB).

☐ Explain the difference between the cash and accrual methods of accounting.

☐ List the types of activities conducted by an auditor.

☐ Explain what a chart of accounts is, and its value to an accounting system.

☐ List the steps in the accounting cycle.

Accounting History

Accounting is not only as old as written language—there is reason to believe that written language may have evolved out of the desire to create accounts. The first physical evidence of accounting transactions was the discovery of 5,300-year-old bone labels inscribed with marks and attached to bags of oil and linen in the tomb of King Scorpion I in Abydos, Egypt (Wiley n.d., 420).

Other ancient societies also used accounting methods. Scribes in Mesopotamia kept records of commerce on clay tablets. In ancient Greece, the account books of bankers show that they changed and loaned money and helped people make cash transfers through affiliate banks in other cities. In ancient Rome, government and banking accounts grew out of records kept by the heads of families.

In fourteenth century Italy, Luca Pacioli disseminated the first type of double entry bookkeeping known as the "Italian Method," which is the basis for double entry accounting that is used today. "Historians generally accept that the Italian method of double entry bookkeeping, based upon making entries of equal amounts to the debit and credit of two different accounts, was the foundation for modern accounting. All modern accounting systems rely upon the principle of duality enshrined in that technique" (Sangster 2016, 299).

Financial and Managerial Accounting

Accounting is the language used in budgeting. It is "the process of identifying, measuring and communicating economic information to various users" (Noreen, Brewer, and Garrison 2008, 11). Accounting is the numerical representation used to express the library's plan for the future as well as the means to control the library's current revenue and expenses, and to explain how resources were used in the past.

Financial accounting is concerned with providing information to stockholders, creditors, and others who are outside the organization. It provides the data needed to judge an organization's profitability and solvency. In contrast, managerial accounting provides staff and administration with information to facilitate planning and control. Managerial accounting provides essential data required to run an organization.

Libraries rely on managerial accounting to provide necessary operational and planning information as well as to help the library prepare its budget. Managerial accounting, which emphasizes the future, provides a number of useful types of information to libraries. Of greatest importance are reports to help library administration plan, direct, motivate, control, and evaluate the performance of the library.

The major differences between the two types of accounting are illustrated in table 2.1.

TABLE 2-1

Financial vs. Managerial Accounting

FACTOR	FINANCIAL ACCOUNTING	MANAGERIAL ACCOUNTING
Emphasis on the Future	Primarily summarizes past financial transactions.	Reflects and forecasts the changes that are constantly taking place in economic conditions, technology, customer needs and desires.
Relevance of Data	Should be observable and verifiable.	Most managers would rather have a good estimate immediately rather than wait for more precise results. Subsequently there is less emphasis on precision.
Precision	All statements must be accurate down to the last penny, which takes time and effort.	Estimates and financial reports may be "rounded off" or based on the best information available at the time.
Segments of an Organization	Concerned with the entire organization as a whole.	May break down the entire library into segments such as a financial report on the costs of reference services.
Generally Accepted Accounting Principles (GAAP)	Financial accounting statements prepared for external users must comply with generally accepted accounting principles (GAAP). External users must have some assurance that reports have been prepared with a common set of ground rules that allows comparability and reduces fraud and misrepresentation.	Not bound by GAAP. For example, a library may want to sell off a piece of excess property. GAAP requires that the land be stated at its original historical cost on financial reports. Perhaps the more relevant information may be the current market price for the property that is ignored under GAAP.
Is It Required?	Financial reporting must be done. Various outside parties such as the Securities and Exchange Commission (SEC) and tax authorities require periodic financial statements.	Financial regulatory bodies most often don't control managerial accounting practices. A university or public library may be required to prepare reports for review by funding authorities, but the reports are not usually reviewed by state or federal agencies.

Adapted from Noreen, Brewer, and Garrison 2008, 7-10.

Basic Accounting Equation

Both financial and managerial accounting depend on the accounting equation that is the foundation for the entire accounting system:

Assets = Liabilities + Owners Equity

or

Assets = Liabilities + Fund Balance

The left side of the accounting equation refers to the assets of the organization. Those items that are valuable economic resources and will provide future benefits to the organization should appear on the left side of the equation.

The right side of the equation is the owner's equity or fund balance and indicates who provided the funds or has a claim to those assets. Creditors may have provided some of the assets, and if so they have a claim to them. Other assets are provided by the owners of the business in the private sector and by the legal "owner" of the library in the public sector. For libraries the owners may be parent organizations such as the university, city, and so on (Porter and Norton 2013, 14–15).

In a for-profit organization, owner's equity is called stockholders' equity. In a non-profit organization such as a library, owner's equity is referred to as net assets or fund balance because that is what remains when liabilities are subtracted from assets.

Generally Accepted Accounting Principles (GAAP) and the Governmental Accounting Standards Board (GASB)

Financial accounting statements prepared for external users must comply with GAAP because external users must have some assurance that the reports prepared are in accordance with a common set of rules. Managerial accounting does not have to comply with Generally Accepted Accounting Principles (GAAP) standards.

Most nonprofit organizations including libraries follow standards established by Governmental Accounting Standards Board (GASB). Established in 1984, the GASB is the independent, private-sector organization based in Norwalk, Connecticut, that establishes accounting and financial reporting standards for US state and local governments that follow Generally Accepted Accounting Principles (GAAP). Financial reporting is a communication between governments and financial report users. The GASB's goal is to set accounting standards that yield information that assists users in making decisions about a government and to help them assess whether it has been accountable for the resources that have been entrusted to it.

The GASB standards are recognized as authoritative by state and local governments, state Boards of Accountancy, and the American Institute of CPAs. The GASB develops and issues accounting standards through a transparent and inclusive process intended to promote financial reporting that provides useful information to taxpayers, public officials, investors, and others who use financial reports (GASB 2016).

The Schaumburg Township District Library's auditor's report references GASB and states:

> Accounting principles generally accepted in the United States of America require that the required supplementary information as listed in the table of contents be presented to supplement the basic financial statements. Such information, although not a part of the basic financial statements, is required by the Governmental Accounting Standards Board who considers it to be an essential part of financial reporting for placing the basic financial statements in an appropriate operational, economic, or historical context. (Baker, Tilly, Virchow, and Krause, LLP 2015, 1)

The Auditing Process

An audit is an examination of records or procedures, and is usually performed by a certified public accountant (CPA) who is trained to evaluate the financial condition of an organization and issue reports that explain it. A financial audit seeks to determine whether an organization has complied with relevant accounting standards, internal procedures, and externally imposed laws and regulations. A performance audit seeks to determine whether an organization is efficient in its use of resources to provide goods and services, and to make suggestions for future improvements.

An independent auditor is engaged to render an opinion on whether an organization's financial statements are presented fairly in all material respects, in accordance with financial reporting framework. An audit conducted in accordance with generally accepted accounting principles (GAAP) and relevant ethical requirements enables the auditor to form that opinion.

In performing an audit, the auditor conducts tests and procedures designed to ascertain the accuracy of the financial information provided by the library. He will examine a representative sample of documents to determine it is reasonable to expect that the procedures and documentation maintained for those selected items are indicative of all records of the library.

To form the opinion, the auditor gathers appropriate and sufficient evidence and observes, tests, compares, and confirms until the auditor is satisfied that she has the complete information required to create an opinion. The auditor then forms an opinion as to whether the financial statements are free of material misstatement, whether due to fraud or error.

Some of the more important auditing procedures include:

- interviewing management and others to gain an understanding of the organization itself, its operations, financial reporting, and known fraud or error
- evaluating and understanding the internal control system
- performing analytical procedures on expected or unexpected variances in account balances or classes of transactions
- testing documentation that supports account balances or classes of transactions
- observing the physical inventory count
- confirming accounts receivable and other accounts with a third party

There are a number of financial tasks that auditors don't do. First and foremost, auditors do not take responsibility for the financial statements on which they form an opinion. The responsibility for financial statement presentation lies squarely in the hands of the organization being audited.

Auditors are not a part of management, which means the auditor will not

- authorize, execute, or consummate transactions on behalf of a client
- prepare or make changes to source documents

- assume custody of client assets, including maintenance of bank accounts
- establish or maintain internal controls, including the performance of ongoing monitoring activities for a client
- supervise client employees performing normal recurring activities
- report to the board of directors on behalf of management
- sign payroll tax returns on behalf of a client
- approve vendor invoices for payment
- design a client's financial management system or make modifications to its source code
- hire or terminate employees (Gelman, Rosenberg, and Freedman 2016)

At the completion of the audit, the auditor may also offer objective advice for improving financial reporting and internal controls to maximize a company's performance and efficiency.

In addition to evaluating the financial system, the CPA may also evaluate the system for maintaining financial records and securing internal control over the library's funds. Although the auditor is contracted to perform services for the library, the CPA must be independent, and her findings should not be influenced by staff, board, or administration. Audits are usually completed once a year, often at the end of the calendar or fiscal year.

Many libraries are required to have an independent audit because of institutional, local, and/or state regulations (Blazek 1996, 45–49).

Cash-Basis and Accrual-Basis Accounting

Cash-basis accounting systems recognize revenues when cash is received and expenses when cash is paid. In contrast, an accrual-basis accounting system recognizes revenues in the year in which they are earned (whether received or not) and expenses in the year that resources are used.

The cash method of accounting is focused on the inflows and outflows of cash. Much like your personal finances, organizations have revenue when they make a deposit and incur an expense when they cut a check. There is little regard to when the revenue was actually earned, or the expense was actually incurred; we just worry about the cash flows.

The accrual method of accounting doesn't worry about cash flow but instead focuses on when revenue was actually earned and when expenses where actually incurred. For example, let's say you use your credit card to purchase office supplies in the month of April and pay for the purchase in May when you receive the credit card bill. Under the accrual method of accounting you would record the expense for supplies in April when the expense is incurred, not in May when the expense is paid.

The other main difference between the two methods is the ability to budget accurately. The accrual method of accounting allows for better budgeting and planning because it looks at when liabilities are incurred and revenue earned rather than when cash is paid. This method puts on the books liabilities that might otherwise be forgotten, like accrued vacation. The cash method doesn't worry about accrued vacation until the bill must be paid. This could create a cash flow issue for a small nonprofit that hasn't planned to pay out an accrued vacation balance and must now cut expenses in other areas to have enough cash to pay the outstanding balance.

The cash method of accounting is the easiest, but not necessarily the most accurate method. If you have paid staff, you should not use the cash method of accounting. Be sure to check your state regulations. Some states require the accrual method of accounting to be used. The cash method of accounting is best used by very small libraries with little or no paid staff, no set programs, and little to no plans for expansion.

The accrual method of accounting should be used by libraries with larger amounts of funding and paid staff and plan to raise additional funds from larger donors such as foundations or government entities. Generally accepted accounting principles also require the use of the accrual method of accounting. If you wish to have an audit done under generally accepted accounting principles, you should use the accrual method of accounting (Coley 2009).

The Balance Sheet

Using the accounting equation, libraries may create a balance sheet, which is a financial report that indicates the financial position of the library at a specific point in time, that is, a precise date. It is a snapshot of the library's financial position. It can be prepared for any day of the year, but it is typically done for the last day of the fiscal year. The Schaumburg Township District Library (STDL) prepares a balance sheet every month. At any point in time when the balance sheet is prepared, it must be "in balance." That is, the assets must equal liabilities and the library's fund balance.

Not-for-profit organizations have long used fund accounting to record and report their financial information. Instead of using the term *net assets* in fund accounting, the owner's equity section of the balance sheet is referred to as the fund balance. The term refers to the remaining balance in the fund, if some or all the assets were used to pay all liabilities. Because not-for-profit organizations do not have owner, "fund balance is a fairly descriptive term" (Finkler, Smith, Calabrese, and Purtell 2017, 420).

The *fund balance* is what results when liabilities are subtracted from assets—the difference between assets and liabilities is a fund balance. A positive fund balance means there are more assets than liabilities; a negative fund balance means just the opposite. This can be complicated by the fact that part of the fund balance is reserved and part unreserved.

A library may have a number of funds that comprise its fund balance. For example, it may have a fund that contains the tax revenues, a donation fund, a trust fund, and so on. Its balance sheet might identify all the individual fund balances or lump them into one fund.

STDL's financial statements will be used to illustrate some of the financial documents. All of its financial statements are available at http://schaumburglibrary.org/about/financial-documents/#incomestatements.

Exhibit 2.1 is the balance sheet for the STDL as of January 31, 2016. If the balance sheet were dated February 15, 2016, it most likely would be different because it would reflect the financial transactions that may have taken place in the fifteen-day period between the two dates.

Note that the library's total assets of $16,560,452 equal the library's liabilities and fund balance. Under the assets side of the equation, the library has a cash position ($500,000) that seems sufficient to pay for such current expenses such as salaries, utilities, and books. It has investments of over $16 million that will be converted to cash as needed to pay for its salaries, materials, and other expenses. It seems to have a healthy fund balance that will pay for future expenses and financial obligations.

The Income Statement

Income statements are reports that reveal the revenues and expenses for a specified period, and the resulting net income or net loss of time. For-profit organizations also refer to the income statement as the profit and loss statement (P&L). The statement measures the excess of revenues over expenses.

Exhibit 2.2 is an income statement from the STDL for the nine-month period from July 1, 2015 to March 31, 2016 that shows the actual revenues and expenses for the prior year (2014/15), the budget for the prior year, the actual budget for the current year (2015/16), and the percentage change for revenues and expenses for both years. The variance between the budgets for the prior year is displayed, as is the year-to-date variance between the budgeted amount and actual amount.

The Statement of Cash Flows

The statement of cash flow is related to the income statement. Cash flow is a measure of the amount of cash received and distributed over a given time period, as opposed to revenues and expenses, which frequently are recognized at a time other than when the actual cash receipt or payment occurs. The statement of cash flows centers on the financial, rather than the operating, aspects of the organization, and discloses where the money comes from and how it is spent. Cash flow determines an organization's viability, which relates to whether the organization is currently generating and will continue to generate enough cash to meet both short-term and long-term obligations. It determines whether the organization can meet its day-to-day obligations (Finkler, Smith, Calabrese, and Purtell 2017, 371).

Most libraries, unlike many for-profit organizations, have a predictable and steady stream of income. In the case of STDL, its balance statement shows it has $5,000,000 in cash or tradable financial paper that may be converted to cash. STDL is able to meet its cash flow obligations based on the amount of cash and financial paper it holds.

Chart of Accounts

A chart of accounts is a numerical list of all accounts used by an organization to record financial transactions. The chart of accounts may be likened to the Library of Congress (LC) or Dewey Decimal Classification (DDC) systems that are used by libraries to organize their book and media collections, but the chart of accounts is designed to organize financial information. An account is a financial record used to accumulate amounts for each individual asset, liability, revenue, and expense used by the library. Just as the DDC has a record for every media item in the library, an account has a record of all the library's financial information organized in specific accounts. The numbering system is a convenient way to identify accounts, which are the basic building blocks of an accounting system. Accounts are records used to accumulate amounts for each individual asset, liability, revenue, expense, and component of an organization.

Unlike the LC or DDC systems, all types of organizations do not use the same chart of accounts, but rather create a set of particular accounts that meet their unique requirements. The first step in setting up a chart of accounts is to determine what financial accounts will be needed to record the transactions of the library. Transactions are recorded into one of these accounts—you can't make entries into accounts that don't exist, or try to fit them into the existing set of accounts. If a transaction does not fit into the existing list of accounts, a new account is created. The chart of accounts becomes the official set of accounts used to record accounting transactions during the year.

The National Center for Charitable Statistics (NCCS) has a chart of accounts (the Unified Chart of Accounts, or UCOA) freely available to any nonprofit organization, accountant, or consultant, which may be a starting point for a library trying to create or revise its chart of accounts. The system is designed so that nonprofits can quickly and reliably translate their financial statements into the categories required by IRS Form 990, the federal Office of Management and Budget, and other standard reporting formats. UCOA also seeks to promote uniform accounting practices throughout the nonprofit sector. Libraries may adapt the chart of accounts to their unique needs by adding and deleting accounts. An example of the account categories for cash include:

1000 Cash:
>   1010 Cash in bank
>   1020 Cash in bank—payroll
>   1040 Petty cash
>   1070 Savings and short-term investments

The UCOA is sponsored by a number of major nonprofit support organizations in addition to NCCS, including the California Association of Nonprofits, Compass Point Nonprofit Services, and the California Society of CPAs. The UCOA may be found at **exhibit 2.3** (NCCS 2016).

Accounting Cycle

The accounting cycle consists of all the steps performed each period to prepare a set of financial statements required or desired by the library. End of period may be a fiscal or calendar year. Some of the steps (e.g., recording transactions) are performed continuously, whereas others (e.g., preparing adjusting entries) are performed only at the end of the accounting period. The work activities of the accounting cycle may be performed by library staff, outsourced to a service provider, or performed by financial staff from the library's parent organization. All the steps must be completed in order to produce reports such as the balance sheet, income statement, and so on.

Table 2.2 summarizes the steps in the accounting cycle.

TABLE 2.2
Steps in the Accounting Cycle

ACTIVITY	WHEN DONE	DESCRIPTION
1. Conduct and analyze information from source documents	Continuously	Source documents are the basis for recording transactions. Transactions take many different forms such as invoices, cash register tapes, time cards, and so on. They provide the evidence needed in an accounting system to record a transaction. Transaction analysis is challenging and requires the ability to think logically about an event and its effect on the financial position of the entry.
2. Journalize transactions	Continuously	Once the transaction is analyzed, it is recorded in the journal. A journal is a chronological record of an organization's transactions. Transactions are entered into the journal manually or automatically.
3. Post transaction to accounts in the ledger	Periodically (or immediately in a computerized system)	Posting is the process of transferring a journal entry to the ledger accounts. Transactions are periodically posted from the journal to the ledger account. A general ledger (sometimes called a set of accounts) is a book, a file, a hard drive, or another device containing all the accounts. Journalizing is the process of "posting" the transactions from the source document to the ledger. Accounts are posted into the account types specified under the Chart of Accounts. Transactions are normally recorded in a general journal, but specialized journals may be used to record repetitive transactions.
4. Prepare work sheets	End of the Accounting Period	A work sheet is a device used at the end of the period to gather the information needed to prepare financial statements without actually recording and posting adjusting entries. A work sheet allows an account to organize the information needed to prepare the financial statements at the end of the period. A work sheet is not a financial statement.
5. Prepare financial statements	End of the Accounting Period	These are reports that convey information about the library's financial position and the results of its activities. The library determines what financial statements it requires and wants.

ACTIVITY	WHEN DONE	DESCRIPTION
6. Record and post adjusting entries	End of the Accounting Period	Adjusting entries are internal transactions and therefore do not affect the cash account. Each entry involves an adjustment to either an asset or a liability with a corresponding change in either revenue or expense. Adjusting entries are not needed if a cash basis is used. Most organizations make adjusting entries monthly.
7. Close the accounts	End of the Accounting Period	When accounts are closed, balances of revenue and expenses are set to zero to begin the next period. Any surplus revenue is transferred to the library's fund balance. This final step prepares the library for the next accounting cycle.

Adapted from Porter and Norton 2013, 182-184.

Summary

An understanding of accounting terms, processes, and activities is required to comprehend and create a library's budget. Because accounting is the language of budgets, a good knowledge of accounting concepts and principles is necessary to prepare and monitor the library's budget and financial operations.

Managerial accounting is the system that generates financial information that improves management, and is the system that is used by most libraries. It enables libraries to answer financial questions such as where they have spent their resources, what their current financial position is, and which scenarios are possible for the future. In order to answer these questions, libraries have to collect, organize, and produce financial reports that enable managers to monitor and control current spending and determine what flexibility exists for future financial expenditures. Adequate financing is required for any library program.

Without the application of accounting techniques, libraries would not be able to organize their financial information into accounts using a chart of accounts, nor take the collected information to produce reports such as balance or income statements. An auditor who prepares independent reports and reviews the accuracy of the financial activities on an annual basis will assure the library its financial records and procedures are accurate.

EXERCISES

1. Explain the value of accounting to any type of organization.
2. Compare and contrast financial and managerial accounting.
3. List the kind of financial and operating information a library might want to have. Explain why.
4. Identify with whom an independent auditor should interact within a library. Who should be the person responsible for selecting the auditor?
5. Consider how disagreements between the auditor and library staff could be resolved. Who should resolve them?
6. Using the unified chart of accounts, create a series of accounts for your library and assign account numbers to them. For example, you may select book and materials expenses.
7. Using the steps in the accounting cycle, list dates and people responsible for completing the steps in your library.

References

Baker, Tilly, Virchow, and Krause, LLP. 2015. Schaumburg Township District Library, Financial Statements as of and for the Year Ended June 30, 2015.

Blazek, Jody. 1996. *Financial Planning for Nonprofit Organizations,* Wiley Nonprofit Law, Finance and Management series. New York: Wiley.

Coley, Hillary. 2009. "Cash vs. Accrual." Greater Washington Society of Certified Public Accountants, Educational Foundation. www.nonprofitaccountingbasics.org/accounting -bookkeeping/cash-vs-accrual.

Finkler, Steven A., Daniel L. Smith, Thad D. Calabrese, and Roberty M. Purtell. 2017. *Financial Management for Public, Health, and Not-for-Profit Organizations.* Thousand Oaks, CA: Sage.

Gelman, Rosenberg and Freedman, Certified Public Accountants. 2016. "What an Auditor Does and Doesn't Do." www.grfcpa.com/resources/publications/auditor-responsibilities/.

Governmental Accounting Standards Board. 2016. "About the GASB." www.gasb.org/cs/Content Server?c=Page&pagename=GASB%2FPage%2FGASBSectionPage&cid=1176168081485.

National Center for Charitable Statistics. 2016. "Unified Chart of Accounts." National Center for Charitable Statistics. http://nccs.urban.org/projects/ucoa.cfm.

Noreen, Eric W., Peter Brewer, and Ray H. Garrison. 2008. *Managerial Accounting.* Boston: McGraw-Hill Irwin.

Porter, Gary A., and Curtis L. Norton. 2013. *Financial Accounting: The Impact on Decision Makers.* 8th ed. Mason, OH: South-Western/Cengage Learning.

Sangster, Alan. 2016. "The Genesis of Double Entry Bookkeeping." *Accounting Review* 91 (1): 299–315. doi: 10.2308/accr-51115.

Wiley, Carol. n.d. "The History of Accounting." AccountingEdu.org. www.accountingedu.org/ history-of-accounting.html.

EXHIBIT 2.1: **Balance Sheet**

SCHAUMBURG TOWNSHIP DISTRICT LIBRARY
BALANCE SHEET
January 31, 2016

	General Fund	Building & Equipment Special Reserve	Working Cash	Total
Assets				
Cash	$323,556	$0	$0	$323,556
Investments (Cost)	4,867,410	5,701,463	5,500,011	16,068,884
Investments (Fair Value Adj)	(1,891)	(6,801)	(6,942)	(15,634)
Grants Receivable		0	0	0
Due From Other Funds	0	0	0	0
Prepaid Expenses	167,201	0	0	167,201
Misc. Receivables	16,445	0	0	16,445
Total Assets	**$5,372,721**	**$5,694,661**	**$5,493,069**	**$16,560,452**
Liabilities				
Accounts Payable	$10,629	$0	$0	$10,629
Accrued Salary	296,730	0	0	296,730
Due To Other Funds		0	0	0
Deferred Revenue	0	0	0	0
Misc. Payables	25,930	0	0	25,930
Total Liabilities	**$333,290**	**$0**	**$0**	**$333,290**
Fund Balance - 7/1/2015	5,706,535	5,775,825	5,468,394	16,950,754
Current Year Revenues Over (Under) Expenditures	(667,103)	(81,164)	24,675	(723,592)
Fund Balance -1/31/2016	5,039,432	5,694,661	5,493,069	16,227,162
Total Liabilities & Fund Equity	**$5,372,721**	**$5,694,661**	**$5,493,069**	**$16,560,452**

(1) Statements are Unaudited

SCHAUMBURG TOWNSHIP DISTRICT LIBRARY
INCOME STATEMENT
JULY 1, 2015 THROUGH MARCH 31, 2016

	Fiscal Year-To-Date as of MARCH 31, 2016					Fiscal Year Ending 6/30/16		
	2014/15 Actual	2015/16 Budget	2015/16 Actual	% Change From Prior Yr	YTD Budget Variance	Budget	Projected	Variance
GENERAL FUND								
REVENUES								
Tax Revenue	$14,369,584	$14,701,760	$14,948,124	4.0%	1.7%	$14,717,500	$14,717,500	0.0%
Replacement Tax	73,188	81,790	110,875	51.5%	35.6%	136,620	$165,195	20.9%
Gifts, Fines and Fees	104,205	115,285	106,289	2.0%	-7.8%	154,000	$154,000	0.0%
Investment Income	82,725	90,000	81,780	-1.1%	-9.1%	120,000	$120,000	0.0%
Per Capita Grant	0	0	0	-	-	130,000	$97,000	-25.4%
ALA Grant	0	0	250	-	-	0	$0	-
Other Grant Revenue	1,335	0	0	-100.0%	-	0	$0	-
Mortgage Payment - Bethel Baptist	99,917	0	0	-100.0%	-	0	$0	-
E-Rate Funding	50,118	55,500	52,767	5.3%	-4.9%	55,500	$55,500	0.0%
Copy Equipment	46,471	45,450	35,011	-24.7%	-23.0%	60,600	$60,600	0.0%
Program Revenue	70,650	91,097	80,171	13.5%	-12.0%	135,100	$135,100	0.0%
Miscellaneous	19,829	23,480	39,949	101.5%	70.1%	31,328	$31,328	0.0%
Unrealized Gain/(Loss) - Invest (1)	1,959	0	7,829	299.7%	-	0	$0	-
Transfer from B & E Special Reserve	0	0	0	-	-	0	$0	-
Total Revenues	$14,919,982	$15,204,362	$15,463,126	3.6%	1.7%	$15,540,648	$15,536,222	0.0%
EXPENDITURES								
Books and Materials								
Books - Adult	$183,817	$290,949	$213,623	16.2%	-26.6%	$381,700	$381,700	0.0%
Reference Materials	258,482	237,722	210,594	-18.5%	-11.4%	270,750	$270,750	0.0%
Business Materials	214,978	221,921	160,856	-25.2%	-27.5%	250,500	$250,500	0.0%
Extension & Literacy Materials	146,647	183,652	137,109	-6.5%	-25.3%	227,903	$227,903	0.0%
Youth Services	78,815	0	0	-15.1%	-	0	$0	-
Kid's Zone	0	120,000	66,910	-	-86.7%	160,000	$160,000	0.0%
Teen Center	0	18,264	16,018	-	28.4%	24,200	$24,200	0.0%
Serials	47,990	59,900	23,452	-51.1%	-60.8%	63,200	$63,200	0.0%
Popular Library Materials	162,240	175,251	120,406	-25.8%	-31.3%	267,500	$267,500	0.0%
Binding	4,070	3,600	0	-100.0%	-100.0%	4,800	$4,800	0.0%
Total Books and Materials	$1,097,038	$1,311,259	$948,968	-13.5%	-27.6%	$1,650,553	$1,650,553	0.0%
Wages and Benefits								
Popular Services	$663,016	$452,275	$465,294	-29.8%	2.9%	$610,606	$610,606	0.0%
Administration	624,339	700,832	668,369	7.1%	-4.6%	946,140	$946,140	0.0%
Circulation	1,101,304	1,134,912	1,054,789	-4.2%	-7.1%	1,532,135	$1,532,135	0.0%
Community Services	134,875	186,126	179,594	33.2%	-3.5%	251,271	$251,271	0.0%
Maintenance	198,139	220,158	218,414	10.2%	-0.8%	297,209	$297,209	0.0%
Reference	882,158	819,421	829,883	-5.9%	1.3%	1,106,227	$1,106,227	0.0%
Access Services	505,241	475,215	449,808	-11.0%	-5.3%	639,824	$639,824	0.0%
Youth Services	512,834	0	0	-100.0%	-	0	$0	-
Kid's Zone	0	494,391	501,088	-	1.4%	667,430	$667,430	0.0%
Teen Center	0	229,374	205,332	-	-10.5%	309,654	$309,654	0.0%
Information Technology	318,489	332,528	319,332	0.3%	-4.0%	448,911	$448,911	0.0%
Hoffman Estates Branch	229,910	230,700	246,374	7.2%	6.8%	311,449	$311,449	0.0%
Hanover Park Branch	289,024	285,891	294,012	1.7%	2.8%	385,953	$385,953	0.0%

1

SCHAUMBURG TOWNSHIP DISTRICT LIBRARY
INCOME STATEMENT
JULY 1, 2015 THROUGH MARCH 31, 2016

	Fiscal Year-To-Date as of MARCH 31, 2016					Fiscal Year Ending 6/30/16		
	2014/15 Actual	2015/16 Budget	2015/16 Actual	% Change From Prior Yr	YTD Budget Variance	Budget	Projected	Variance
Virtual Branch	0	39,402	67,310	-	-9.0%	$53,196	$53,196	0.0%
Sunday Services	302,938	339,490	308,912	2.0%	-	$447,766	$447,766	0.0%
Merit Increment	11,410	0	11,630	1.9%	-	$130,000	$130,000	0.0%
Special Projects	12,925	15,855	929	-92.8%	-94.1%	$19,413	$19,413	0.0%
Short-Term Disability	47,602	37,503	66,874	40.5%	78.3%	$50,000	$50,000	0.0%
Personnel Benefits	1,339,136	1,390,814	1,332,005	-0.5%	-4.2%	$1,862,426	$1,862,426	0.0%
Total Wages and Benefits	$7,173,341	$7,384,888	$7,219,950	0.6%	-2.2%	$10,069,610	$10,069,610	0.0%
Administrative Expenses								
Utilities	$341,421	$384,642	$305,259	-10.6%	-20.6%	$518,561	$518,561	0.0%
Insurance	108,828	156,834	143,383	31.8%	-8.6%	210,178	210,178	0.0%
Unemployment Claims	0	6,000	322	-	-94.6%	8,000	8,000	0.0%
Legal Fees	7,536	13,500	8,538	13.3%	-36.8%	27,650	27,650	0.0%
Furniture, Equipment & Vehicles	101,920	52,790	20,740	-79.7%	-60.7%	54,640	54,640	0.0%
Library Supplies	163,506	216,230	151,535	-7.3%	-29.9%	284,750	284,750	0.0%
Maintenance Services & Repairs	296,677	515,987	267,095	-10.0%	-48.2%	639,858	639,858	0.0%
Staff Development	64,207	141,944	90,189	40.5%	-36.5%	187,793	187,793	0.0%
Promotional Expenses	73,751	91,034	85,594	16.1%	-6.0%	126,150	126,150	0.0%
Library Programs	248,571	231,316	229,181	-7.8%	-0.9%	298,015	298,015	0.0%
Repairs/Service Contracts	35,565	61,321	12,453	-65.0%	-79.7%	72,935	72,935	0.0%
Special Projects	125,350	15,000	5,100	-95.9%	-66.0%	15,000	15,000	0.0%
Computer Operations	581,880	1,387,856	791,223	36.0%	-43.0%	1,436,612	1,436,612	0.0%
Legal Notices	1,563	2,000	428	-72.6%	-78.6%	2,000	2,000	0.0%
Total Administrative	$2,150,775	$3,276,453	$2,111,042	-1.8%	-35.6%	$3,882,140	$3,882,140	0.0%
Other Expenses								
Contingency	$12,436	$54,250	$30,888	148.4%	-43.1%	$66,750	$66,750	0.0%
Research and Development	14,604	18,750	16,149	10.6%	-13.9%	25,000	25,000	0.0%
Capital Projects	5,670	0	0	-100.0%	-	0	$0	-
Building Improvements	10,368	54,410	34,188	229.7%	-37.2%	54,410	54,410	0.0%
Art & Special Project Purchases	0	3,750	2,950	-	-21.3%	5,000	5,000	0.0%
Audit Fees	8,000	13,500	10,500	31.3%	-22.2%	13,500	13,500	0.0%
Total Other Expenses	$51,078	$144,660	$94,675	85.4%	-34.6%	$164,660	$164,660	0.0%
Total Expenses	$10,472,232	$12,117,261	$10,374,635	-0.9%	-14.4%	$15,766,965	$15,766,965	0.0%
Revenues Over (Under) Expenditures	$4,447,750	$3,087,100	$5,088,491	14.4%	64.8%	($226,317)	($230,743)	2.0%
Fund Balance - July 1, 2015		5,706,534	5,706,534				5,706,534	
Fund Balance - Ending		$10,795,025	$10,795,025				$5,475,791	
DEBT SERVICE FUND								
REVENUES								
Tax Revenue	$0	$0	$0	0.0%	0.0%	$0	$0	0.0%
Interest Income	0	0	0	0.0%	0.0%	0	0	0.0%

2

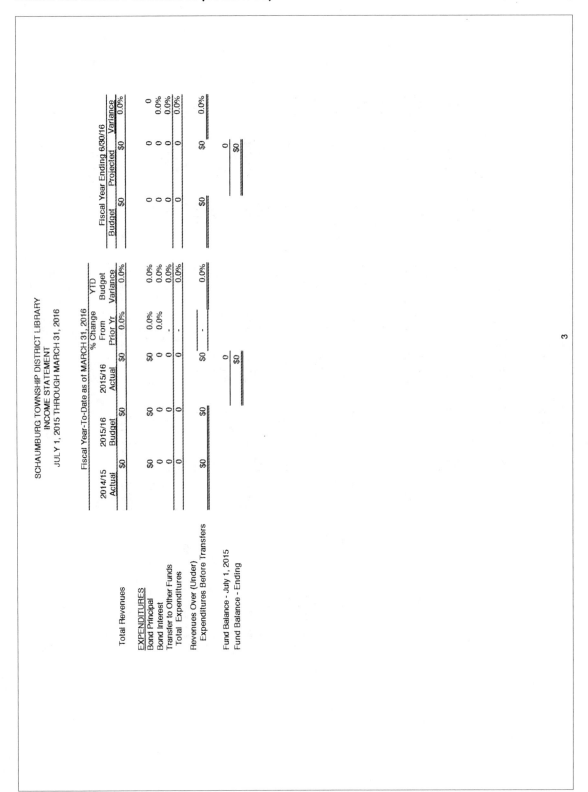

SCHAUMBURG TOWNSHIP DISTRICT LIBRARY
INCOME STATEMENT
JULY 1, 2015 THROUGH MARCH 31, 2016

Fiscal Year-To-Date as of MARCH 31, 2016

	2014/15 Actual	2015/16 Budget	2015/16 Actual	% Change From Prior Yr	YTD Budget Variance		Fiscal Year Ending 6/30/16		
---	---	---	---	---	---	---	Budget	Projected	Variance
Total Revenues	$0	$0	$0	0.0%	0.0%		$0	$0	0 0.0%
EXPENDITURES									
Bond Principal	$0	$0	$0	0.0%	0.0%		0	0	0 0.0%
Bond Interest	0	0	0	0.0%	0.0%		0	0	0 0.0%
Transfer to Other Funds	0	0	0	-	0.0%		0	0	0 0.0%
Total Expenditures	0	0	0	-	0.0%		0	0	0 0.0%
Revenues Over (Under) Expenditures Before Transfers	$0	$0	$0	-	0.0%		$0	$0	0 0.0%
Fund Balance - July 1, 2015		0	0					0	
Fund Balance - Ending		$0	$0					$0	

3

SCHAUMBURG TOWNSHIP DISTRICT LIBRARY
INCOME STATEMENT
JULY 1, 2015 THROUGH MARCH 31, 2016

		Fiscal Year-To-Date as of MARCH 31, 2016				Fiscal Year Ending 6/30/16		
	2014/15 Actual	2015/16 Budget	2015/16 Actual	% Change From Prior Yr	YTD Budget Variance	Budget	Projected	Variance
BUILDING & EQUIPMENT SPECIAL RESERVE FUND								
REVENUES								
Transfer from Debt Service Fund	$0	$0	$0	-	0.0%	$0	$0	0.0%
Unrealized Gains/(Losses) (1)	70,025	0	26,477	-62.2%	-	0	26,477	-
Total Revenues	$70,025	$0	$26,477	-62.2%	-	$0	$26,477	-
EXPENDITURES								
Furniture & Equipment	$0	$55,703	$20,242	-	-63.7%	$66,185	$66,185	0.0%
Special Projects	19,452	$64,833	48,821	151.0%	-24.7%	107,268	$107,268	0.0%
Building Improvements	456,079	$437,500	85,746	-81.2%	-80.4%	1,123,296	$1,123,296	0.0%
Transfer to General Fund	0	0	0	0.0%	0.0%	0	$0	0.0%
Total Expenditures	$475,530	$558,036	$154,809	-67.4%	-72.3%	$1,296,749	$1,296,749	0.0%
Revenues Over (Under) Expenditures	($405,505)	($558,036)	($128,332)	31.65%	-77.0%	($1,296,749)	($1,270,272)	-2.0%
Fund Balance - July 1, 2015			5,775,824				5,775,824	
Fund Balance - Ending			$5,647,494				$4,505,552	
WORKING CASH FUND								
REVENUES								
Unrealized Gains/(Losses) (1)	$35,085	$0	$28,786	-18.0%	-	$0	$28,786	-
Total Revenues	35,085	0	28,786	-18.0%	-	0	28,786	-
EXPENDITURES	0	0	0	0.0%	0.0%	0	0	0.0%
Revenues Over (Under) Expenditures	$35,085	$0	28,786	-18.0%	-	$0	28,786	-
Fund Balance - July 1, 2015			5,468,394				5,468,394	
Fund Balance - Ending			$5,497,180				$5,497,181	

(1) Investments are carried at Fair Market Value. This represents unrealized gain / (loss) until investments mature or are called for redemption.

(2) Statements are Unaudited.

4

Unified Chart of Accounts
Cross-Referenced to Selected Not-For-Profit Reporting Requirements
version 3.0

Page 1

Balance Sheet or Statement of
Financial Position Accounts (1000-3999)

Balance Sheet Account Coding
XXXX
Line item [→]

version 3.0 Account Number		Form 990 Line Item	Form 990 EZ Line Item	OMB A-122 Cost Principles	United Way of America Accounting Guide
1	Assets				
1000	Cash:				
1010	Cash in bank-operating	45	22	n/a	1000-1099
1020	Cash in bank-payroll	45	22	n/a	1000-1099
1040	Petty cash	45	22	n/a	1000-1099
1070	Savings & short-term investments	46	22	n/a	1100-1199
1100	Accounts receivable:				
1110	Accounts receivable	47a	24	n/a	1200-1299
1115	Doubtful accounts allowance	47b	24	n/a	1200-1299
1200	Contributions receivable:				
1210	Pledges receivable	48a	24	n/a	1300-1399
1215	Doubtful pledges allowance	48b	24	n/a	1300-1399
1225	Discounts - long-term pledges	48a	24	n/a	1300-1399
1240	Grants receivable	49	24	n/a	1300-1399
1245	Discounts - long-term grants	49	24	n/a	1300-1399
1300	Other receivables:				
1310	Employee & trustee receivables	50	24	n/a	1200-1299
1320	Notes/loans receivable	51a	24	n/a	1200-1299
1325	Doubtful notes/loans allowance	51b	24	n/a	1200-1299
1400	Other assets:				
1410	Inventories for sale	52	24	n/a	1400-1499
1420	Inventories for use	52	24	n/a	1400-1499
1450	Prepaid expenses	53	24	n/a	1500-1599
1460	Accrued revenues	47a	24	n/a	1200-1299
1500	Investments:				
1510	Marketable securities	54	22	n/a	1700-1799
1530	Land held for investment	55a	22	n/a	1800-1899
1540	Buildings held for investment	55a	22	n/a	1800-1899
1545	Accum deprec - bldg investment	55b	22	n/a	1800-1899
1580	Investments - other	56	22	n/a	1900-1999
1600	Fixed operating assets:				
1610	Land - operating	57a	23	n/a	1800-1899
1620	Buildings - operating	57a	23	n/a	1800-1899
1630	Leasehold improvements	57a	24	n/a	1800-1899
1640	Furniture, fixtures, & equip	57a	24	n/a	1800-1899
1650	Vehicles	57a	24	n/a	1800-1899
1660	Construction in progress	57a	24	n/a	1800-1899
1700	Accum deprec - fixed operating assets:				
1725	Accum deprec - building	57b	23	n/a	1800-1899
1735	Accum amort - leasehold improvements	57b	24	n/a	1800-1899
1745	Accum deprec - furn,fix,equip	57b	24	n/a	1800-1899
1755	Accum deprec - vehicles	57b	24	n/a	1800-1899
1810	Other long-term assets	58	24	n/a	1900-1999
1850	Split-interest agreements	58	24	n/a	1900-1999
1910	Collections - art, etc	58	24	n/a	1900-1999
1950	Funds held in trust by others	58	24	n/a	1900-1999
	Total assets	59	25	n/a	n/a

Unified Chart of Accounts
Cross-Referenced to Selected Not-For-Profit Reporting Requirements
version 3.0

Page 2

Balance Sheet Account Coding
XXXX
Line item

version 3.0 Account Number		Form 990 Line Item	Form 990 EZ Line Item	OMB A-122 Cost Principles	United Way of America Accounting Guide
2	**Liabilities**				
2000	Payables:				
2010	Accounts payable	60	26	n/a	2000-2099
2020	Grants & allocations payable	61	26	n/a	2200-2399
2100	Accrued liabilities:				
2110	Accrued payroll	60	26	n/a	2100-2199
2120	Accrued paid leave	60	26	n/a	2100-2199
2130	Accrued payroll taxes	60	26	n/a	2100-2199
2140	Accrued sales taxes	60	26	n/a	2100-2199
2150	Accrued expenses - other	60	26	n/a	2100-2199
2300	Unearned/deferred revenue:				
2310	Deferred contract revenue	62	26	n/a	n/a
2350	Unearned/deferred revenue - other	62	26	n/a	2500-2599
2410	Refundable advances	62	26	n/a	2500-2599
2500	Short-term notes & loans payable:				
2510	Trustee & employee loans payable	63	26	n/a	2400-2499
2550	Line of credit	65	26	n/a	2400-2499
2560	Current portion - long-term loan	65	26	n/a	2400-2499
2570	Short-term liabilities - other	65	26	n/a	2400-2499
2610	Split-interest liabilities	65	26	n/a	2400-2499
2700	Long-term notes & loans payable:				
2710	Bonds payable	64a	26	n/a	2600-2699
2730	Mortgages payable	64b	26	n/a	2600-2699
2750	Capital leases	64b	26	n/a	2600-2699
2770	Long-term liabilities - other	64a	26	n/a	2600-2699
2810	Gov't-owned fixed assets liability	65	26	n/a	2600-2699
2910	Custodial funds	65	26	n/a	2600-2699
	Total liabilities	66	26	n/a	n/a
3	**Equity**				
3000	Unrestricted net assets:				
3010	Unrestricted net assets	21 & 67	21 & 27	n/a	3000-3999
3020	Board-designated net assets	21 & 67	21 & 27	n/a	3000-3999
3030	Board designated quasi-endowment	21 & 67	21 & 27	n/a	3000-3999
3040	Fixed operating net assets	21 & 67	21 & 27	n/a	3000-3999
3100	Temporarily restricted net assets:				
3110	Use restricted net assets	21 & 68	21 & 27	req	3000-3999
3120	Time restricted net assets	21 & 68	21 & 27	req	3000-3999
3200	Permanently restricted net assets:				
3210	Endowment net assets	21 & 69	21 & 27	n/a	3000-3999
	Total net assets	21 & 73	21 & 27	n/a	n/a
	Total liabilities & net assets	74	n/a	n/a	n/a

Unified Chart of Accounts
Cross-Referenced to Selected Not-For-Profit Reporting Requirements   Page 3
version 3.0

Income Statement or Statement of
Financial Activities Accounts (4000-9999)

Income Statement Account Coding
XXXX-xxx

Line Item ↑ ↑ tivity Code

version 3.0 Account Number		Form 990 Line Item	Form 990 EZ Line Item	OMB A-122 Cost Principles	United Way of America Accounting Guide
4	**Contributions, Support**				
4000	Revenue from direct contributions:				
4010-***	Individual/small business contributions	1a	1	n/a	4000-4099
4020-***	Corporate contributions	1a	1	n/a	4000-4099
4070-***	Legacies & bequests	1a	1	n/a	4300-4399
4075-***	Uncollectible pledges - estimated	contra 1a	1	n/a	4000-4099
4085-***	Long-term pledges discount	contra 1a	1	n/a	4000-4099
4100	Donated goods & services revenue:				
4110-***	Donated professional services-GAAP	Part IV-A & 82b	n/a	match/in-kind	4000-4099
4120-***	Donated other services - non-GAAP	Part IV-A & 82b	n/a	match/in-kind	n/a
4130-***	Donated use of facilities	Part IV-A & 82b	n/a	match/in-kind	n/a
4140-***	Gifts in kind - goods	1d	1	match/in-kind	4000-4099
4150-***	Donated art, etc	1d	1	match/in-kind	4000-4099
4200	Revenue from non-government grants:				
4210-***	Corporate/business grants	1a	1	match/$	4000-4199
4230-***	Foundation/trust grants	1a	1	match/$	4000-4199
4250-***	Nonprofit organization grants	1a	1	match/$	4000-4199
4255-***	Discounts - long-term grants	contra 1a	1	match/$	4000-4199
4300	Revenue from split-interest agreements:				
4310-***	Split-interest agreement contributions	1a	1	n/a	4000-4199
4350-***	Gain (loss) split-interest agreements	20	1	n/a	4000-4199
4400	Revenue from indirect contributions:				
4410-***	United Way or CFC contributions	1b	1	match/$	4700-4799
4420-***	Affiliated organizations revenue	1b	1	match/$	4500-4599
4430-***	Fundraising agencies revenue	1b	1	match/$	4800-4899
4500	Revenue from government grants:				
4510-***	Agency (government) grants	1c	1	grant/match	5500-5999
4520-***	Federal grants	1c	1	grant/match	5500-5999
4530-***	State grants	1c	1	grant/match	5500-5999
4540-***	Local government grants	1c	1	grant/match	5500-5999

Unified Chart of Accounts
Cross-Referenced to Selected Not-For-Profit Reporting Requirements
version 3.0

Page 4

Income Statement Account Coding
XXXX-xxx

Line item _____→   _____→ tivity Code

version 3.0 Account Number		Form 990 Line Item	Form 990 EZ Line Item	OMB A-122 Cost Principles	United Way of America Accounting Guide
5	**Earned revenues**				
5000	Revenue from government agencies:				
5010-***	Agency (government) contracts/fees	2 & 93(g)	2	n/a	5000-5499
5020-***	Federal contracts/fees	2 & 93(g)	2	grant/match	5000-5499
5030-***	State contracts/fees	2 & 93(g)	2	grant/match	5000-5499
5040-***	Local government contracts/fees	2 & 93(g)	2	grant/match	5000-5499
5080-***	Medicare/Medicaid payments	2 & 93f	2	grant/match	5000-5499
5100	Revenue from program-related sales & fees:				
5180-***	Program service fees	2 & 93(a)	2	match/$	6200-6499
5185-***	Bad debts, est - program fees	2 & 93(a)	2	match/$	6200-6499
5200	Revenue from dues:				
5210-***	Membership dues-individuals	3 & 94	3	n/a	6000-6099
5220-***	Assessments and dues-organizations	3 & 94	3	n/a	6100-6199
5300	Revenue from investments:				
5310-***	Interest-savings/short-term investments	4 & 95	4	n/a	6500-6599
5320-***	Dividends & interest - securities	5 & 96	4	n/a	6500-6599
5330-***	Real estate rent - debt-financed	6a & 97a	8	n/a	6500-6599
5335-***	Real estate rental cost - debt-financed	6b & 97a	8		
5340-***	Real estate rent - not debt-financed	6a & 97b	8		
5345-***	Real estate rental cost - not debt-financed	6b & 97b	8		
5350-***	Personal property rent	6a & 98	8		
5355-***	Personal property rental cost	6b & 98	8	n/a	6500-6599
5360-***	Other investment income	7 & 99	4	n/a	6500-6599
5370-***	Securities sales - gross	8a-(A) & 100	5a	n/a	6600-6699
5375-***	Securities sales cost	8b-(A) & 100	5b	n/a	6600-6699
5400	Revenue from other sources:				
5410-***	Non-inventory sales - gross	8a-(B) & 100	5a	40	6600-6699
5415-***	Non-inventory sales cost	8b-(B) & 100	5b	40	6600-6699
5440-***	Gross sales - inventory	10a & 102	8	n/a	6400-6499
5445-***	Cost of inventory sold	10b & 102	8	n/a	6400-6499
5450-***	Advertising revenue	11 & 103	8	n/a	6900-6999
5460-***	Affiliate revenues from other entities	11 & 103	8	n/a	6900-6999
5490-***	Misc revenue	11 & 103	8	n/a	6900-6999
5800	Special events:				
5810-***	Special events - non-gift revenue	9a & 101	6a	n/a	4200-4299
5820-***	Special events - gift revenue	1a & (9a)	1 & (6a)	n/a	4200-4299
6	**Other revenue**				
6800	Unrealized gain (loss):				
6810-***	Unrealized gain (loss) - investments	Part IV-A	n/a	n/a	6600-6699
6820-***	Unrealized gain (loss) - other assets	Part IV-A	n/a	n/a	6600-6699
6900	Net assets released from restriction:				
6910-***	Satisfaction of use restriction	n/a	n/a	n/a	n/a
6920-***	LB&E acquisition satisfaction	n/a	n/a	n/a	n/a
6930-***	Time restriction satisfaction	n/a	n/a	n/a	n/a
	Total revenue, gains, & other support	12	9	n/a	n/a

Unified Chart of Accounts
Cross-Referenced to Selected Not-For-Profit Reporting Requirements
version 3.0

Page 5

Income Statement Account Coding
XXXX-xxx

Line item [ ] [ ] ctivity Code

version 3.0 Account Number		Form 990 Line Item	Form 990 EZ Line Item	OMB A-122 Cost Principles	United Way of America Accounting Guide
7	**Expenses - personnel related**				
7000	Grants, contracts, & direct assistance				
7010-***	Contracts - program-related	22	10	9	9100-9199
7020-***	Grants to other organizations	22	10	9, 39	9100-9199
7040-***	Awards & grants - individuals	22	10	39	9100-9199
7050-***	Specific assistance - individuals	23	10	34	8900-8999
7060-***	Benefits paid to or for members	24	11	34	?
7200	Salaries & related expenses:				
7210-***	Officers & directors salaries	25	12	7, 32	7000-7099
7220-***	Salaries & wages - other	26	12	7, 32	7000-7099
7230-***	Pension plan contributions	27	12	7, 36	7100-7199
7240-***	Employee benefits - not pension	28	12	7, 13, 49	7100-7199
7250-***	Payroll taxes, etc.	29	12	7	7200-7299
7500	Contract service expenses				
7510-***	Fundraising fees	30	13	39	8000-8099
7520-***	Accounting fees	31	13	39	8000-8099
7530-***	Legal fees	32	13	39	8000-8099
7540-***	Professional fees - other	43	13	39, 44	8000-8099
7550-***	Temporary help - contract	43	13	39	8000-8099
7580-***	Donated professional services - GAAP	Part IV-B, 82b	n/a	12	8000-8099
7590-***	Donated other services - non-GAAP	Part IV-B, 82b	n/a	12	n/a

Unified Chart of Accounts
Cross-Referenced to Selected Not-For-Profit Reporting Requirements
version 3.0

Page 6

Income Statement Account Coding
XXXX-xxx

Line item ← → tivity Code

version 3.0 Account Number		Form 990 Line Item	Form 990 EZ Line Item	OMB A-122 Cost Principles	United Way of America Accounting Guide
					0
8	**Non-personnel related expenses**				
8100	Nonpersonnel expenses:				
8110-***	Supplies	33	16	28	8100-8199
8120-***	Donated materials & supplies	33	16	12	8100-8199
8130-***	Telephone & telecommunications	34	16	6	8200-8299
8140-***	Postage & shipping	35	15	6, 54	8300-8399
8150-***	Mailing services	35	15	6	8300-8399
8170-***	Printing & copying	38	15	28, 33, 41	8600-8699
8180-***	Books, subscriptions, references	38	15	30, 41	8600-8699
8190-***	In-house publications	38	15	28, 33, 41	8600-8699
8200	Facility & equipment expenses:				
8210-***	Rent, parking, other occupancy	36	14	37, 46	8400-8499
8220-***	Utilities	36	14	19, 46	8400-8499
8230-***	Real estate taxes	36	14	51	8400-8499
8240-***	Personal property taxes	36	14	51	8400-8499
8250-***	Mortgage interest	36	14	23	8400-8499
8260-***	Equipment rental & maintenance	37	14	27, 46	8500-8600
8270-***	Deprec & amort - allowable	42	16	11, 15	9500-9599
8280-***	Deprec & amort - not allowable	42	16	11, 15	9500-9599
8290-***	Donated facilities	Part IV-B, 82b	n/a	12	8400-8499
8300	Travel & meetings expenses:				
8310-***	Travel	39	16	44, 45, 55, 56	8700-8799
8320-***	Conferences, conventions, meetings	40	16	29, 34	8800-8899
8500	Other expenses:				
8510-***	Interest-general	41	16	23	9200-9299
8520-***	Insurance - non-employee related	43	16	5, 22	9300-9399
8530-***	Membership dues - organization	43	16	30	9400-9499
8540-***	Staff development	43	16	44, 53	9400-9499
8550-***	List rental	43	16	23	9400-9499
8560-***	Outside computer services	43	16	39	8000-8099
8570-***	Advertising expenses	43	16	1	9400-9499
8580-***	Contingency provisions	43	16	8	9400-9499
8590-***	Other expenses	43	16	20, 35, 43	9400-9499
8600	Business expenses:				
8610-***	Bad debt expense	43	16	3	9400-9499
8620-***	Sales taxes	43	16	51	9400-9499
8630-***	UBITaxes	43	16	51	9400-9499
8650-***	Taxes - other	43	16	51	9400-9499
8660-***	Fines, penalties, judgments	43	16	10, 16	9400-9499
8670-***	Organizational (corp) expenses	43	16	31, 44, 45, 47, 50	9400-9499
	Total expenses	44	17	n/a	n/a
9	**Non-GAAP expenses**				
9800	Fixed asset purchases				
9810-***	Capital purchases - land	capitalized	capitalized	11, 15	LB&E
9820-***	Capital purchases - building	capitalized	capitalized	11, 15, 42	LB&E
9830-***	Capital purchases - equipment	capitalized	capitalized	11, 15	LB&E
9840-***	Capital purchases - vehicles	capitalized	capitalized	11, 15	LB&E
9910-***	Payments to affiliates	16	16	9	9600-9699
9920-***	Additions to reserves	n/a	n/a	n/a	n/a
9930-***	Program administration allocations	n/a	n/a	n/a	n/a

3

Library Budget Development
Process and Participants

Learning Objectives of This Chapter Are to:

☐ Describe the function of a budget calendar and how to prepare one.

☐ Understand what questions in the budget process must be answered in order to prepare a budget.

☐ Be able to use a budget checklist.

☐ Review alternative approaches that libraries use to prepare their budgets.

☐ Understand how teams work together in the budget process.

Budget Calendar

The starting point in the library's initial budgeting process is the creation of a budget calendar. A budget calendar is a schedule of activities that should be completed in order to create and develop a budget. It is a policy guideline that identifies tasks and assigns target completion dates for the budgetary process, and lists the individuals and groups responsible for each of the identified tasks.

The steps in developing the budgeting calendar are shown in table 3.1.

TABLE 3.1

Steps in Developing a Budget Calendar

STEP	COMMENTS
1. List the major budget development tasks	All of the tasks required to complete a budget should be listed in chronological order. This requires a review of the library's goals and objectives to determine if any major changes are needed that might have budgetary impact. In addition it requires policy reviews and data gathering including: • Updating income and expense estimates • Determining if there are salary and price increases for existing programs projected during the upcoming fiscal year • Establishing income and expense goals for departments and programs • Determining if there are additional programs that need to be included in the upcoming budget that were not in last year's budget • Identifying programs or activities that may be eliminated or modified in the new budget • Establishing spending priorities for the coming budget year for existing and any possible new programs
2. Establish overall time frames and specific deadlines	A beginning and end date is established for all the tasks to make sure that the budget will be ready and approved for the new fiscal year. This requires "counting back" from the budget approval date to allow time to accomplish all the required tasks. Specific dates for each step need to be cited.
3. Identify those responsible for each task	A person or team must be assigned and given responsibility for all the tasks that need accomplishing, and a deadline for completing these tasks should be noted.
4. Seek review and comment from board and staff	Staff should be active participants in the budget process, and help shape the budget that is presented to the library's administrative decision-making body.
5. Revise and distribute the final budgeting calendar	Everyone involved in the budget process needs to know the process and key dates and their responsibilities.

Adapted from Dropkin, Halpin, and La Touche 2007, 43-45.

Table 3.2 is a sample budget calendar for a medium-sized public library with an administrative board and a fiscal year that begins in July.

This hypothetical example illustrates the activities that must be taken to complete a budget, and need to be customized for the type of library and the organization and administrative structure.

TABLE 3.2

Sample Budget Calendar, Medium-Sized Public Library

DATE	ACTIVITY
1/20	Library management team (director, assist director, and fiscal services director) meet to discuss goals and objectives for the upcoming fiscal year and list changes that may be required in the new budget. This may include programs to be added and/or dropped.
1/25	Library director meets with the board's budget committee to discuss possible changes in the upcoming fiscal year.
2/1	Budget work sheets and instructions are distributed to the library's department heads (reference head, circulation director, and so on).
2/2 – 3/6	Library department heads prepare detailed budget work sheets detailing their budget requests.
3/7	Library department heads submit their budget work sheets to the library's management team.
3/15	Library management team reviews budget requests from the department heads and prepares a draft budget.
3/20 – 4/2	Community meetings are held to present the draft budget and receive feedback from the community. These meetings may be conducted by the library management and/or board.
4/10	Library management team reviews the draft budget and may make revisions based on community input.
4/20	Library management team presents the budget to the board's budget committee, and receives suggestions for budget revisions.
5/5 – 5/20	Library board reviews the revised budget, and after approval presents the budget at a number of community meetings.
6/2	Library board approves the final revised budget.
7/1	Approved budget is implemented for the new fiscal year.

Budget Process Questions

Library budgets are the result of collaborations among a number of internal and external stakeholders. Some of the key questions that must be answered during the budget process are:

- What will be the dollar amount of the library's budget?
- How is the dollar amount determined?
- Is there an internal library budget committee to develop the budget, and if so, who are members?
- Who from outside the library participates in the budgetary process?
- What type and how many meetings are held to prepare and review the budget?
- Is the current year's budget built from last year's budget or is a new type of zero-based budget developed each year?
- If there are internal conflicts about spending priorities, how are they decided?
- Who makes the final decision from the library on the budget?
- Is further review from the university, city manager, or administrative board needed after library staff agrees on a budget?
- Is there an appeal process if the library believes the budget is not adequate?
- What is the process to control the adopted budget during the year?

Budget Checklist

A budget checklist as shown in Table 3.3 is a useful tool to get budget planning started.

TABLE 3.3
Budget Checklist

QUESTION	COMMENTS
1. How is the library's funding determined?	Funding authorization usually comes from the parent institution or as part of a budget ordinance for special district libraries.
2. Has a budget calendar been established?	Budget calendars establish "milestones" in the budget process triggering what has to be done, when it needs to be done, by whom. The calendar also functions as a control for measuring progress.
3. What sort of budget (s) will be created?	Options include an overall library operating budget, a budget for a section of the library, a special projects budget, or a capital budget for purchasing equipment and/or facilities.
4. What type of budgetary techniques will be used?	Flexible budgeting, performance budgeting, zero-based budgeting, and forecasting are some possible options.

QUESTION	COMMENTS
5. In addition to the annual operating budget, does the library prepare a long-range (5 year) budget?	It is good to have both an operational as well as long-range budget prepared each year. The long-range budget may be a way of phasing in new programs or activities, and help guide future annual budgets. It is recommended that if operating and long-range budget systems are used, that they be prepared six months apart. The long-range budget does not require as much detail.
6. Who are the members of the library's budget team and what are their roles?	Depending on the size of the library, budgeting may be done by the director alone, an internal committee, or by a special section in the library devoted to budgeting and finance.
7. Who has the responsibility to make the final decision on the budget?	May be the director, parent institution, or a board.
8. Does the budget agree with the vision, mission, and goals of the library?	Budgeting is the tool to allocate resources required to support the library's mission, goals, and objectives.
9. Do any of the library's policy guidelines need to be updated because of decisions made during the budget process?	Depending on changes suggested in the budget, income projections, expenses projections, and cash-flow projections may need to be revised.
10. How are costs and expenses determined?	Realistic measures of costs and expenses are required for budget allocation and need to be updated with the latest financial information.
11. How will internal and external stakeholders be involved in the budgetary development process?	May range from participation on the budget development team to attendance at meetings where budget alternatives are discussed.
12. How will budgetary decisions be documented?	Budget work-sheets, files, and minutes need to be kept to document how budgetary decisions were made.
13. Are accrediting and/or requirements changing that may require a reallocation of library resources?	New mandatory requirements imposed by state, local, or institutional organizations may change the allocation of budget priorities. For example, a requirement to make bathrooms accessible may require the reallocation of funding from other library programs to meet the new building code requirement.
14. How is the budget formally approved and implemented?	Usually approval is from the group that provides funding authorization for the library. Implementation requires management overseeing the budget and incorporating the new budget into the accounting system.
15. How will the budget be monitored and controlled during the fiscal year?	May require weekly, monthly, and quarterly reports comparing actual income and expenses against budgets. Real time "dashboards" are increasingly being used to monitor budgetary activities.
16. Are there contingency plans in place in case there is a reduction or increase in library revenues during the fiscal year?	Change is inevitable and as part of the budgeting process there may be a need for budgetary plan changes during the fiscal year if economic conditions deteriorate or improve, or if a financial emergency arises.

How Is the Dollar Amount of the Library's Budget Allocation Determined?

The library's budget allocation is a critical point in budgetary planning because it determines how much funding is available to the library. Libraries receive funding because they are part of a larger institution such as a university or city, or because the library has its own special taxing district. The process in which funds are obtained varies widely from library to library, and the three libraries used as case studies illustrate three different methods of funding. (Chapter 5 will provide more detail on the types of budgets used by libraries, and chapter 6 reviews additional funding sources that libraries may use.) This chapter reviews how funding allocations are determined, and who participates in determining how the budget will be developed.

San Diego State University

At San Diego State University (SDSU), the fiscal year begins on July 1, and ends on June 30. The budget process begins approximately one year in advance of the fiscal year with the State of California allocating a budget to the California State University (CSU) system. The CSU conducts budget consultations with campus presidents from July through September where priorities and enrollment targets are determined. Around November, the trustees approve the CSU budget request. From January through May the CSU Budget Office reviews the governor's budget and issues budget letters to the CSU campuses. Revisions may occur and then a final budget letter is sent to campuses once the governor enacts the budget in June.

Once SDSU receives its allocation from the CSU, it begins allocating a budget to various divisions. Critical needs and strategic initiative funding, as well as any necessary budget reductions, are identified by divisional vice presidents and presented to the President's Budget Advisory Committee (PBAC). PBAC consists of SDSU's provost, vice presidents, the president's chief of staff, the president of the associated students' organization, the chair of the senate committee on academic resources and planning, the senate chair, and a senate representative. PBAC serves in an advisory capacity and makes a recommendation regarding distribution of the budget to the president, who then approves the SDSU campus budget. The divisions then allocate the budget to their departments based on divisional goals (Anglin 2016).

As a department under the academic affairs office, the SDSU Library and information access department (hereafter referred to as the Library) receives its budget allocation from the provost's office. In order to appeal the budget received and to request additional funds the Library makes a written request to the academic affairs office and will receive a written response. The Library's director of budget and fiscal operations is the liaison in taking the allocated amount from the provost's office and converting it into the Library's budget. For the most part the Library is able to spread its budget across the various accounts it uses at its discretion, with the exception that salary funds should stay within salary accounts; the same holds true for operations funds.

The SDSU Library receives funding from the state, student fees, and various on-campus sources to meet the needs of students and faculty. Donations are also received and managed through the San Diego State University Research Foundation. These funds are restricted according to how their sources have indicated they must be used, and so the Library may have an obligation to report how the funds were spent. Depending on the source, some remaining funds not spent in the prior year may be carried forward into the new budget year. An example of this would be when funds were committed for a construction project that began in the prior year but was not completed or billed until after the prior year closed. Because the expense is not paid until the new year, the funds set aside in the prior year carry forward and pay off the expense once it is billed in the new year.

Chula Vista Public Library

The City of Chula Vista has a strong city manager form of government and a weak mayor and city council. Although the city manager serves at the pleasure of the mayor and council, she controls the budgets of the various city departments including the Chula Vista Public Library (CVPL). The city manager sends out a budget letter via one of the manager's deputies that provides budget direction to enable the library to develop its budget. For the fiscal year (FY) 2015/16, the stipulation is that departments develop a baseline budget that begins with the current year's budget and is adjusted according to actual spending in the current year, inflation, projections for new expenditures and any additional capital expenditures that are expected.

Some highlights of the city manager's budget letter are:

- The baseline budget for Personnel Services includes funding for all council-authorized positions with the exception of "frozen" positions. The personnel services budget has been adjusted to reflect cost-of-living adjustments and updated pension system rates, and the most current projections for health care costs.
- Supplies and services were carried over flat from the last fiscal year.
- Utility budgets have been adjusted based on changes in usage due to weather and facility demand (Kachadoorian 2015).

The direction from the city manager to maintain a baseline budget enables the library to begin its budget process. It is an interactive process with library staff interacting with the city manager's designated budget analysts and personnel throughout the budget process.

Probably the biggest budget decision for library staff came in 2009 when a decision was made to preserve the materials budget at the expense of cutting hours. The public was unsatisfied with that decision, which hurt the library's viability. The newly appointed library director proposed turning more of the budget allocation into open hours and cutting the material budget. This decision has been well received by the public.

The CVPL receives budget input from its three formal support groups; the Board of Library Trustees, the Executive Board of the Friends of the Chula Vista Library, and the Chula Vista Public Library Foundation. The library director meets with them regularly, keeping the three groups informed on library issues and programs, so that they have a good understanding of what is taking place at the library and what is needed. Over the past couple of years, the three support groups have initiated joint meetings so they can get to know each other better and present a united front to the city council to support the library's budget through letters, e-mails, personal visits, and presentations. The library support groups meet monthly, and the library also gets input from the four individual Friends chapters representing the different branches in the community. Library administration also pays attention to citizen comments and complaints that are received throughout the year.

Another chartered city commission that provides input to the library budget is the Growth Management Oversight Commission (GMOC). This is an influential city commission that establishes thresholds for service and monitors each of about twenty departments and service categories to see that thresholds are met. One of the important things that the GMOC does is to provide "suggested standards" to the departments it monitors. The library has been out of compliance with the commission's square-feet-per-capita threshold for thirteen years. GMOC does not have any statutory power to force compliance but it is very vocal about the library's shortages. The library director had the opportunity of addressing the commission for the past six years, and it understands that library service is more than a matter of square feet per capita but involves operations and staffing levels.

There are tremendous conflicts in the city and the community about budget priorities. The public safety department is very influential in promoting its priorities, and it has strong unions that make their voices felt at the council level. The older west side and the newer east side of town don't see things the same way—citizens of each think the other is getting the better deal as far as investment, street repair, amenities, attention, and so on. You could summarize the conflict as "preserve the existing versus develop the new." Conflicts are decided at the council level by a majority vote. In November 2014, the city voted to have council members elected by district rather than at large. Future council decisions may be influenced by a regional, rather than an overall city approach to budget decisions.

After the library submits its budget, the city manager, the two deputy city managers, and the finance department evaluate it in closed-door meetings. Revisions may be made to the budgets submitted by the departments. The city manager sends his proposed budget to the city council by the end of May. Council members and the mayor can change or amend it before they vote to accept it. During this process, citizens and members of the council discuss aspects of the budget in council sessions to draft a final document that can be approved with four votes. This can take place over three or four public council meetings, with the deadline of June 30 for final budget decisions (Waznis 2015).

Schaumburg Township District Library

Unlike San Diego State University (SDSU) or the Chula Vista Public Library (CVPL), the Schaumburg Township District Library (STDL) is able to levy its own tax levy ordinance (Library District Act [75 ILCS 16/1-1 et seq.]) as a special district in Illinois. The library has an administrative board that makes the final decision on the budget allocation. Under the act:

- Public library districts are created by an election or a conversion of a preexisting library.
- Public library district board trustees are elected at the consolidated election and consist of seven trustees.
- Public library district board trustees hold office for six years unless the board adopts a resolution that the terms of its trustees shall be four years.
- Public library districts are required to elect a president, a treasurer, and a secretary.

The library board submits an annual document, the "Schaumburg Township District Library Ordinance," which requests a tax for the dollar amount that is estimated to be needed and levied upon all taxable property within the corporate limits of this District, in accordance with the Appropriation Ordinance previously enacted; said tax to be levied to defray the expenses and liabilities of this District for the fiscal year. The ordinance specifies how much money is required to finance salaries and benefits, library materials, administrative expenses, and special projects (Board of Library Trustees 2015). **Exhibit 3.1** is a copy of the ordinance filed with Cook County.

To calculate the tax levy ordinance, the library board must determine the amount needed to fund services and the amount available from various revenue sources. The difference is raised through property taxes and this amount is the tax levy. Passage of the tax levy ordinance must be delivered to the Cook County clerk by the second Tuesday in December, and requires that the library district carefully calculate property tax revenues needed to fund services.

The Illinois tax cap (the Property Tax Extension Limitation Law, or PTELL) provides for property tax increases that are limited to the lesser of 5 percent or the increase in the national Consumer Price Index (CPI) for the year preceding the levy year. The limitation can be increased for a taxing body with voter approval (a referendum). The CPI produces monthly data on changes in the prices paid by urban consumers for a representative basket of goods and services as published by the United States Department of Labor, Bureau of Labor Statistics (McClure 1990).

The property tax extension in the levy is determined by Cook County that determines the equalized assessed value (EAV) as follows: First, the assessed value is determined by multiplying the fair market value of a parcel of real estate assigned by the assessor by the assessment percentage set by Illinois law. Next, the assessed value is multiplied by the state equalization factor to determine the equalized assessed value of the parcel.

Any applicable exemptions are deducted from the equalized assessed value to determine the equalized assessed value after exemptions. Finally, the equalized assessed value after deductions is multiplied by the tax rate to determine the parcel's tax liability.

The STDL is on a July 1–June 30 fiscal year. There are no municipal officials or county officials involved in the budget process; only the autonomous, self-governing, taxing body of the STDL Board participate. Tax bills are sent out in August and March and revenues are received in September and April. Mid-fiscal year (November/December), the STDL is notified by Cook County what the tax levy increase will be for the following fiscal year, and there was an increase in revenue of 0.8 percent from FY 2015/16 to FY 2016/17.

Budget Development Team Participants

Now that an approximate amount of revenues has been established, the next step in the budgetary process is to allocate the funds to support the mission, goals, and objectives of the library programs, activities, and resources. This is primarily an internal process, although there may be participation from the library's parent organization.

Participation in budget development team varies from library to library, but usually consists of the library director, key deputies, and the person assigned to manage the financial operations of the library. Other library staff may be assigned to the team as needed. For example, if a new program being considered by the library is a makerspace, the person assigned to head up the function may be consulted to suggest staffing, equipment, space, and materials required to make the program a success.

Members of the team may participate as part of their job description. For the team to be effective a number of other factors should be considered.

- The team must have adequate leadership and structure to develop the budget. If the director is heading up the team, she must allocate the necessary time and resources to the task.
- A climate of trust must exist in the team. The goal of budget development is to create a budget that best meets the overall needs of the library and not just one department or division.
- Members are included not only because of their job roles, but also because of their abilities to contribute to budget development. Participants must be creative and willing to take risks.
- The personalities of team members are important. The best team members have a high degree of conscientiousness as well as being open to experience. They should be willing to work hard, listen to other points of view, and accomplish what is best for the entire library.
- Most teams work best with no more than five to nine members.
- Staff at all levels should be consulted for their opinions on what works in the current budget and what might be changed by reallocating resources to new programs and activities.

San Diego State University

Differing methods are used in creating the SDSU Library's budget by account. For many of the Library's accounts (e.g., telephone, supplies, and postage) past history and current market trends can be used to determine an appropriate budget amount. Because it has large computer lab facilities, a worker space, and multiple group study rooms with technology, the Library also has multiple IT maintenance and support agreements. These are kept in an IT database from which the value can be determined for the budget by applying an average increase over the prior year. The same holds true for the collection, subscriptions, and various management activities such as human resources and payroll, interlibrary loan and outsourced contracts (elevator maintenance, copiers, and so on) required for library operations. The budget for the books account varies by year depending on funds available to the Library and may come with usage restrictions based on the source of the funds and current campus strategic initiatives. Other accounts such as those for work orders, services, and equipment are dependent on what projects the Library is planning for the year. For these, the director of budget and fiscal operations works closely with library and facilities representatives to determine the projects and estimated costs.

Once a draft budget is created, the dean will review it and changes may be made. The draft will then be shared with the Library's management team, which consists of representatives from all areas of the Library and includes the dean, associate dean, director of access services and human resources, director of library information technologies and digital initiatives, and the director of budget and fiscal operations. Based on input from the management team additional changes may be made to the draft budget. After management team review the budget will be shared with the library council that serves in an advisory capacity to the dean, who is the final decision-maker. Council's input will be considered, and additional changes may be made. At this point, the Library's budget will be final and will be shared with all Library staff.

SDSU has a university senate library committee that is chaired by a faculty member and consists of representatives from the colleges and Library. This committee meets during the academic year to discuss issues associated with the Library as well as to provide information for distribution to interested constituencies across the campus. The committee has only an advisory role and not a policy role regarding the budget. On occasion faculty members have advocated to the influential the faculty senate for additional funds for the Library.

Over the course of the year, the director of budget and fiscal operations and the budget analyst are carefully tracking actual spending and forecasting commitments against the budget for the various funding sources. The director of budget and fiscal operations frequently updates the management team about how the Library is tracking to budget and the amount of funds remaining. Various presentations are also made over the course of the year to the library council and Library as a whole. The Library will also report various financial information as requested to Academic Affairs (Spearman 2016).

Chula Vista Public Library

The Chula Vista Public Library has a management committee responsible for the overall administration of the library that also functions as the budget team. This internal committee consists of the library director, two principal librarians, three branch managers, and the library's senior management analyst. The internal budget committee is a small cohesive team and operates in an atmosphere of mutual respect, so generally members can talk about differences and get to a place where all support the final decision.

The library management analyst constantly monitors the budget during the fiscal year. The library has a quarterly review with the assigned analyst from the finance department to make sure it is on track, and funds can be moved via the midyear budget adjustment. The library also can add funds, such as donations or grants, via a council agenda item at any time. Discretionary funds are available on a limited basis if a unique opportunity or a critical facilities problem suddenly develops (Waznis 2016).

Schaumburg Township District Library

The Schaumburg Township District Library has an internal budget committee consisting of the executive director, deputy director, finance director, and human resources director. The four-member library budget committee meets frequently, both formally and informally, from January 15 to May 15. It reviews programmatic and capital needs and provides a framework for department directors to submit their budget requests. In early March, the finance director meets with and presents budget work sheets to each department director. **Exhibit 3.2** is an example of a work sheet distributed to department directors. The four-member budget committee meets with department directors in mid-April to review submitted requests. All initiatives must be related to and support the Library's plan of service (akin to a strategic plan, but materially different), and its mission, vision, and values statements. Nobody outside of the library is involved in the internal budget decisions.

Because the library is a taxing district, there are no municipal officials involved in the budget process, only the autonomous, self-governing, taxing body of the library board.

The library uses a zero-based budget in which every budgetary item is evaluated for performance, demand, and need. The committee often has conflicts about budget priorities and data-driven evaluation measures are used to prioritize budget items. The executive director makes the final decisions on the budget.

The library board holds three public budget committee meetings during which budget recommendations are reviewed. All department directors attend all meetings to answer community questions.

The library's finance director prepares monthly income statements, balance sheets, bill lists, and investment portfolio reports for the library board. She reviews budget performance monthly with the administration and department directors (Sarnoff 2016).

Summary

Budgeting is the process that turns the library's mission and goals into tangible programs by allocating financial resources. It requires that management and staff develop a calendar that lists the steps required to create a budget, and identifies who is responsible for each step in the process. Libraries vary to a great degree in how they are funded, but all should review any questions in their budget processes and the budget checklists to make sure there are no omissions in their processes.

EXERCISES

1. Prepare a budget calendar for a library of your choice listing activities, people responsible, and milestone dates. Describe all the steps in the development of your calendar.
2. Answer the budgetary process questions for your selected library.
3. For your selected library, provide answers to the budget checklist questions.
4. For the library you selected in exercise 1, explain how the dollar amount of the library's budget allocation is determined.
5. Using the library that you selected in exercise 1, assume that a new local building code requires accessible bathrooms at a cost of $60,000. What is the process you would use to make a recommendation on how to pay for the unexpected cost?
6. Compare and contrast the similarities of the budget approaches used by SDSU, CVL, and the SDTL.

References

Anglin, Yolanda. 2016. "SDSU Budget 101—Day 1: More Than You Ever Wanted to Know." San Diego State University. July 14, 2016.

Board of Library Trustees. 2015. Schaumburg Township District Library Ordinance. In *Ordinance no. 2015/2016-4*.

Dropkin, Murray, Jim Halpin, and Bill La Touche. 2007. *The Budget-Building Book for Nonprofitis: A Step-by-Step Guide for Managers and Boards*. 2nd ed, Guidebook series, New York: John Wiley and Sons, Inc.

Kachadoorian, Maria. 2015. Baseline Budget for Fiscal Year 2015–16.

McClure, Steve. 1990. "What Municipal Officials Should Know about the Tax Levy Cycle." *Illinois Municipal Review*.

Sarnoff, Stephanie. 2016. "Schaumburg Township District Library Budget Communication." Schaumburg, IL.

Spearman, Sallee. 2016. "San Diego State University Library Budgetary Process." San Diego: San Diego State University.

Waznis, Betty. 2015. Strategic Vision Progress Report July 2015. Chula Vista, CA: Chula Vista Public Library.

Waznis, Betty. 2016. "Chula Vista Public Library Budget Process."

**SCHAUMBURG TOWNSHIP DISTRICT LIBRARY
ORDINANCE NO. 2015/2016-4**

DETERMINATION OF MONEY TO BE RAISED BY TAXATION – 2015 TAX LEVY

WHEREAS, the Illinois Municipal Budget Law, 50 ILCS 3301/1, et seq., as amended, requires all Illinois municipal corporations to adopt a Combined Annual Budget and Appropriation Ordinance specifying the objects and purposes of expenditures; and the Illinois Public Library District Act, 75 ILCS 16/35-5 et. seq., 75 ILCS 16/30-85, and other relevant statutes provide procedures for the passage of a Budget and Appropriation Ordinance and a Tax Levy Ordinance; and

WHEREAS, pursuant to the above and other statutes, an ordinance has been prepared in tentative form and made available for public inspection at least thirty (30) days prior to the adoption thereof, and a public hearing on said Budget and Appropriation Ordinance has been held prior to final action thereon; and notice of said hearing was published at least thirty (30) days prior to said meeting in a newspaper published within the District; and said Ordinance was passed prior to passage of this Levy Ordinance; and a certified copy of said Ordinance will be posted and published as required by law prior to the adoption of the final tax levy ordinance; and said Budget and Appropriation Ordinance will be filed with the County Clerks of all counties affected thereby; and a "Certified Estimate of Anticipated Revenues" will be filed within thirty (30) days of the adoption; and

WHEREAS, the "Truth in Taxation Act", 35 ILCS 200/18-60, requires the corporate authority of each taxing district to determine the estimated amount necessary to be raised by taxation for the current year at least twenty (20) days prior to the adoption of the its aggregate tax levy.

Section 1. The Ordinance No. 2015/2016-3 of this Board, "Combined Annual Budget and Appropriation Ordinance for Library Purposes for the Fiscal Year 2015/2016," is hereby incorporated by reference.

Section 2. A tax in the sum of FIFTEEN MILLION TWO HUNDRED THIRTY-ONE THOUSAND FIVE HUNDRED AND FIVE AND NO/100 DOLLARS ($15,231,505.00) is estimated to be needed and levied upon all taxable property within the corporate limits of this District, in accordance with the Appropriation Ordinance previously enacted; said tax to be levied to defray the expenses and liabilities of this District for the fiscal year beginning July 1, 2015 and ending June 30, 2016, for the specific objects and purposes indicated as follows:

2015/2016 SCHAUMBURG TOWNSHIP DISTRICT PUBLIC LIBRARY TAX LEVY

I. LIBRARY MATERIALS

4000	Books – Adult		$381,700.00
4100	Reference Materials		270,750.00
4200	Materials – Business		250,500.00
4300	Materials – Extension		227,903.00
4400	Materials –Youth Services		184,200.00
4600	Serials		63,200.00
4700	Popular Library Materials		267,500.00
4800	Binding		4,800.00
		Subtotal	$1,650,553.00

II. SALARIES AND BENEFITS

5000	Access Services	639,824.00
5000	Administration	946,140.00
5000	Circulation	1,532,136.00
5000	Programming & Outreach	251,271.00
5000	Fiction, Movies & Music	610,606.00
5000	Virtual Branch	53,196.00
5000	Hanover Park Branch	385,953.00
5000	Hoffman Estates Branch	311,449.00
5000	Information Technology	448,911.00
5000	Maintenance	297,209.00

5000	Reference	1,106,227.00
5000	Youth Services	977,084.00
5001	Sunday Services	447,766.00
5002	Merit Increments	0.00
5003	Special Projects	19,413.00
5004	Short-Term Disability Payments	50,000.00
5200	Personnel Benefits	8,195.00
5201	Deferred Comp – Matched	65,940.00
5202	Dental	41,500.00
5203	Medicare	110,353.00
5204	Medical Insurance	616,701.00
5205	Social Security	276,597.00
5206	Health Care Tax	250.00
5207	Employee Picnic	1,400.00
5300	Personnel Benefits – Retirement Plan Contributions	735,490.00
	Subtotal	$9,933,611.00

III. ADMINISTRATIVE EXPENSES

6000	Utilities	$ 518,561.00
6100	Insurance	210,178.00
6101	Unemployment Claims	8,000.00
6200	Legal Fees	27,650.00
6300	Furniture & Equipment	54,639.00
6400	Library Supplies	284,750.00
6500	Maintenance Services	539,588.00
6505	Building Repairs	100,270.00
6600	Staff Development	187,793.00
6700	Promotional Materials	110,400.00
6705	Marketing	15,750.00
6800	Library Programs	0.00
6900	Repairs/Service Contracts	72,935.00
7000	Information Technology – Special Projects	15,000.00
7003	Computer Hardware	581,256.00
7004	Service Contracts	571,727.00
7005	Service Fees	53,500.00
7006	Software	189,019.00
7007	Computer Supplies	41,110.00
7008	Research and Development	25,000.00
7200	Legal Notices	2,000.00
9200	Audit Services	13,500.00
	Subtotal	$3,622,626.00

IV. SPECIAL PROJECTS

8100	Contingency	$ 0.00
8300	Capital Projects	0.00
8305	Building Improvements	24,715.00
8500	Art & Special Project Expenses	0.00

Subtotal	$	24,715.00

V. BUILDING FUNDS:
    9000 Building Notes Fund $ 0.00
    9100 Building and Equipment Fund
          (accumulated per 75 ILCS 16/40-50)   0.00
          Subtotal   0.00

TOTAL GENERAL FUND $15,231,505.00

VI. FUNDS LEVIABLE IN EXCESS OF LIBRARY
    TAX RATE:
    1. Illinois Municipal Retirement Fund (pursuant to
        40 ILCS 5/21-105 and 5/21-121) 0.00
    2. Social Security and Medicare Fund (pursuant to
        40 ILCS 5/7-171) 0.00
    3. Insurance, Liability, Risk Management, and Environmental
        Protection Fund (pursuant to 745 ILCS 10/9-107) 0.00
    4. Audit Fees Fund (pursuant to 50 ILCS 310/9) 0.00
    5. Reserve Fund for the construction, equipment and repair
        of buildings acquired for library purposes, and for repairs
        and alterations of library buildings and equipment
        (pursuant to 75 ILCS 16/40-50) 0.00
    6. Building, Equipment & Maintenance .02% Fund: 0.00
        (pursuant to 75 ILCS 16/35-5(b) 0.00
    7. Bond and Interest Fund to retire bonds pursuant to
        referendum of November 7, 1995 0.00

    Subtotal – Special Funds Levies 0.00

VII. FUNDS ON HAND: End of fiscal Year (Working
    Cash Fund) 0.00

VIII. BUILDING FUND: Construction of a new library
    building pursuant to Referendum held November 7, 1995 0.00

TOTAL TENTATIVE LEVY – ALL FUNDS $15,231,505.00

    <u>Section 3</u>.   All unexpended balances of proceeds received annually from public library taxes not in excess of statutory limits may be transferred to the Special Reserve Fund heretofore established according to 75 ILCS 16/40-50, pursuant to plans developed and adopted by this Board, and said unexpended balances shall be accumulated in this Fund for the purpose

of erecting a building to be used as a library or to purchase a site for the same, or to purchase a building, or to build an addition thereto, to furnish necessary equipment therefore, to acquire library materials such as books, periodicals, films, recordings and electronic data storage and retrieval facilities in connection with either the purchase or construction of a new library building or the expansion of an existing library building, or for the emergency expenditures for the repair of an existing library building or its equipment, or to do any or all of these things.

Section 4.   Except as otherwise provided by law, no further appropriations shall be made at any other time within such fiscal year, provided that this Board may from time to time make transfers between the various items in any Fund, or appropriations in excess of those authorized by the budget in order to meet an immediate and unforeseen emergency, by a two-thirds (2/3) vote of all the trustees, as provided by 75 ILCS 16/30-90, et. seq., provided that nothing in this Section shall be construed to permit transfer between Funds required by law to be kept separate. Any remaining balances, in amounts up to 20% of those appropriations, after the close of the fiscal year shall be available until August 30th for the authorization of the payment of obligations incurred prior to the close of the fiscal year, and until September 30th for the payment of such obligations or for the transfer of unexpendable balances thereof to be accumulated, as provided by 75 ILCS 16/30-90 and 16/40-50.

Section 5.   The Secretary of this Board shall file, on or before the last Tuesday in December a certified copy of the approved Levy Ordinance and shall certify the several amounts that this District has levied with the County Clerk of each county affected by this Levy; and the Secretary of this Board shall also file, on or before the third Tuesday in December, certified copies of this Ordinance and the Budget and Appropriation Ordinance with the Library or

Libraries operated by this District, and to make said Ordinances available for public inspection at all times.

Section 6. Upon filing said certified copy hereof with such County Clerk, the rate percent shall be ascertained and the tax extended as provided by law against property in this District; and the tax so levied and assessed shall be collected and enforced in the same manner and by the same officers as the general taxes in this District and county, and shall be paid over to the Treasurer of this Board by the officers collecting the same.

Section 7. This Board hereby certifies that all applicable provisions of 35 ILCS 200/18-55 et. seq., as amended, ("the Truth-in-Taxation Law") will be complied with in passing the final property tax levy.

Section 8. Any "Building, Equipment and Maintenance .02% Fund" levied pursuant to 75 ILCS 16/35-5, et. seq. is not subject to the "PTELL" or "Tax Cap" provisions of 35 ILCS 200/18-185 et seq., 200/18-85 et seq., and 35 ILCS 200/18-205 et seq.

Section 9. The Board has established a Working Cash Fund, pursuant to 75 ILCS 16/35-35 and 16/30-95, as a separate and additional special fund for the sole purpose of enabling the library board to have in its funds, at all times, sufficient money to meet demands thereupon for ordinary and necessary and committed expenditures for library purposes. Pursuant to the aforesaid fund having been created, the proceeds have been deposited in a special and separate fund, and shall be carried over from year to year without, in any manner, reducing or abating a future annual library tax levy, and shall not be deemed a current asset available for library purposes; and the proceeds of such fund may be transferred from the local library Working Cash Fund to the general library fund, and disbursed therefrom in anticipation of collection of taxes lawfully levied for general library purposes; and such taxes when collected, and after payment of tax warrants, shall be drawn upon to reimburse the Working Cash Fund; and all of the above

pursuant to Para. 16/35-35, the aforesaid statutes and other statutes appertaining thereto. Any

interest accruing from the investment of these funds shall be transferred to the General Fund to

be applied to meet ordinary and necessary and committed expenses pursuant to 30 ILCS 350/9(c)

and related statutes.

PASSED by the Board of Library Trustees of the Schaumburg Township District Library, Cook County, Illinois, on the 21st day of September, 2015.

AYES: _____

NAYS: _____

ABSENT AND NOT VOTING: _____

_____
President, Board of Library Trustees
Schaumburg Township District Library

((Seal))

ATTEST:

_____
Secretary, Board of Library Trustees
Schaumburg Township District Library

State of Illinois   )

) SS

County of Cook   )

I, the undersigned, do hereby certify that I am the duly qualified Secretary of the Board of Library Trustees of the Schaumburg Township District Library, Cook County, Illinois; and as such am the keeper of the records and files of the Board of Library Trustees of said District.

I do further certify that attached hereto is a full, true and complete copy of a certain ordinance passed, approved and adopted by the Board of Library Trustees on this 21st day of the month of September in the year 2015, captioned:

Ordinance No. 2015/1016-4
Determination of Money To Be Raised By Taxation – 2015 Tax Levy

I do further certify that the deliberations of the members of said Board of Library Trustees of Schaumburg Township District Library on the adoption of said ordinance were taken openly; that said meeting was held at a specified time and place convenient to the public, that the vote on the adoption of said ordinance was taken openly; that notice of said meeting was duly given to all newspapers, radio or television stations and other news media requesting such notice; and that said meeting was called and held in strict accordance with the provisions of "An Act in Relation to Meetings," approved July 11, 1957, as amended, and that said Board of Library Trustees has complied with all of the applicable provisions of said Act and its procedural rules in the adoption of said ordinance.

IN WITNESS THEREOF, I hereunto affix my official signature and the seal of said Schaumburg Township District Library this 21st day of the month of September in the year 2015.

_____

Secretary, Board of Library Trustees
Schaumburg Township District Library
130 S. Roselle Road
Schaumburg, Cook County, State of Illinois

EXHIBIT 3.2: **Budget Work Sheet Template**

XYZ Department

Click buttons below to access budget tabs

Personnel Services

Account	Line Item	Jul	Aug	Sep	Oct	Nov	Dec	Jan	Feb	Mar	Apr	May	Jun	Total	2015	2014	2013
5000-1-1-09-01	Salaries	20,000	20,000	20,000	20,000	20,000	20,000	20,000	20,000	20,000	20,000	20,000	20,000	240,000	239,242	235,000	234,000
5000-1-1-09-04	Salaries ILL	5,100	5,100	5,100	5,100	5,100	5,100	5,100	5,100	5,100	5,100	5,100	5,100	61,200	61,340	61,240	61,100
	Total Salaries	25,100	25,100	25,100	25,100	25,100	25,100	25,100	25,100	25,100	25,100	25,100	25,100	301,200	300,582	296,240	295,100

Other

Account	Line Item	Jul	Aug	Sep	Oct	Nov	Dec	Jan	Feb	Mar	Apr	May	Jun	Total	2015	2014	2013
4100-1-1-09-01	ILL Replacements	250	250	250	250	250	250	250	250	250	250	250	250	3,000	2,575	2,435	2,345
6300-1-1-09-01	Small Furniture and Equi	0	0	0	0	500	0	0	0	750	0	0	0	1,250	1,112	1,010	1,110
6408-1-1-09-01	Supplies	1,000	1,000	1,000	1,000	1,000	1,000	1,000	1,000	1,000	1,000	1,000	1,000	12,000	12,575	15,260	13,350
6600-1-1-09-01	Staff Dev.	0	0	750	500	0	0	0	750	0	0	0	0	2,000	1,475	1,350	1,200
6900-1-1-09-01	Repairs	0	0	0	0	0	0	0	500	600	0	0	0	1,000	750	700	720
7003-1-1-09-01	Hardware & Peripherals	0	600	0	0	0	600	0	0	0	0	0	0	1,800	1,200	1,200	1,200
7004-1-1-09-01	Software Subscriptions	0	0	0	500	500	0	0	0	0	0	0	600	1,100	1,025	1,015	1,020
7005-1-1-09-01	Technology Consulting	0	0	0	0	0	0	0	0	0	0	0	0	0	0	0	0
	Total Other	1,250	1,850	2,000	1,750	2,250	1,850	1,250	2,500	2,600	1,250	1,250	1,850	20,150	20,712	20,535	20,945
	Total	26,350	26,950	27,100	26,850	27,350	26,950	26,350	27,600	27,700	26,350	26,350	26,950	321,350	321,294	316,775	316,045
	Grand Total XYZ Department	26,350	26,950	27,100	26,850	27,350	26,950	26,350	27,600	27,700	26,350	26,350	26,950	321,350	321,294	316,775	316,045

Buttons (left side): Salaries | Salaries ILL | Materials | Furniture and Equipment | Supplies | Staff Development | Repairs | Hardware & Peripherals | Software | Technology Consulting

Buttons: Narrative | 2015 Budget | Personnel Req Form

4

Library Performance Measures and Operating Ratios

Learning Objectives of This Chapter Are to:

☐ Understand the value of standards, inputs, outputs, processes, satisfaction and outcomes in helping determine how much to budget and how to allocate the budget into spending categories.

☐ Appreciate why most professional library organizations believe that outcomes are the best measure of customer satisfaction.

☐ Know the value of benchmarking and how to create a set of libraries that may be used as a benchmarking (peer comparison) set.

☐ Discover the wealth of data sources that deal with library operations and budgets available through ACRL*Metrics*, the Public Library Data Set, EDGE, and state and local data-collection sources.

☐ Realize how ratio analysis can illustrate the differences in budgets in various types and sizes of libraries.

☐ Recognize the importance of analyzing local university and community needs in crafting a budget.

ALTERNATIVE WAYS THAT LIBRARIES ARE ABLE TO OBTAIN FUND-ing for their operations have been discussed, with examples from the San Diego State University (SDSU) library, Chula Vista Public Library (CVPL), and the Schaumburg Township District Library (STDL). The roles that staff and internal and external stakeholders play in the budget develop-ment process have also been reviewed. The next question when preparing a budget is to calculate its size based on the funds available and the way funds are distrib-uted among the competing elements that make up library service. For example, should library open hours be sacrificed in order to maintain the books and materials budget? After all, if a book is not ordered and added to the collection it may not be possible to do so later, given today's shorter publishing runs. Yet, if hours are sacrificed in order to maintain collections but the library is closed, students, faculty, and the public may become discontented, as happened in the City of Chula Vista.

Standards, Inputs, Outputs, Processes, Satisfaction, and Outcomes

The author has served as a building and management consultant to a number of libraries and has learned that client questions tend to center on "how much" and "how many." Questions like, "How big should our building be? How much should we spend on books and media? How do our staffing levels compare to comparable libraries?" are always asked. In response to these questions, three general approaches are suggested: standards, benchmarking, and programmatic needs.

Standards

The American Library Association (ALA) no longer has a list of prescriptive standards for libraries in America.

> Instead, what ALA has to offer are processes to develop outcome-based measures for a library or a set of tools that will enable benchmarking a service for your particular community. Such benchmarks can also be used to set an initial range for a new building or collection size to enable continued planning. The reason for this is that each library serves a different community with different needs. For example, a public library serving a community with many young families wants and needs a library with different facilities and services than a library serving a similar size population with a high percentage of empty-nesters and retirees. Similarly, an academic library that serves a mostly residential population of students would have different needs than one that serves a set of com-muter students. (ALA 2016, 366)

Eliminating standards may be a good approach because every library serves a unique community and budgets must be crafted to meet the library's customers. And yet, in presenting a budget, other departments in a community or in an academic organization often refer to existing guidelines because they support a convincing argument and are easily understood by administrators. For example, a police chief might state during her budget meeting that the department has 1.5 officers per capita for the community served, but in her experience 2 officers are needed to lower crime. She might also point out that 2.0 officers per capita is a guideline that is used in an adjoining community. Administrators and politicians understand this argument and can use it to justify budget requests to their constituencies. The author once heard a coastal city's chief lifeguard make a convincing argument to the city council for more personnel based on a professional lifeguard association guideline that determined how many lifeguards were needed for feet of protected shoreline. He even had the president of the Australian lifeguard association testify in support of the lifeguard/feet of shore guideline. When library administrators present their budget to a governing body, some of its members may find it difficult to understand outcome measures such as changes in knowledge, skills, attitude, behavior, status, or condition. Members of the library's governing body, whether a provost or a city council member, typically like measures they can understand and justify to their constituency. They like to keep it simple and standards and guidelines help to do so.

Some libraries continue to employ standards and guidelines that help shape library budgets and building projects. For example, when he was a consultant to the Riverside Public Library, the author discovered it had a standard that required 0.6 square feet of library space per capita.

Inputs and Outputs

Inputs are resources that contribute to development and delivery of programs and services. They are the traditional measure of the "things" required to meet user needs. Inputs are the resources libraries use, including tangible assets such as staff, physical collections, and facilities as well as less tangible assets like library websites, digital collections, and wireless networks (Lyons and Lance 2009).

Outputs measure the actual use of the library, and may include metrics such as library visits, circulation, hours of public access, computer use, the number of orientation classes offered to new students, and how many story hours conducted.

Traditional measures quantify a library's raw materials or potential to meet user needs (*inputs*) and the actual use of library collections and services (*outputs*). Input and output statistics reveal changes in what libraries do over time. For example, they provide a longitudinal look at the number of books purchased and circulated per year. Traditional approaches to measuring inputs and outputs focus on physical library resources. Libraries are slowly building a consensus on what should be measured, and how to measure inputs and outputs in the digital environment. The goal is to develop standard definitions that facilitate gathering digital library data that can be compared with traditional library data from its own institution and from others (Covey 2002).

Some input measures could be size of budgets (staff, collections, operations), number of staff, collections sizes, types of media in the collection, number and sizes of facilities, size of communities (for public libraries) and number of students (for universities), and infrastructure (hours, seats, computers). Typical output measures include circulation of materials (print, electronic, interlibrary loan), reference/information service inquiries answered, use of facilities as measured by gate counts, number of programs and instruction sessions held and attendance at the sessions, use of the library's website, use of electronic databases, and so on.

Measuring inputs and outputs requires answering these questions:

- What are you measuring? A precise definition is necessary.
- How often will you gather the data?
- How often will you report and review the data?
- Which format will you use to present the data?
- Are there any comparable levels of performance against which to compare the results?
- Who is responsible for gathering and measuring the data?

Sometimes input or output measures can bring unwanted notoriety to a library. The *San Diego Union Tribune* reported that the San Diego Public Library ranked fifteenth in California in books checked out per capita, which is not the type of publicity the SDPL wants after spending $200 million on a new main library a few years ago.

Processes and Satisfaction

Processes are activities that turn inputs into outputs. They are a sequence of interdependent and linked procedures that at every stage consume one or more resources to convert inputs into outputs. Process measures are the specific steps in a process that lead—either positively or negatively—to a particular outcome metric. Some typical process measures in a library might be time and efficiency (e.g., time to catalog a book), costs and economy (e.g., cost per article download), quality and accuracy, quantity and workload, and infrastructure measures (e.g., facilities, computing). Inputs focus on how large or how much, outputs focus on usage, and processes focus on time, efficiency, costs, and quality (NISO 2010).

Every process should have a balanced set of measurements (Key Performance Indicators—KPIs) against which its performance can be tracked, communicated, and improved. There are three types of measurement required: input measures, output measures, and satisfaction measures.

Process measures improve quality and cost by enabling libraries to reduce the amount of variation in service delivery. Establishing process metrics at potential points of variation in a service process enables monitoring and reducing inappropriate variation (Burton n.d.).

Input measures enable you to assess the basic performance of the process itself. Output measures enable you to assess the quality of the intermediate or final outputs. Both can be measured without involving the customer(s) of the process.

Satisfaction measures are direct assessments of the customer's view of the process, which can only be gathered by interacting with or interviewing the customer. In many ways they are like outcomes. But they are different--outcomes measure a change experienced by a library user, whereas satisfaction measures indicate how happy or satisfied, or how unhappy or unsatisfied the user is with his library experience.

Here are some examples of how inputs, outputs, and satisfaction work together.

INPUT MEASURES	OUTPUT MEASURES	SATISFACTION
Number of reference librarians available to the public per hour the library is open and resources available to the reference staff	Number of reference questions answered	Random surveys of customers' satisfaction with the quality and accuracy of the information they receive and the friendliness of the reference staff
Number of facility seats available, comfort of the seats, and attractiveness of the facility environment (e.g., the number of building amenities such as a store, restaurant, and so on)	Ratio of library seats occupied during the day to the number of seats available	Customer satisfaction with the quantity and quality of library seating and facility amenities

Outcomes

Outcomes are the effects that the library has on an individual or the population served by the library. Many consider them the best way to measure the impact of library service.

According to the Institute of Museum and Library Services (IMLS), although

> academic knowledge and skills are foundations, learning is broader. It includes the cognitive, social, and physical; the practical, entertaining, and personal; the formal and informal; and many more domains and settings. Learning represents knowledge, attitudes, skills, and behaviors that support individual success in our complex world—in short, outcomes. Outcomes allow us to know something about the extent to which we have (or haven't) reached our audiences. Information about outcomes allows us to strengthen our services. Equally important, it communicates the value of museums and libraries to the broadest spectrum of those to whom we account. Without data, it's been said, "you're just another guy with an opinion." (IMLS 2016)

From a user point of view, outcomes are what the library provides, such as a loaned book, an answer to a reference question, or a seat in the library. Outcome measures are behavioral and cognitive changes that may occur to library customers when they use the services and resources of the library. There is no direct relationship linking output and outcome measures. Who knew that Karl Marx occupying a seat in the British Museum Library (output measure of taking a seat) would result in the outcome measure of producing *Das Kapital*. Data on outputs (services provided) come from libraries, whereas data on outcomes (personal changes experienced) come from users. In order to know the cognitive and behavioral outcomes that users experience, they must be surveyed, and even then the person being questioned may not fully recognize the changes that may result from library use. Also problematic is that library service outputs—at least as they are usually reported by libraries to state library agencies and IMLS—tend to be generic: the total number of visits, circulation, program attendance, etc. Without knowing the purpose of each visit, the subject of the materials borrowed, or the specific questions asked, it is hard to match output to the possible outcome. In their LJ Index 2014 Star Libraries article, Ray Lyons and Keith Curry Lance present an excellent discussion of outputs and outcomes that explains the differences and similarities between the two measures (Lyons and Lance 2009).

Carolyn A. Anthony describes how output measures are used in a summer reading program. She writes, "think about the consequences if the public library program were to significantly reduce the summer slide or even help students increase their reading skills over the summer. Teachers who typically spend the first six weeks of the school year reviewing lessons from the prior year might need to spend only two or three weeks of the new year on review, gaining three or four additional weeks to work on new skill development" (Anthony 2014).

Outcome measures enable libraries to view all their services and activities through the lens of library users. It is the library's customers who determine if the library is performing up to the expected service level. Better libraries go beyond what is expected to delight library customers.

Benchmarking

Benchmarking is a method to compare the quantitative aspects of library service for your library against those of a similar set of libraries. Benchmarking involves gathering data using a variety of selected measures, such as population served, budget, and governance, and assessing how the library compares with these benchmarked or peer libraries. It provides a systematic approach to identifying the activities with the greatest potential for improvement based on the comparison with similar libraries (Noreen, Brewer, and Garrison 2008, 266).

Benchmarking can be applied against any product, process, function, or approach in business. Common focal points for benchmarking initiatives include measures of time, quality, cost effectiveness, and satisfaction. The intent of benchmarking is to compare your own operations against competitors' and to generate ideas for improving processes, approaches, and technologies to reduce costs, increase profits, and strengthen customer loyalty and satisfaction. Benchmarking is an important component of continuous improvement initiatives (Reh 2016).

> Benchmarking is a quality assessment tool that operates effectively in a strategic planning environment. Etymologically, the term *benchmark* comes from a surveyor's mark to establish elevation. In business, and particularly in total quality management (TQM), a benchmark means a standard of excellence against which other similar outcomes are measured or judged. For higher education, several ideas are often pulled together in the use of the term. The most inclusive one is assessment of different ways to determine the effectiveness of programs. Two related ideas are process benchmarking to compare processes and comparative analysis to improve results. Comparative analysis focuses on what was accomplished, whereas process benchmarking examines the workflow to help a planning unit improve its effectiveness and/or efficiency. (St. Clair 2006)

A library system might select five to ten peer libraries that serve similar customers based on population size, square miles of service area, demographic characteristics of the community, commuting students versus those living on campus, and so forth. For example, the SDSU Library might select five or six similar libraries in the California State University System for benchmarking comparison, and the CVPL could select public libraries of similar size based on population served.

The value of benchmarking in the budget process is that it provides comparisons to indicate if the library's budget is comparable to other libraries, and if not why. It is "community wisdom" that describes how much other libraries are spending and how they are spending their resources.

Benchmarking is much easier to implement today because of the growth of automated systems. Collecting the information described in the ACRL and PLA systems below is only possible by the systematic collection of data. "Big Data" in all industries has changed how organizations understand and serve their customers. The same is true for libraries. Information on internal operations and processes, library customers—their preferences, and the way they use the library—is critical to developing efficient and effective library services. Knowing whom we serve, how customers use our libraries, and how we employ resources will enable library decision-makers to provide better library programs (Robbins and Judge 2017, 11–14).

Steps in the Benchmarking Process

Because any process, product, function in a business can be benchmarked, methodologies vary. Typically, a benchmarking process will:

- Define the subject of the benchmarking study. Will it evaluate all areas of the library or specific areas such as budgets, facilities, technology?
- Select and define the measures that will be included.
- Select the comparison set of libraries that will be studied.

- Assess the data and identify differences and gaps between your library and the benchmarked set.
- Analyze the root causes of the differences or gaps.
- If is necessary to make changes based on the information received, define an improvement initiative complete with goals and objectives.
- Communicate the goals to all the library's stakeholders.
- Implement the improvement initiative and measure results.
- Report on the results, identify improvements, and repeat the process.

Criteria for Selecting a Benchmarking Set

Libraries may utilize two types of benchmarking: competitive benchmarking restricts the search for best practices to libraries, whereas function benchmarking endeavors to determine best practices regardless of industry (Dess, McNamara, and Eisner 2017, 366).

The author was part of a planning team for a new library project in the United Arab Republic. Our team developed a set of benchmarked libraries in North America and in Europe to serve as comparisons. Both comparison sets are attached as **exhibit 4.1** (North America) and **exhibit 4.2** (Europe). These were useful in setting a capital and operating budget for the proposed library in Al Ain (Meyer Scherer and Rockcastle, Rohlf Associates, and PA Library Consulting 2011)

Libraries can benchmark almost any type of input, output, or process. The choice of what to benchmark depends on what information the library is seeking, the ability to gather that information, and the cost of acquiring the benchmarking data.

Data Sources

As suggested, libraries should attempt to develop a set of similar libraries that may be used for comparison. This provides a continuous set of information that may be compared over a period of time. It is valuable to review the data periodically as well as when the library must make a budgetary or operational decision. The Association of College & Research Libraries (ACRL), Public Library Association (PLA), Edge, state library associations, and regional library associations are a rich source of library comparison information.

ACRLMetrics

ACRL provides comprehensive data that may be used in benchmarking studies. ACRL-*Metrics* is a "click-only" reporting function that enables peer benchmarking and multi-year trend analysis. It is a web-based online subscription service providing on-demand, 24x7 secure browser access, comprehensive customized report outputs, and easy repurposing, sharing, and publishing of report outputs. It provides turnkey, benchmarking templates based on ratios recommended in *Viewing Library Metrics from Different Perspective: Inputs, Outputs and Outcome* (Dugan, Hernon, and Nitecki 2009. Almost any desired type of data is measured in the online service. Much of the data comes from National Center for Educational Statistics (NCES), which is the "primary federal entity for collecting and analyzing data related to education in the United States. and other nations. It is the home of the Library Statistics Program, which provides the data for ACRL*Metrics*." (ACRL and Counting Opinions 2011)

Christopher Stewart has written two articles about ACRL*Metrics*. The first describes what it is and the types of reports it can help generate for libraries and the second (Stewart 2011, 2012) provides six tables that list many items that are valuable to incorporate into a benchmarking study.

The first two tables in the 2011 article list key ratios and percentages and efficiency ratios.

Stewart's table 1 presents fifteen selected key ratios and percentages from the National Center for Education Statistics' (NCES) academic libraries survey collection including sixteen ratios and percentages such as librarian full-time equivalents (FTEs) per 1000 circulation and percentage of staff expenditures on salaries and wages.

Stewart's table 2 shows thirteen selected efficiency measures from NCES academic libraries survey collection such as circulation per librarian FTE, weekly reference transactions per librarian FTE, and so on.

The ratios and percentages from tables 1 and 2 are found in **exhibit 4.3.**

Stewart's tables 3 through 6 illustrate application of the system with reports on peer group (i.e., comparable libraries) generated for Big Ten institutions using ACRL*Metrics*. The four tables show e-books held in 2010 (table 3); total library expenditures per student, 2010 (table 4); six-year graduation rates and total library expenditures per student, 2004 to 2010 (table 5); and comparison of university instructional staff and library staff levels, 2004 to 2010 (table 6).

Public Library Data Services

The Public Library Data Service (PLDS) Statistical Report, a PLA project, is designed to meet the needs of public library administrators and others for timely and effective library-specific data that highlights and supports a wide variety of management decisions. Published annually, the PLDS report presents exclusive, timely data on finances, library resources, annual use figures, and technology from public libraries across the United States and Canada. In addition to these topics, each year's edition contains a special survey highlighting information on one service area or topic (e.g., statistics or strategic planning). The first report was issued in 1988 in paper format, and since 2011 it has been only available online by subscription.

More than 1,000 libraries participate in the report by completing questionnaires that report financial, statistical, and operating information. Counting Opinions (SQUIRE) Ltd. on behalf of the PLA now conducts the survey. Counting Opinions provides an online service for capturing data and accessing results. The subscription service offers access to the longitudinal PLDS data sets from FY 2002 (Reid 2016).

The subscription online database features a dynamic, web-based format, with searchable data exportable into Excel or CSV file formats, and linked data from other report sections. Users can create customized tables and PLDS datasets. The data is accessed through the online data portal PLAmetrics, a service much like ACRL*Metrics* (PLA 2016).

Libraries that don't have the time or expertise to create a report may purchase a customized PLAmetrics report. The data collected for the PLDS report is versatile and can be manipulated to provide a customized report about how your library compares to other libraries. An hourly fee is charged to compile the customized report.

Edge

Edge is a management and leadership tool that assists libraries in the growth and development of technology services. The Urban Libraries Council led Edge's creation; it was developed by a national coalition of leading library and local government organizations and funded by the Bill and Melinda Gates Foundation. Through a suite of tools, Edge supports libraries in making strategic decisions and identifying areas for improvement. The Edge Toolkit provides libraries with an overview of current public services and community engagement. From operations to partnerships and programming, the toolkit generates recommendations for implementing best practices to align with future growth and community priorities. It also provides useful resources to demonstrate the library's community service to community leaders.

Through completing the Edge Assessment, libraries evaluate their current services and identify opportunities for improvement and evaluate the library's public technology services. Through the assessment tool, libraries learn about other libraries' best practices in technology-related services for their communities and determine what steps they should take to improve their public technology programming. The eleven Edge benchmarks are organized in three major areas: community value, engaging the community, and organizational management. All of the benchmarks pose evaluative questions that are not only valuable for evaluating existing services but also in planning new technology services (Edge 2016).

State and Local Resources

Many state educational agencies and state libraries provide library data that is useful for comparison. One example is the Library Research Service (LRS) in Colorado. LRS is an office of the Colorado State Library, which is a unit of the Colorado Department of Education. The agency generates library statistics and research for library and education professionals, public officials, and the media. LRS reports and analyzes statistics on school, public, and academic libraries, and conducts studies on major library issues that are reported in two online publications: Fast Facts, and the Closer Look Studies. It also offers templates for user surveys as well as other library financial, operational, and statistical information.

Data is organized by statistic and group, and can be refined by library, population group, and legal basis. Results can be exported in a spreadsheet format that enables numerical manipulation to meet user needs. LRS is a gold mine of information for any type of library (Colorado State Library 2016).

Operating and Financial Ratios

Most ratio analysis done in the private sector is centered on profitability, whereas in the public sector customer satisfaction is the primary goal. Another limiting factor is that most libraries are funded by governmental or quasi-governmental agencies, which makes cash flow less important than it is in some other types of nonprofits (e.g., a Meals on Wheels organization). One value of ratios for libraries is that they allow libraries of different sizes to compare financial status and operations. Another plus is that it allows libraries to measure their financial health.

A ratio is a comparison of one number to another. In financial ratio analysis, numbers ae taken from the library's financial statements. Ratios are used because the comparison between two numbers generates information that is more useful than either or both of the numbers separately.

One problem with ratios is that different people and sources frequently don't compute them in exactly the same ways, which leads to some confusion. When computing ratios some questions to consider are:

- How is it computed?
- What is it intended to measure, and why might we be interested?
- What is the unit of measurement?
- What might a high or low value be telling us? How might such values be misleading?
- How could this measure be improved? (Dess, McNamara, and Eisner 2017, 442)

Let's take an example of a library that has a statement of financial conditions that shows it has current assets of $610,000 and current liabilities of $140,000. Current assets are assets that are expected to be realized in cash, or sold or consumed, during the operating cycle or within one year if the cycle is shorter than one year. Current liabilities are obligations that will be satisfied within the next operating cycle or within one year if the cycle is shorter than one year. The current ratio equals current assets divided by current liabilities. Generally, the higher the current ratio, the more liquid is the organization. What this means in this example is that the library has 4.4 dollars of assets for 1 dollar of liabilities ($610,000/$140,000 = 1.4). Is this good or bad? This is where the library may want to look at historical data to see if there have been changes over the years, or perhaps compare that ratio to similar libraries (Porter and Norton 2013, G-3).

There are many ratios that may be calculated from the library's financial statements such as the current ratio (cash + receivables + inventories/accounts payable + advance from grantors), as well as many others that measure liquidity, efficiency, risk and capacity, and comparison ratios such as total revenues and population.

A list of possible metrics to use in ratio analysis may be found in a *Sample List of Quantitative Metrics for Libraries,* which includes approximately eighty measures for

- library size and patron base
- transactions (circulation and reference)
- budget, resource allocation, and value of print and digital materials
- facilities and foot traffic
- virtual foot traffic
- education and outreach
- operations (White, Vjas, and Krugman 2013)

The information gathered through services such as ACRL*Metrics* and PLAmetrics may be used not only to compare similar libraries through benchmarking studies, but also through ratio analysis to compare unlike libraries based on size or type. Comparisons can be made over a historical time period or against norms for the library industry.

Using one of the ACRL*Metrics* ratios, *percent of operating expenditures on collections,* for three case study libraries presents the following comparisons.

SCHAUMBURG TOWNSHIP DISTRICT LIBRARY
>Total budget = $15,540,648
>Materials budget = $1,645,044
>$1,645,044 / $15,540,648 = 11 percent of the budget for collections.

CHULA VISTA PUBLIC LIBRARY
>Total Budget = $3,900,000
>Materials budget = $55,000
>$55,000 / $3,900,000 = 1 percent of the budget for collections.

SAN DIEGO STATE UNIVERSITY
>Total budget = $11,622,311
>Materials budget = $2,900,934
>$2,900,934 / $11,622,311 = 25 percent of the budget for collections

Using this ratio, we are able to compare two public libraries and one academic library for the current year. Schaumburg Township is probably closer to the norm for comparable libraries, whereas the materials budget for Chula Vista is low (reflecting the decision to respond to citizen requests for more hours, which are financed through a lowered materials budget). San Diego State University (SDSU) has a very strong materials budget based on total budget.

Programmatic Needs

Standards, inputs, outputs, processes, satisfaction, outcomes and benchmarking provide a library with tools to evaluate its operations against peer libraries and standards. This enables it to decide if its programs and activities are comparable to similar libraries.

However, some libraries may prefer to emphasize different programs than their peers based on environmental, political, or social reasons. An example of this was when Clara Stanton Jones, the first African American woman president of the American Library Association and director of the great Detroit Public Library (DPL), decided to make a radical shift in the services offered by the DPL. Based on her knowledge of the community served, she realized that the existing library programs were not meeting the informational needs of the changing population of Detroit. She reallocated budgeted resources and staff from existing programs to a new type of library service—The Information Place (TIP). TIP was a community information service that provided current information to Detroiters on how to find a job, get food stamps, resolve landlord-tenant disputes, and so on. The author was on the staff of the library and observed resistance from some staff, who felt that the reallocation of the budget to TIP from traditional library services was wrong because they believed the library should not be in the community information business. They felt that the library's purpose was to serve people who were looking for books and media for educational and recreational reasons. In the end, the author believes that Ms. Jones made the right decision because she realized that because there was a finite amount of resources available to the library, they should be employed where they could best serve Detroiters.

What Can We Afford?

The value of performance measures, standards and guidelines, benchmarking, and other techniques is to provide a library with information on how it compares to peers and other types of libraries. This industry wisdom is beneficial because it indicates whether a library is allocating its scarce resources as other libraries do, and if not, why. CVPL decided to allocate more of its budget to open hours at the expense of its materials budget because that was what the community seemed to want. Determining how to spend scarce budget dollars results in dilemmas like Chula Vista's, and the budget decision often requires hard choices. In the end, the question is what can we afford. Chapter 3 describes the process that libraries employ to arrive at a budget bottom line amount as to what they can afford.

EXERCISES

1. Select a library that you know and analyze five inputs and outputs for that library.
2. For the library you selected, describe how you would measure outcomes for two of their services.
3. For the library you selected, create a benchmark (peer comparison set) and choose five measures for comparison.
4. Select five of the key ratios and percentages and efficiency ratios in exhibit 4.3 and analyze the library of your choice.
5. Assume your supervisor has asked you to evaluate and write a report on the adequacy and quality of library service offered to your customers. Create an outline of how you would proceed and what information you might need.

References

American Library Association. 2016. "Library Standards." www.ala.org/tools/atoz/library-standards.

Anthony, Carolyn A. 2014. "Moving Towards Outcomes." *Public Libraries Online* (May/June).

Association of College & Research Libraries, and Counting Opinions. 2011. "ACRL*Metrics*" Presentation, ACRL Conference, Philadelphia, PA.

Burton, Tom. n.d. "Why Process Measures Are Often More Important Than Outcome Measures in Healthcare." www.healthcatalyst.com/process-vs-outcome-measures-healthcare.

Colorado State Library. 2016. "Welcome to Library Research Service." https://www.lrs.org/data-tools/public-libraries/annual-statistics/.

Covey, Denise Troll. 2002. *Usage and Usability Assessment: Library Practices and Concern*. Digital Library Foundation.

Dess, Gregory G., Gerry McNamara, and Alan B. Eisner. 2017. *Strategic Management: Text and Cases*. 8th ed. New York: McGraw Hill Education.

Dugan, Robert E., Peter Hernon, and Danuta A. Nitecki. 2009. *Viewing Library Metrics from Different Perspectives*. Santa Barbara, CA: ABC Clio.

Edge. 2016. "Edge Assessment Workbook." www.libraryedge.org/sites/default/files/Edge_Assessment_Workbook.pdf.

Institute of Museum and Library Services. 2016. "Outcome Based Evaluations." https://www.imls.gov/grants/outcome-based-evaluations.

Lyons, Ray, and Keith Curry Lance. 2009. "America's Star Libraries." *Library Journal* 134 (3): 26.

Meyer Scherer and Rockcastle, Ltd., Robert H. Rohlf Associates, and PA Library Consulting. 2011. "Al Ain Public Library Conceptualization Study." Minneapolis, MN.

National Information Standards Organization. 2010. *Measure, Assess, Improve, Repeat: Using Library Performance Metrics*. In NISO 2010 Events: NISO. www.niso.org/news/events/2010/.

Noreen, Eric W., Peter Brewer, and Ray H. Garrison. 2008. *Managerial Accounting*. Boston: McGraw-Hill Irwin.

Porter, Gary A., and Curtis L. Norton. 2013. *Financial Accounting: The Impact on Decision Makers*. 8th ed. Mason, OH: South-Western/Cengage Learning.

Public Library Association. 2016. "PLDS and PLAmetrics." www.ala.org/pla/publications/plds.

Reh, F. John. 2016. "You Can't Manage What You Don't Measure." https://www.thebalance.com/you-can-t-manage-what-you-dont-measure-2275996.

Reid, Ian. 2016. "The 2015 Public Library Data Service Statistical Report: Characteristics and Trends." *Public Libraries* 55 (4): 24–33.

Robbins, Stephen P., and Timothy A Judge. 2017. *Organizational Behavior*. 17th ed.: New York: Pearson.

St. Clair, Gloriana. 2006. "Benchmarking and Restructuring." Association of College & Research Libraries. www.ala.org/acrl/publications/booksanddigitalresources/booksmonographs/pil/pil49/stclair.

Stewart, Christopher. 2011. "An Overview of ACRLMetrics." *Journal of Academic Librarianship* 37 (1): 73–76.

———. 2012. "An Overview of ACRLMetrics, Part II: Using NCES and IPEDs Data." *The Journal of Academic Librarianship* 38 (6): 342–45.

White, Karen, Kris Vjas, and Karen Krugman. 2013. "Sample List of Quantitative Metrics for Libraries." *Computers in Libraries* (April 9).

	Boston, MA	Denver, CO	Seattle, WA	Nashville, TN	Vancouver, BC	Austin, TX	Columbus, OH	Jacksonville, FL	AVERAGES
Reasons for inclusion in benchmark	1,2,3,4, 6,7	1,3,6,7,	1,2,3,5, 6	1,2,3,4, 6	1,2,3,4, 5,6	1,3,6,7	1,3,6	1,2,3,4, 5,6	
Total population served by library	589,141	598,707	602,000	626,144	628,621	765,957	843,582	891,192	**693,168**
Size of main library (m2)	86,400	50,114	33,723	27,871	32,500	10,278	23,728	27,640	**36,532**
M2 of main library space per capita	0.147	0.084	0.056	0.045	0.052	0.013	0.028	0.031	**0.053**
Size of primary service area (m2)	231	401	218	1300	114	671	888	2175	**750**
Number of branches	26	22	26	20	21	21	21	20	**22**
Total collection size	16,341,122	2,165,256	2,294,601	1,670,715	2,254,154	1,455,793	2,185,192	3,147,971	**3,939,351**
Holdings per capita	27.74	3.62	3.81	2.67	3.59	1.90	2.59	3.53	**6.18**
Number of computers	442	566	790	525	1042	360	2,000	1,000	**841**
Number of computers per 1,000 capita	0.75	0.95	1.31	0.84	1.66	0.47	2.37	1.12	**1.18**
Full time equivalent staff	487	447	527	317	509	350	583	459	**460**
Average hours main library open per week	68	56	62	47	65	66	56	67	**61**
Expenditures per capita	$64.64	$59.33	$83.84	$37.12	$57.15	$31.68	$53.67	$42.99	**$52.50**
Visitors per capita	2.7	2.0	3.4	0.9	9.4	0.7	1.1	1.1	**2.6**
Circulation per capita	5.77	16.17	19.97	6.62	15.72	5.48	19.5	10.27	**18.27**

Reasons for inclusion in benchmark

1. Size of population served.
2. Diversity of population served.
3. Presence of higher education institutions.
4. Cultural awareness and promotion in the city.
5. Rapid growth in the area.
6. Availability of the data.
7. City was benchmark in McKinsey & Co. report.

BENCHMARK LIBRARY	EXPENDITURES PER CAPITA (IN AED)
Boston, MA	237.24
Denver, CO	217.74
Seattle, WA	307.68
Nashville, TN	136.24
Vancouver, BC	209.75
Austin, TX	116.27
Columbus, OH	196.97
Jacksonville, FL	157.79
Average	192.68
Exchange rate	*3.67 (as of 01/01/2011)*

North American Cities Annual Operating Costs in AED per Capita

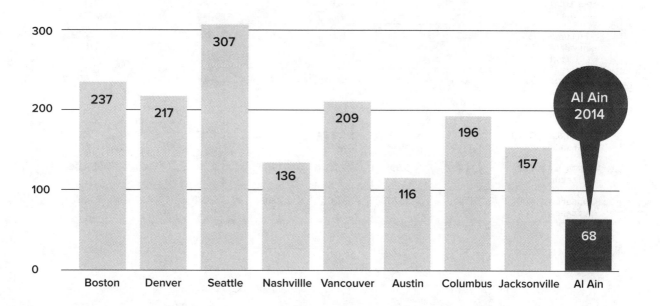

	Oslo, NO	Helsinki, FI	Stuttgart, DE	Zaragoza, ES	Riga, LV	Amsterdam, NL	Marseilles, FR	AVERAGES
Reasons for inclusion in benchmark	1,2,3,6	1,3,4,6	1,2,3,6	1,2,3,4,6	1,3,4,5,6	1,2,3,5,6	1,2,3,4,5,6	
Total population served by library	538,411	564,874	592,915	606,895	717,371	784,754	852,396	**665,374**
Size of main library (m2)	23,150	10,000	22,320	15,492	15,322	28,000	11,000	**17,898**
M2 of main library space per capita	0.043	0.018	0.038	0.026	0.021	0.036	0.013	**0.027**
Size of primary service area (m2)	454	686	207	1,063	307	219	240	**454**
Number of branches	20	36	25	24	45	28	8	**27**
Total collection size	1,378,361	1,935,999	1,265,883	523,000	1,055,979	1,869,730	1,150,627	**1,311,368**
Holdings per capita	2.56	3.43	2.12	0.79	1.50	2.38	1.63	**2.06**
Number of computers	87	367	175	83	256	600	206	**253**
Number of computers per 1,000 capita	0.16	0.65	0.30	0.14	0.36	0.76	0.24	**0.37**
Full time equivalent staff	194	508	171	125	254	200	291	**249**
Average hours main library open per week	53	58	59	64	62	84	40	**60**
Expenditures per capita	€ 30.67	€ 52.72	€ 23.88	€ 6.94	€ 5.80	€ 38.23	€ 15.26	**€ 24.78**
Visitors per capita	4.82	11.20	3.89	2.83	1.70	2.29	1.66	**4.06**
Circulation per capita	4.08	17.01	10.75	1.41	4.65	2.04	3.27	**6.17**

Reasons for inclusion in benchmark

1. Population served: number.
2. Population served: diversity.
3. Presence of higher education institutions.
4. Cultural awareness and promotion in the city.
5. Area served is experiencing rapid growth.
6. Availability of the data.
7. City was benchmark in McKinsey & Co. report.

BENCHMARK LIBRARY	EXPENDITURES PER CAPITA (IN AED)
Oslo, NO	150.59
Helsinki, FI	258.85
Stuttgart, DE	117.25
Zaragoza, ES	34.07
Riga, LV	28.47
Amsterdam, NL	187.70
Marseille, FR	74.90
Average	121.69
Exchange rate	4.91 (as of 01/01/2011)

European Cities Annual Operating Costs in AED per Capita

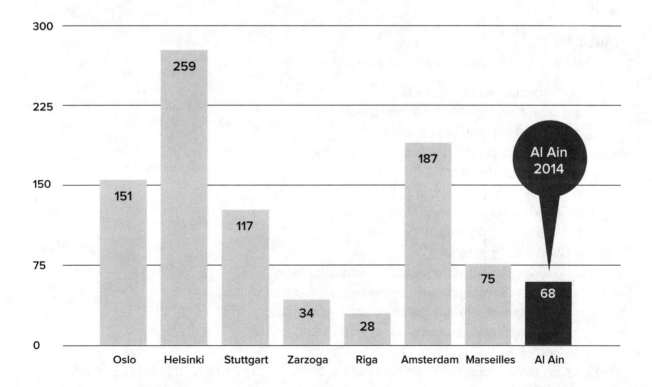

Following are selected ratios, percentages, and efficiency measures from Christopher Stewart's article on ACRL*Metrics* (Stewart 2012, 3)

TABLE 1.
Selected key ratios and percentages from NCES academic libraries survey collection

1. Total staff expenditures per FTE staff
2. Expenditures on salaries and wages per FTE
3. FTEs per 1000 circulation
4. Librarian FTEs per 1000 circulation
5. % of FTEs with librarian title
6. % of FTEs all other paid staff
7. % of staff expenditures on benefits
8. % of staff expenditures on salaries and wages
9. % of operating expenditures on collections
10. % of operating expenditures on electronic materials
11. % of operating expenditures on employee benefits
12. % of operating expenditures on books and other materials
13. % of operating expenditures on audiovisual
14. % of operating expenditures on staff expenditures
15. Benefits per staff FTE

TABLE 2.
Selected efficiency measures from NCES academic libraries survey collection

1. Circulation per librarian FTE
2. Circulation per other professional staff
3. Circulation per student assistant
4. Circulation per staff FTE
5. Circulation turnover
6. Weekly visits per librarian FTE
7. Weekly visits per other professional staff
8. Weekly visits per student assistant
9. Weekly visits per staff FTE
10. Weekly reference transactions per librarian FTE
11. Weekly reference transactions per professional staff
12. Weekly reference transactions per student assistant
13. Weekly reference transactions per staff FTE

Stewart, Christopher. 2012. "An Overview of ACRL*Metrics*, Part II: Using NCES and IPEDs Data." *The Journal of Academic Librarianship* 38 (6):342-345.

5

Budgeting and Forecasting

Learning Objectives of This Chapter Are to:

☐ Show the relationship of budgets to the vision, mission, and goals of the library.

☐ Understand how a budget is "built up" from each department, division, or program of the library to an overall master budget.

☐ Recognize how each library division or department creates its own separate budget and how these budgets are integrated into the overall operating budget.

☐ Know the components of the master budget and the operating budget, financial budget(s), and other budgets as needed.

☐ Identify and understand the strengths and weaknesses of the four major budgeting techniques of line item, program, performance, and zero-based budgets.

Budgeting

Chapter 1 defined a budget as a "plan driven by the vision, mission, goals and objectives of the library." It is a quantitative plan for acquiring and using resources over a specified time period. Budgets also function as control mechanisms in that once the budget is approved, it is monitored to make sure the plan is being followed. Control involves the steps taken by management to increase the likelihood that all parts of the library are working together to achieve the goals developed and approved by the library's administrative organization. A good budgeting system employs both planning and control, because without effective control the entire process is a waste of time and effort.

Some of the many benefits that organizations realize from budgeting are (Noreen, Brewer, and Garrison 2008, 92):

1. Budgets are the way to take the library's vision, mission, and goals and turn them into programs and services.
2. Budgets serve as a communication device so that the library's plans and priorities are clearly known by all stakeholders.
3. Budgets force managers to think about and plan for the future. Without the necessity to prepare a budget, many managers would devote all their time to dealing with daily emergencies.
4. The budgeting process provides a means of allocating resources to those parts of the library where they will be used most effectively.
5. Budgets coordinate the activities of the entire library by integrating the plans of the various programs, departments, and divisions. Budgeting helps to ensure that everyone in the library has agreed to the overall plan.
6. Budgets define goals and objectives that can serve as benchmarks for evaluating subsequent performance.

Types of Budgets

A library may employ a number of budgets that are best suited to its planning and monitoring needs. The basic budget is a comprehensive look at the entire library's overall project of revenues and financial support and its expected expenditures. However, almost endless adaptations of the basic budget form can be created for particular planning and assessment needs. Some of these possibilities include:

- annual, quarterly, and/or monthly projections of income and expenditures for the entire library as well as its various divisions (e.g., technical services), branches, and programs
- revenue projections by type including fines, revenues from the district, and allocations from the provost

- individual project, department, branch, or other cost-center projections such as an orientation program for new students or a summer reading club
- cost to deliver service to a student or member of the public (e.g., cost to circulate a book)
- capital budgets for major equipment such as a new automation system, a building addition, or a new building
- a cash flow projection to make sure that the library is able to meet its expenses throughout the year
- fund-raising revenues and expenses
- special reserves for items like debt service or a reserve fund for future capital projects
- budgets for ancillary services like a bookstore or coffee shop (Blazek 1996, 69–70)

Master Budget

The master budget, sometimes called the comprehensive budget, incorporates and summarizes all the entire budget types listed above for the next budget period. The main elements include the operating budget, financial budget, and other budgets as needed, including a capital budget, special program budget, and so on (figure 5.1). The operating and financial budgets present a plan of service for the next fiscal year.

FIGURE 5.1
Master Budget

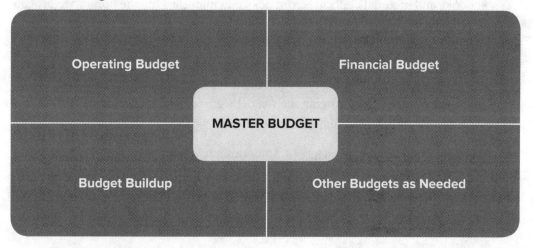

Operating Budget

The operating budget is a plan for the expected revenues and expenses for the next year. It includes anticipated income by source and amount, the amounts of individual line-item expenses, and totals by major budget categories such as salaries, fringe benefits, and media. The operating budget should include a summary of budget highlights; explanations of changes in incomes, expenses, and services; any actions affecting personnel (such as raises, promotions, and the creation or elimination of positions); and any other changes to current budget or current operations (Dropkin, Halpin, and LaTouche 2007, 68–69).

An operating budget for the Schaumburg Township District Library (STDL) for 2015/2016 shows both the revenue sources as well as the major expenditure categories. An explanation of budget changes for operations, revenues, and expenditures is attached as **exhibit 5.1**. The budget presented to the administrative board is attached as **exhibit 5.2** (Sarnoff 2016, 6–8).

The STDL is a district library, which means that most of its revenue comes from property taxes that the district board levied in Schaumburg Township. Of the total budget, $15,540,648, 95 percent ($14,717,500) is derived from tax revenues. Over the last three years revenues have not increased or decreased significantly. This probably signifies that the community has not had significant growth in new property during the period and/or the district board has decided to keep library budget at existing levels.

Expenditures for STDL may be divided into four major categories: personnel, books and materials, administrative costs, and service and reserve funds. Descriptions of the fund categories are:

- Personnel costs. For almost all libraries, the largest expenditure category is personnel services, which consists of salaries, benefits, and other human resource costs. STDL divides personnel costs into the departments and divisions of the library, including administration and youth services.
- Books and materials. All costs for books and materials for the library are broken down into categories such as adult books, reference materials, and so on.
- Administrative costs. These are the costs to keep the library operating, including utilities, insurance, and building repairs.
- Debt services and building and equipment reserves. Not all libraries have reserve funds to pay for items such as debt service and reserves and expenditures for equipment, building improvements.

Benchmarking was discussed in chapter 4. Sometimes it is illuminating to compare ratios. Table 5.1 shows ratios (rounded) for the SDTL's and the Chula Vista Public Library's three major budget categories expenditures. Debt service is not included because it is not significant for CVPL.

TABLE 5.1

Benchmarking

BUDGET CATEGORY	STDL DOLLAR AMOUNT	STDL PERCENT OF BUDGET	CHULA VISTA PL DOLLAR AMOUNT	CHULA VISTA PL PERCENT OF BUDGET
Personnel	$10,069,611	65%	$3,349,253	86%
Books & Materials	$1,650,553	11%	$97,000	2%
Administrative	$3,882,141	24%	$461,433	12%
Total	$15,602,305	100%	$3,907,686	100%

The percentage differences between the two libraries have to do with the decision to offer more open hours of service at the CVPL at the expense of the book and materials budget. The percentage difference in the administrative costs of the two libraries may be due to CVPL being part of a larger city government, and STDL being its own taxing district. Some of the administrative costs in Chula Vista may be absorbed by the parent authority.

The question of what the percentage of each of the budget categories should be has probably vexed librarians since the start of the very first libraries. In 1910, the *North Carolina Library Bulletin* reported that:

> Library boards are often puzzled about the proper division of the funds at their disposal. Given an income of $1,000 or $2,000 a year, for instance, how much of it should be spent for salaries, how much for books, periodicals, and binding, and how much for heat, light, furniture, insurance, and so on? The ALA committee on library administration recently conducted an investigation of the budgets of seventeen representative libraries, each holding from 5,000 to 10,000 volumes. It was found that these libraries as a whole are spending 25 percent of their total income on books, periodicals, and binding; 45 percent on salaries of librarians; and 30 percent for other expenditures.
>
> According to this ratio a library with an income of $2,000 a year would spend $900 for salaries, $500 for books, etc., and $600 for other expenses. (NC Library Commission 1910)

The quarterly journal *New York Libraries* (1913), commented on this division of the library budget:

> In our judgment these proportions might be varied slightly to the advantage of the library and the community, by increasing the percentage devoted to library salaries, as it is the quality and skill of the librarian more than any other factor in your library equipment, that will determine the value of the library to the community. An acute German critic has laid down the rule that the efficiency and grade of a library may be generally judged by

the proportion of income devoted to salaries, as in low-grade libraries this ratio is almost invariably low.

In 1978, Jacob and Sallinger conducted a comprehensive historical review of budget allocation studies of materials versus staff in academic libraries from 1945 to the 1960s. They looked at budget ratios of academic libraries in an attempt to discover what trends there might be in personnel/materials budget ratios and examined the figures for a group of libraries in 1967 and again in 1975. For each period they used the National Center for Educational Statistics college and university library volumes for that period as a source. In order to keep the number of libraries manageable, they arbitrarily selected libraries with a minimum collection of 400,000 volumes in 1967. They identified differences in rural areas where the cost of living may be lower and in those libraries that had strong unions. They concluded that there was not much change in the percentages in the eight-year period. They concluded that "since adequate staffing has been a necessity for excellence of performance in libraries, administrators have usually sought a sufficient budgetary component for personnel. To spend "two for one" (i.e., two dollars for personnel as against one for resources) has been considered a necessary evil if good service were to obtain" (Jacob and Sallinger 1978).

Deciding the correct ratios of personnel/books and materials/administration are not the only issue that must be considered when budgeting. Each of the three elements of library service may be analyzed to determine the most effective and efficient service level for a particular library. Lyons and Blosser present a quantitative model for allocating materials budgets using the Comprehensive Allocation Process (CAP), which is a reproducible decision-making structure for the allocation of new collections funds, the reallocation of funds within stagnant budgets, and budget cuts in the face of reduced funding levels. The system was designed to overcome the common shortcomings of current methods, and its philosophical foundations include the values of accountability, transparency, and efficiency. It features a conceptual framework, quantitative data, qualitative evidence, and data analysis and allocation techniques (Lyons and Blosser 2012)

Decisions about personnel allocations, including the mix of professional, paraprofessional, and support staff, need to be reviewed as well. The physical layout of the library, services provided, and organizational structure have an impact on personnel costs. For example, on a tour of the joint San Jose State University/San Jose Public Library, the author noted that the library offered three levels of reference service: a general reference desk on the main floor staffed by paraprofessionals and supervised by a professional librarian, a series of "reference consultation pods" on the second floor staffed by librarians, and smaller desks on the other five floors staffed by subject bibliographers. Other methods of providing the same service may cost more or less than the organizational structure selected in San Jose.

Libraries should periodically check their budget allocation percentages for personnel/books and materials/administration to compare how they measure up against similar libraries. All budget decisions come from the vision, mission, goals, and objectives of the library and the amount of the three major budget categories needs to reflect the planning choices that were made.

Financial Budgets

Financial budgets consist of a cash budget and a capital budget. The cash budget plans for cash receipts and payouts. The capital budget plans for major and minor expenditures that will be made during the budget period (e.g., a new computer system or an addition to the library building).

For libraries that use cash-basis accounting, which is typical for most libraries, the cash budget is identical to the operating budget. Cash budgets forecast when revenues will be received and expended. Information from the cash budget allows libraries to know when they will need cash for payrolls, to pay vendors, and so on. Cash budgets allow libraries to schedule and allocate their revenues as required during the budgetary period. Accurate scheduling may allow the library to realize a higher rate of return on the cash in the bank until it is required. Cash flow and cash budgets will be reviewed in chapter 8.

Capital Budgets

Capital budgets usually aren't required every year but only when a major financial expenditure is required. Capital expenditures are those that will be used for more than one fiscal year, are used for a long time (in the case of a building, up to fifty years) and the acquisition cost is typically large. Capital budget decisions are made for a number of reasons. Libraries decide to make capital expenditures based on a number of factors.

- Will the capital acquisition reduce costs? For example, will a materials handling system, which automatically returns books to sections of the library where they are stored, be lower than the cost of staff to return them physically? In order to compute this cost comparison, the useful life of the materials handling system capital and operating costs must be compared to the staff costs over a period of years to determine payback. However, cost rationality does not always rule in making the decision. The author was a consultant to an architect working on a project in Angola, and my job was to determine the size of the building and provide adjacencies for library activities. My calculation called for a building of approximately 300,000 square feet, and I suggested a building of five to six stories. The client rejected this and requested a building of thirty stories for two reasons: because he wanted to have the building serve as a beacon from miles away and to provide the maximum number of jobs for the local university population by having service desks on all thirty floors.
- Is a physical building expansion (or a new building) required to meet current service requirements or an enhanced level of customer service and/or convenience?

This decision can't be as easily quantified as is calculating materials handling or a computer system.

- Should the library lease or buy the capital equipment? Because this decision may be complex, the library may require a consultant to help quantify and understand the cost and policy alternatives.
- How are screening and preference decisions made? A screening decision on undertaking a capital project requires a threshold of what the return of the expenditure will be. Some universities and municipalities will only undertake a capital project if a sufficient rate of return for the investment meets the standard for the parent organization. Preference decisions relate to specific vendors, and most libraries have a requirement to award contracts to the lowest possible vendor.

Capital budgets will be discussed in more detail in chapter 7.

Other Budgets

From time to time there is a need for a special budget. For example, the library may be planning a special exhibit to celebrate an event such as an art exhibit or loan of a special collection such as the First Folio on loan from the Folger Shakespeare Library. **Exhibit 5.3** is a sample budget for an exhibit (Dropkin, Halpin, and La Touche 2007, 149). Other examples might be a budget for an unplanned HVAC (heating, ventilation, air conditioning) replacement during the year. Some libraries leave a reserve in their budgets of up to ten percent to cover unplanned expenses.

Budget Buildup

In many libraries, the master budget is constructed by gathering budgets from divisions or departments in the library. **Exhibit 5.4** is a template that the STDL administration sends out to all the library's departments (STDL 2016).

The library is organized into departments: access services; administration; circulation; community engagement; fiction, movies, and music; information technology; reference; and youth services. Each of these departments completes the template and returns the completed document to library administration, where the budget requests are reviewed, modified, and approved. An example of an approved departmental budget for a portion of the community engagement department is attached as **exhibit 5.5.**

Budgeting Techniques or Formats

Budget techniques "establish the rules by which the budgeting game is played (the decision rules)" and also "create the standards by which success is measured (rules of evidence)" (Marti 2013). It is important to establish formats for library budgeting because they determine how financial information is structured, the kind of information required to justify budget requests, and what kind of questions are asked during the budget review process.

There are a number of techniques that may be used to create a budget, that may be classified into four general types of approaches: line item, program, performance, and zero-based. The four approaches may be modified and combined into a hybrid budget containing elements of one or more of the techniques (Morgan and Robinson 2002)

Line-Item Budgets

The examples from the STDL all represent line items. A line-item budget is an accounting method that lists all of an organization's expenditures based on the department or cost center; see, for example, the various budget lines listed in exhibit 5.5 for the community engagement department. Each department's expenditures are given a separate line on the budget. This method helps library staff determine the exact source of their expenses, and is a quick way of identifying specific budget items.

A line-item budget is a simple budget that builds on the revenues and expenses from previous years, and adjusts them for minor changes in the new fiscal year budget. It is also called a historical budget, because libraries typically use historical revenues and expenses to prepare the budget for the current period. A library can create a new budget by using what it has done before if it doesn't plan to make any major changes.

Some advantages of line-item budgets are:

- *Simplicity*: The major advantage of line-item budgeting is that it is simple. It is easy to budget for each area or department of a library based on historical expenditures. If the amount of these expenditures has been consistent over a period of years, line-item budgeting can offer a simple and reliable means of anticipating expenses for the coming year. The simplicity can also save time and effort in budget preparation, because much of the necessary data is readily available.
- *Easy justification*: Because proposed expenditures are based on historical needs, there is often little dispute among departments within the organizations, as the trends have been well established over time. If one department requests an abnormal increase over previous years, the department head is forced to support the request.
- *Flexibility*: Line items use the same categories that appear on the financial statements and are easy to understand. Its flexibility and simplicity may prove more effective than other budget methods in many situations. Managers and supervisors can solicit input from staff, ensuring its broad usage and adoption as the library's primary planning vehicle. This is the case at the STDL.

The main disadvantage of relying only on a line-item analysis in building a budget is that it may create only a superficial analysis of expenditures. Budget preparers may simply accept the status quo, assuming that because this budgeting method worked well in previous fiscal years, it will continue to be effective for the coming year. This assumption may ignore opportunities to take an in-depth look at each line item to determine if the proposed expenditure is truly necessary or if funds could be allocated more efficiently (Joseph 2016).

Program Budgets

The line-item budget lists total department appropriations by items on which the library will spend funds; in contrast, a program budget displays a series of mini-budgets that show the cost of every activity that the library will perform (Morgan and Robinson 2002). A program budget reflects the goal-oriented nature of budgeting and the long-range consequences of decisions commonly used with strategic plans. In a line-item budget scenario, if you are asked to cut expenses by 15 percent, it is very hard to visualize, anticipate, and explain the impact on the services and products that you provide. In a line-item budget cutting 15 percent from a periodical budget only means that you will be forced to spend less, and which you might do through cancellations, not adding new titles, and perhaps reducing hours. The impact on quality of service is hard to foresee. Using a program budget, you should be able to forecast the impact of the cuts in terms of usage and access.

A program budget lets you identify expenditures in each cost center, and work with manageable budgeting units that together make up the total budget. Basically, you are preparing a series of mini-budgets, comprising line-item breakdowns within each program budget category, grouped by desired outcomes. Once you have assessed the needs of your customers, and defined the programs and services to be funded, you should create a cost-center budget for each program so that all costs related to the program will appear together. All staff, materials, and administrative expenses to maintain the cost center should be estimated. The steps in a program budget process are:

1. Distinguish between recurring and nonrecurring costs.
2. Distinguish between personnel and non-personnel costs.
3. Associate personnel with the programs they provide.
4. Allocate non-personnel costs to programs.
5. Associate revenues with programs (Fabian, Johnson, and Kavanagh 2015, 10).

When preparing a program budget, estimate alternative levels of activity and identify the costs for each level. For example, you might compare the alternative costs and benefits of keeping the library open additional hours and forecast the expenses for the additional hours and consider the benefit that may result from enhanced service and customer satisfaction. Next, analyze the effectiveness of various alternatives in meeting the library's objectives. Finally, identify the most cost-effective alternatives and rank the various programs, starting with those without which the library cannot function or fulfill its mission.

An example of a program budget grouping all expenditures needed to provide product or functions may be found in exhibit 5.5, which is a "mini-budget" for an STDL branch. It lists all the costs associated with the branch. If the library is forced to reduce expenditures and decides to close the branch in order to reach a new reduced budget target, some impacts of the cut can be anticipated. Circulation, customer visits, support from the branch's Friends may be reduced, and other service outlets may have their workload increased, and so on.

A program budget offers many advantages. It emphasizes services and activities, not dollars. It focuses on the results of what those dollars purchase, and it translates goals into dollars and dollars into measurable quantitative products. You may extend programs to different departments within the library and prepare a budget that identifies costs for each department. A program budget matches budget requests with tangible programs, products, and services. It forces a periodic review of how the library is spending its money and provides tangible evidence to the provost, library board, or whomever monitors whether the library is trying to reach its goals and objectives. With a program budget as your working plan, you can evaluate achievements, because costs are tied to results. Program budgets make the changing needs of the library easier to understand and articulate (Seer 2000).

A program budget is more time-consuming and challenging to develop than a line-item budget. In order for it to be effective, the library must have a predefined accounting structure that dictates how expenditures are coded and defined. Sometimes all the information required is not available, or the library does not have sufficiently trained staff to analyze traditional budget figures and extrapolate the relevant information needed to develop a meaningful program budget. Once good cost information is in place, preparing a program budget becomes significantly easier.

Performance Budgets

There are many definitions of performance budgeting (PB), which is also known as entrepreneurial budgeting, activity-based budgeting, outcomes-based budgeting, planning-programming budgeting, and results-based budgeting. In general, it implies the incorporation of performance measures into the budget process.

Performance budgeting is the same as program budgeting, except that a measure of performance is included to link the line-item program budget expenditures to the library's program goals.

In performance budgeting, full accrual based costs, revenues, and funding appropriations are linked to specifications of planned and actual performance in terms of outputs and outcomes, thereby increasing the quality of departmental performance reporting (Martí 2013). As McGill (2001, 5) writes:

> The United States General Accounting Office (1997) presents a historical review of performance budgeting. It argues that since 1950, the federal government has attempted four government-wide initiatives designed to better align spending decisions with expected performance—what is commonly known as "performance budgeting" (PB). Consensus exists that all these efforts have failed to shift the focus of the federal budget process from its long-standing concentration on the items of government spending to the results of its programs.

Despite this failure, it draws one conclusion. PB refers generally to the process of linking expected results to budget levels but not to any particular approach. Thus, there is no definitive PB process. Yet, both the concept and techniques of PB have evolved considerably since 1950. First was from the Hoover Commission in 1949. The second was the planning-programming budgeting-system (PPBS), championed by President Johnson from 1965. The third was management by objectives (MBO) initiated in 1973 by President Nixon. The last was zero-base budgeting (ZBB) championed by President Carter. All have led to the latest thrust: the Government Performance and Results Act (GPRA). Each of these initiatives established unique procedures for linking resources with results. (McGill 2001, 5)

The original aim of PB for those organizations that adopted this innovation was to purge budgeting of its line-item focus on the cost of inputs and instead to base spending decisions on the work to be performed. PB proponents argued that line-item budgeting impedes government performance by basing allocations on the cost of inputs rather than on the work being performed and by compelling government agencies to comply with burdensome spending rules that constrict managerial discretion.

A performance budget has the following characteristics:

- It presents the major purpose for which funds are allocated and sets measurable objectives.
- It tends to focus on changes in funding rather than on the base (the amount appropriated for the previous budget cycle).
- It identifies programs and agencies that are seeking similar outcomes, thereby drawing such interrelationships to the legislature's attention.
- It offers agencies the flexibility to reallocate money when conditions merit, rewarding achievement and possibly imposing sanctions for poor performance (NCSL 2016).

The main objective of PB is to increase accountability, and accountability requires accurate information. The main advance in PB processes has been in the sophistication of performance measurement and the use of computers to keep track of and manipulate information. This is PB's most conspicuous characteristic. Libraries have invested significant resources to define outputs, outcomes, impacts, benefits, targets, and so on, which enables to better identify the relationship between these measures and the service outcomes the library provides.

Steps in developing a PB are:

1. Identification of a complete set of performance measures or indicators to help objectively evaluate program performance. There are three main types of output indicators: indicators of output quantity, indicators of output quality, and indicators of efficiency. Output quantity indicators measure the volume of service provided. Output quality indicators provide information on the extent to

which the service or activity is likely to achieve its intended outcome. Some quality indicators are easier to measure objectively than others. Output efficiency is delivering library services at the lowest possible cost measured against a standard of what good service is. It is a relationship between output quantity against output quality.

2. Once the set of performance measures has been identified, the next step is to determine which organizational units contribute to activities and how to allocate those activities to the corresponding programs. Sometimes the allocations are straightforward, especially when all operating unit costs are directly allocated to the cost of the program or sub-program. The allocation of indirect costs is less straightforward. For example, the costs of administrative units, such as purchasing and finance, must be allocated to programs. Another accounting challenge is not only to be able to perform the initial allocation for budgeting purposes, but also to keep track of the actual expenditures by program. This can only be achieved by systematically capturing actual hours or expenses via tagging activity and program related elements in time management, purchasing, contracts, and other related systems.

3. The final step in the PBB process is to develop a Program Evaluation Process (PEP), a framework that allows the organization to prioritize and score program budgets effectively during the budget cycles and conduct periodic performance reviews during the year's budget execution phases (Neubrain 2016).

Shick listed some of the limitations of PB, writing that the take-aways from this limited historical window into performance budgeting's first arrival are:

1. PB is a tough sell in good times and harder in bad times.
2. By itself, PB cannot compensate for a shortage of fiscal space.
3. PB cannot reverse the decline in public trust, but it is hamstrung by low regard for political leaders and institutions.
4. Robust growth would improve the political market for PB-driven budget allocations, but PB cannot itself ignite needed growth.
5. Valuing performance yields better results than merely going through the procedural motions of PB.
6. Purging input data is not a precondition for effective implementation of PB, but consolidating line items may be. (Schick 2013, 7)

Another major disadvantage of performance budgeting is the relative cost between two divisions in the library. Supplies and workload may differ from one library department to the next, which makes allocation of costs more challenging. Some department heads may exaggerate their successes to ensure better funding during the next budget cycle.

The main advantage of PB is that it focuses less on the existing base budget and annual incremental improvements, and more on the library's mission, goals, and objectives and the long-term alternative means for achieving them. PB should be directly tied into creating a process that essentially establishes a procedure for distributing available resources equitably among the many competing or potential programs according to the library's plan.

Zero-Based Budgets

Zero-based budgets (ZBB) require that all expenditures be justified in each new period, as opposed to explaining only the amounts requested in excess of the previous period's funding, as is done in line-item budgeting. Line-item budgeting assumes that the activity being budgeted is worthwhile and should continue. ZBB questions this assumption and requires that every activity being considered be justified as to its cost and effectiveness. It is not inaccurate to say that ZBB is a type of PB, but it also has its own unique characteristics. The previous year's budget is thrown out and a new one is built from scratch. This means that programs, activities, departments, and positions may be eliminated. This might lead to radical change in the library as new programs are launched and old programs that are no longer considered effective are eliminated. ZBB confronts conventional thinking and resource allocations by challenging every line item and assumption, including the most sacred of cows.

Zero-based budgeting was created in the 1960s when a staff control manager at Texas Instruments published an article in the *Harvard Business Review* describing the use of a

> systematic and formalized method of budgeting in that company. Budgets were to be formulated at the "ground level" by an organization's managers, and not merely by its budget staff. A little known first-term governor from a southern state saw the article on "ZeroBase Budgeting" and invited its author, Peter Pyhrr, to implement the system in his state. To coin a phrase, the rest is history. The enthusiasm generated for this new system spilled over into other states and also into local governments. The governor became president of the United States and went on to mandate the adoption of the system (as he had promised in his campaign) in the federal government. (Draper and Pitsvada 1981, 76)

Just as President Jimmy Carter fell from favor, so did zero-based budgeting. It was considered to be a fad, and most organizations that adopted it replaced it with more traditional methods of budgeting. But ZBB is now making something of a resurgence. A 2011 Government Finance Officers Association (GFOA) survey shows that an increasing number of leading public budget practitioners (44 percent of all respondents) are considering ZBB, and just over 20 percent of those surveyed (representing both small and large governments) say they are now using ZBB, at least in part. The best explanation as to why this is happening is because the "zero" sends a message that taxes and spending will be kept in check (Kavanagh 2012).

ZBB asks a difficult but necessary question; "if we were starting anew, would we include this program or activity?" No activity or person is safe from a critical examination to determine if that activity or person is the best use of the library's limited resources. The purpose of ZBB is to:

- confront conventional thinking and resource allocations by challenging every line item and assumption
- align resources with the mission of the library
- re-envision the library and ask what activities and resources will truly be needed for it to thrive under future environmental conditions
- fund key strategic activities while removing non-value, costly programs
- justify proposed activities and resources
- build a comprehensive fact base of current services, functions, programs, and expenses
- use a "blank sheet of paper" approach to build the ideal state
- envision what the library will be like in the future by requiring justification for all activities, set budgets and full-time employee levels, redesigning the library and planning for implementation (Rigby 2015)

In beginning the ZBB process, managers should ask these five questions:

1. Should a given program, activity, or position be continued, or would other activities be more important or appropriate?
2. If the program, activity, or position is justified, should it continue operating in the same manner, or should it be modified?
3. If it should be modified, how will it be modified, when, and by whom?
4. How much should the organization spend on the program, activity, or position being studied?
5. Does the proposed change have political backing within the organization, or are we wasting our time trying to make this change? (Dropkin, Halpin, and Touche 2007, 92)

Implementing ZBB requires the development of decision packages. Administration first identifies units in the library for which budgets are prepared. These could be departments, divisions, branches, program categories, program elements, and so on. This is the starting point for identifying decision units for ZBB. Decision units should have a specific manager who should be clearly responsible for the operation of the program. The units must have well-defined and measurable objectives.

After the identification of appropriate decision units, the next step is to prepare a document that describes the objectives or purposes of each decision unit and the actions that could be taken to achieve it. This document is called a decision package. The decision unit must have well-defined and measurable objectives and clearly identifiable costs. There are two types of decision packages. The first is the mutually exclusive decision package, the purpose of which is to identify for each decision unit the alternative ways of performing its functions so as to enable management to choose the best alternative. One such alternative could be to abolish the decision unit and not to perform its functions at all. The second approach is the incremental decision package. Here, each manager identifies different levels of effort (and associated costs) and their impact on the function, ranging from the minimum level, below which it would be impossible to perform the function; a base level, which reflects the current level of activity; and an improvement level, which shows the effect of increases over the current level (Finkler, Smith, Calabrese, and Purtell 2017).

Once the decision packages have been prepared, they are ranked on a scale of 1 to a ceiling of as many levels as desired. Those with the highest score are funded, and those with a score below the available funding threshold are eliminated. To get to this point, libraries must have expertise in ZBB and decision packages, be able to quantify the cost and benefits of their operations, and be willing to expend a lot of time and effort.

Advantages of ZBB include:

- Programs and activities that are no longer valuable can be eliminated during the budget process. It makes one look at activities in a challenging way.
- Libraries are able to quickly respond to changes in the environment each year when programs and activities are reviewed.
- It requires library managers, boards, university officials, and others to question the status quo.

Limitations of ZBB include:

- The availability of budget staff to develop forms and training for ZBB is crucial. The process requires time and money that most smaller libraries can't afford.
- Increased paper work and/or online forms.
- Managers must have the necessary analytical skills and capacity to engage in ZBB analysis.
- It requires accurate cost and performance information.
- If the library is facing a large budget deficit and needs to come to a solution quickly, ZBB may not be the answer because of the time required to implement the system.

President Jimmy Carter and ZBB were a match made in heaven. Carter's engineering background, interest in quantifying every possible aspect of his presidential responsibilities, and his desire to provide the best possible government at the least possible cost made ZBB his natural choice. President Carter was a policy wonk, and ZBB fit him just like the sweaters he wore in the White House to reduce energy costs, but most libraries have neither the time, expertise, or any interest in using such a complicated system.

Forecasting

Revenue forecasting is key to budget creation. It will be reviewed in chapter 6. The amount of revenue generated by a library sets the limits on its budget.

Summary

The master budget consists of the operating budget, financial budget(s), and any other budgets as needed. It is usually built up by having each library division or department create its own separate budget. These budgets are reviewed, modified if required, and become part of the operating budget.

In preparing a budget, four main budget techniques are used ranging from the simplest to the most complex: line item, program, performance, and zero-based budgets. Some of the techniques may be combined to create a hybrid budget format. The choice of one type of budgeting technique over another is based on what the library hopes to accomplish in its budgeting process; sometimes the technique is driven by political factors.

EXERCISES

1. Describe how a library's budget relates to its vision, mission, goals, and objectives.
2. Select a library with which you are familiar, and create a budget for one of its departments or divisions. Estimate the costs of materials, personnel, and administrative items (every cost that is not personnel or materials).
3. Choose two libraries that you know, and break their budgets into the major categories of personnel, materials, and administration. Calculate the percentages assigned to each category, and explain any variances. Use the same exercise for a different type of library (academic, public, school, or special).
4. Create a budget for a special exhibit at a library you know.
5. Of the four budgeting techniques, explain which you favor and why.
6. If the library is required to cut back its budget by 15 percent, what budgeting technique will work best?
7. Consider how politics might impact the budgeting process.

References

Blazek, Jody. 1996. *Financial Planning for Nonprofit Organizations,* Wiley Nonprofit Law, Finance and Management series. New York: Wiley.

Draper, Frank, and Bernard Pitsvada. 1981. "ZBB—Looking Back After Ten Years." *Public Administration Review* 41 (1): 76–83.

Dropkin, Murray, Jim Halpin, and Bill La Touche. 2007. *The Budget-Bulding Book for Nonprofitis: A Step-by-Step Guide for Managers and Boards.* 2nd ed., Guidebook series: John Wiley and Sons, Inc.

Fabian, Chris, Jon Johnson, and Shayne Kavanagh, 2015. "The Challenges and Promise of Program Budgeting." *Government Finance Review* 31 (15): 9–12.

Finkler, Steven A., Daniel L. Smith, Thad D. Calabrese, and Roberty M. Purtell. 2017. *Financial Management for Public, Health, and Not-for-Profit Organizations.* Thousand Oaks, CA: Sage.

Jacob, Emerson, and Florence Sallinger. 1978. "Staff vs. Books in Academic Library Budgets." *Library Journal* 103 (18): 2.

Joseph, Chris. 2016. "Advantages and Disadvantages of a Line-Item Budget." http://smallbusiness.chron.com/advantages-disadvantages-lineitem-budget-25461.html.

Kavanagh, Shayne. 2012. "ZBB IS BACK!" *Public Management* (00333611) 94 (3): 14–17.

Lyons, Lucy Eleonore, and John Blosser. 2012. "An Analysis and Allocation System for Library Collections Budgets: The Comprehensive Allocation Process (CAP)." *The Journal of Academic Librarianship* 38 (5): 294–310.

Martí, Caridad. 2013. "Performance Budgeting and Accrual Budgeting." *Public Performance and Management Review* 37 (1): 33–58.

McGill, Ronald. 2001. "Performance Budgeting." *The International Journal of Public Sector Management* 14 (5): 376–90.

Morgan, Douglas, and Kent Robinson. 2002. *Handbook on Public Budgeting:* Portland State University, Hatfield School of Government, State of Oregon edition.

National Conference of State Legislatures. 2016. "Performance Based Budgeting Fact Sheet." www.ncsl.org/research/fiscal-policy/performance-based-budgeting-fact-sheet.aspx.

Neubrain. 2016. "Performance Based Budgeting: Methodology and Tools." http://docplayer.net/13920968-Performance-based-budgeting-methodology-and-tools.html.

New York Libraries: A Quarterly Devoted to the Interests of the Libraries of the State (3–4). proportions+might&source=bl&ots=g8Rm4DCLrz&sig=z2j62bPNZwI4I6iFLY-OTDgGJKY&hl=en&sa=X&ved=0ahUKEwiO5Y6o4eHXAhWj7YMKHau8Bs4Q6AEIMTAB#v=onepage&q=In%20our%20judgment%20these%20proportions%20might&f=false.

Noreen, Eric W., Peter Brewer, and Ray H. Garrison. 2008. *Managerial Accounting.* Boston: McGraw-Hill Irwin.

North Carolina Library Commission. 1910. "Apportionment of the Library Income." *North Carolina Library Bulletin* 1 (10): 123.

Rigby, Darrell K. 2015. *Management Tools 2015: An Executive's Guide.* Boston: Bain and Company, Inc.

Sarnoff, Stephanie. 2016. Schamburg (Illinois) Township District Library 2015/2016 Operating Budget.

Schaumburg Township District Library. 2016. "Financial Documents." Schaumburg Township District Library https://www.schaumburglibrary.org/financials.

Schick, Allen. 2013. "The Metamorphoses of Performance Budgeting." *OECD Journal on Budgeting* (2): 1–33. doi: 10.1787/budget-13-5jz2jw9szgs8.

Seer, G. 2000. "Special Library Financial Management: The Essentials of Library Budgeting." *The Bottom Line* 13 (4): 186–92.

Operational Changes

There have been various organizational changes reflected in the 2015/2016 budget. Following is a brief summary of these changes:

- The Popular Services Department has been renamed Fiction, Movies & Music.
- The Teen Center has been moved from the Popular Services/Fiction, Movies & Music Department to the Youth Department.
- The Youth Department now shows the Kids Zone as a separate area of the Youth Department.

The combined operating budget for the fiscal year beginning July 1, 2015 and ending June 30, 2016 totals $16,328,748. This is a 2.6% decrease from the 2014/2015 budget. The General Fund is showing a budget of $15,766,965, an increase of 2.0%. The Building & Equipment Reserve Fund is showing expenditures of $561 783, a decrease of 56.7%.

The 2015/2016 operating budget includes a 2% salary increase for employees not at the top of their salary range, and an I% increase for those employees who are at the top of their range. The budget also reflects three new part-time positions and various salary adjustments to several positions.

Combined revenues from all funds are projected at $15,540,648 for 2015/16. Therefore, there is a projected operating deficit of $788,100 for the upcoming fiscal year. There is, however, $3.9 million of fund balance expected to be on hand as of June 30, 2015 in the General Fund, plus another $6 million in the Building and Equipment Reserve Fund.

The operating budget shows the General Fund's fund balance decreasing $226,317 on revenues of $15,540,648 and expenditures of $15,766 965. Fund balance at June 30, 2016 is projected at $3,644,331, which represents 23.5% of budgeted expenditures. The fund balance benchmark set by the Board is 15% so the projected operating deficit does not push the Library into a fund balance shortfall.

Following is a summary of the operating budget by fund:

2015/2016 OPERATING BUDGET

FUND	BEGINNING FUND BALANCE	REVENUES	EXPENDITURES	SURPLUS (DEFICIT)	ENDING FUND BAL.
General	$ 3,870,648	$15,540,648	$15,766,965	$ (226,317)	$3,644,331
Building & Equipment Reserve	6,074,531	0	561,783	(561,783)	5,512,748
Working Cash	5,373,013	0	0	0	5,373,013
Total Budget	$15,318,192	$15,540,648	$16,328,748	$ (788,100)	$14,530,092

Revenues

The only fund showing revenues being projected for 2015/2016 is the General Fund. The Working Cash Fund and Building and Equipment Reserve Fund do not receive revenues, as there is a policy that all investment earnings of those two funds are recorded in the General Fund. For the 2015/2016 fiscal year, General Fund revenues are expected to total $15.5 million. This is a 1.3% increase over the current year's budget, and a 0.7% increase over the current projections for 2014/2015 budget.

The following table compares the 2015/2016 operating budget revenue projections to the prior year's budget and projected figures.

GENERAL FUND REVENUES 2015/2016

REVENUE	2014/2015 BUDGET	2014/2015 PROJECTED	2015/2016 BUDGET	PERCENT CHANGE *
Property Tax Revenue	$14,446,842	$14,517,378	$14,717,500	1.9%
Intergovernmental	255,000	268,850	266,620	4.6%
Fines & Fees	154,600	154,000	154,000	(0.4)%
Investment Income	125,000	120,000	120,000	(4.0)%
User Charges	170,600	195,650	195,700	14.7%
Miscellaneous	186,907	188,520	86,828	(53.5)%
Total Revenues	$15,338,949	$15,444,398	$15,540,648	1.3%

Percentage change represents change from prior year's budget.

Property tax revenue is expected to total $14.7 million for 2015/2016, an increase of 1.9% over the prior year. We are assuming a 1.5% increase in both the 2014 and 2015 tax levy extensions.

Intergovernmental revenues of $266,620 are 4.6% higher than the prior year's budget. The increase can be attributed to our adjusting estimated replacement tax revenue to reflect historical trends.

User charge revenue is being budgeted at $195,700, a 14.7% increase over the current year's budget. This increase is based on actual program revenue exceeding budget for the past few years.

Miscellaneous revenue is showing a 54% decrease from the current year. The primary reason for the decrease is that the final payment to be made by Bethel Baptist Church on the purchase of the old library property was made in November of 2014, resulting i n the loss of the $100,000 budgeted in FY 2014/2015.

A breakdown of a revenues can be found on pages 10 and 11 of the Operating Budget.

Expenditures

General Fund expenditures are budgeted at $15,766,965 for 2015/2016, representing an increase of $302,896, or 2.0%, over the 2014/2015 budget. Following is a table comparing the 2015/2016 budget to the budget and projected figures for 2014/2015.

GENERAL FUND EXPENDITURES 2015/2016

EXPENDITURE	2014/2015 BUDGET	2014/2015 PROJECTED	2015/2016 BUDGET	PERCENT CHANGE *
Books & Materials	$1,670,328	$1,670,328	$1,650,553	(1.3)%
Wages & Benefits	10,042,506	9,910,540	10,069,611	0.3%
Administrative Costs	3,496,339	3,472,561	3,882,141	11.0%
Other Expenses	254,896	244,896	164,660	(35.4)%
Total Expenditures	$15,464,069	$15,298,325	$15,766,965	2.0%

Percent change reflects change from 2014/2015 budget.

- The wages & benefits budget of $10,069,611 makes up more than 60% of the Library's total budget. As previously mentioned, the budget includes a 2.0% increase for employees not at the top of their salary range, and a 1.0% increase for those at the top of their range. Included in the budget are three new part-time positions, and salary adjustments for several employees.
- Administrative costs are increasing $385,802, or 11.0%, over 2014/2015. Insurance expense is increasing by $73,387 (or 54%) due to higher workers compensation premiums resulting from worse than normal workers compensation claim experience. Furniture & equipment expense of $54,639 is 62% lower than the prior year. Library program expense is budgeted at $298,015, a decrease of 11%. Repairs/Service contract expense is increasing by $26,565 due to repairs identified as being necessary this coming year. Computer operations expenditures are increasing $428,490, or 42%.

SCHAUMBURG TOWNSHIP DISTRICT LIBRARY
2015/2016 OPERATING BUDGET SUMMARY

	2012/2013 Actual	2013/2014 Actual	2014/2015 Budget	2014/2015 Projected	2015/2016 Budget	Percent Change Over 14/15 Budget
GENERAL FUND						
REVENUES						
Tax Revenue	$14,177,652	$13,488,259	$14,446,842	$14,517,378	$14,717,500	1.9%
Replacement Tax	129,598	135,819	125,000	136,620	136,620	9.3%
Grant Revenue	165,761	342,884	130,000	132,230	130,000	0.0%
Gifts, Fines and Fees	149,086	152,274	154,600	154,000	154,000	-0.4%
Investment Income	123,154	123,184	125,000	120,000	120,000	-4.0%
E-Rate Funding	19,023	51,735	55,500	55,500	55,500	0.0%
Copy Revenue	59,072	60,153	60,600	60,600	60,600	0.0%
Program Revenue	147,531	124,341	110,000	135,050	135,100	22.8%
Miscellaneous	25,991	30,008	31,490	33,103	31,328	-0.5%
Insurance Reimbursement	122,136	0			0	#DIV/0!
Mortgage Payment - Bethel Baptist	272,319	272,319	99,917	99,917	0	-100.0%
Total Revenues	**$15,391,323**	**$14,780,976**	**$15,338,949**	**$15,444,398**	**$15,540,648**	**1.3%**
EXPENDITURES						
Books - Adult	$295,763	$299,296	$294,000	$309,000	$381,700	29.8%
Reference Materials	321,259	298,339	331,525	322,525	270,750	-18.3%
Business Materials	259,830	275,211	303,000	303,000	250,500	-17.3%
Extension	154,515	191,451	232,903	224,903	227,903	-2.1%
Youth Services	89,707	189,585	171,500	171,500	184,200	7.4%
Serials	44,758	45,543	68,200	68,200	63,200	-7.3%
Popular Library Materials	240,489	247,827	266,400	266,400	267,500	0.4%
Binding	1,372	1,955	2,800	4,800	4,800	71.4%
Total Books and Materials	**$1,407,693**	**$1,549,207**	**$1,670,328**	**$1,670,328**	**$1,650,553**	**-1.2%**
Fiction, Movies & Music	$735,931	$876,044	$888,848	$888,848	$610,606	-31.3%
Administration	921,471	926,773	894,399	863,298	946,140	5.8%
Circulation	1,481,408	1,454,738	1,537,481	1,537,481	1,532,136	-0.3%
Programming and Outreach	253,895	163,499	174,896	174,896	251,271	43.7%
Virtual Branch	0	0	0	0	53,196	#DIV/0!
Maintenance	215,456	243,270	280,218	280,218	297,209	6.1%
Reference	776,842	1,024,831	1,195,575	1,195,575	1,106,227	-7.5%
Access Services	819,896	607,235	693,435	693,435	639,824	-7.7%
Youth Services	651,853	654,270	688,995	688,995	977,084	41.8%
Information Technology	492,831	462,769	426,202	426,202	448,911	5.3%
Hoffman Estates Branch	326,266	302,118	307,915	307,915	311,449	1.1%
Hanover Park Branch	318,058	346,821	391,593	391,593	385,953	-1.4%
Sunday Services	378,966	409,091	432,710	434,408	447,766	3.5%
Merit Increments	120,751	124,789	130,000	130,000	130,000	0.0%

SCHAUMBURG TOWNSHIP DISTRICT LIBRARY
2015/2016 OPERATING BUDGET SUMMARY

	2012/2013 Actual	2013/2014 Actual	2014/2015 Budget	2014/2015 Projected	2015/2016 Budget	Percent Change Over 14/15 Budget
Special Projects	4,391	4,450	24,912	24,912	19,413	-22.1%
Personnel Benefits	1,763,287	1,782,179	1,975,327	1,872,764	1,912,426	-3.2%
Total Personnel Budget	**$9,261,302**	**$9,382,877**	**$10,042,506**	**$9,910,540**	**$10,069,611**	**0.3%**
Utilities	$456,302	$474,464	$483,407	$497,747	$518,561	7.3%
Insurance	156,258	143,777	136,791	169,506	210,178	53.6%
Unemployment Claims	0	0	8,000	8,000	8,000	0.0%
Legal Fees	36,925	37,329	25,250	27,144	27,650	9.5%
Furniture & Equipment	109,220	126,934	143,850	125,666	54,639	-62.0%
Vehicles	0	21,209	0	0	0	#DIV/0!
Library Supplies	240,496	208,102	256,913	246,848	284,750	10.8%
Maintenance Services	605,349	571,981	541,798	529,918	539,588	-0.4%
Building Repairs	0	0	188,500	188,500	100,270	-46.8%
Staff Development	131,100	132,722	179,668	161,468	187,793	4.5%
Promotional Materials	115,653	104,405	111,250	108,850	110,400	-0.8%
Marketing	0	0	8,750	8,750	15,750	80.0%
Library Programs	338,810	309,264	334,070	332,295	298,015	-10.8%
Repairs/Service Contracts	10,475	41,578	46,370	45,170	72,935	57.3%
Special Projects	0	0	21,000	125,351	15,000	-28.6%
Computer Operations	529,390	769,319	1,008,122	895,348	1,436,612	42.5%
Legal Notices	2,001	1,827	2,600	2,000	2,000	-23.1%
Total Administrative	**$2,731,979**	**$2,942,911**	**$3,496,339**	**$3,472,561**	**$3,882,141**	**11.0%**
Projects	$0	$0	$0	$0	$0	#DIV/0!
Contingency	12,342	17,905	50,000	40,000	66,750	33.5%
Research & Development	0	30,324	25,000	25,000	25,000	0.0%
Capital Projects	1,147,231	21,189	0	0	0	#DIV/0!
Building Improvements	0	365,544	161,896	161,896	54,410	-66.4%
Teen Center	835,938	0	0	0	0	#DIV/0!
Art & Special Project Purchases	11,675	653	5,000	5,000	5,000	0.0%
Audit Fees	15,325	15,550	13,000	13,000	13,500	3.8%
Total Other Expenses	**$2,022,511**	**$451,165**	**$254,896**	**$244,896**	**$164,660**	**-35.4%**
Total Expenditures	**$15,423,485**	**$14,326,160**	**$15,464,069**	**$15,298,325**	**$15,766,965**	**2.0%**
Revenues Over (Under) Expenditures Before Transfers	($32,162)	$454,816	($125,120)	$146,073	($226,317)	80.9%

2

SCHAUMBURG TOWNSHIP DISTRICT LIBRARY
2015/2016 OPERATING BUDGET SUMMARY

3

	2012/2013 Actual	2013/2014 Actual	2014/2015 Budget	2014/2015 Projected	2015/2016 Budget	Percent Change Over 14/15 Budget
Transfer From Bldg & Equipt Res.	0	381,633	0	0	0	#DIV/0!
Fund Balance - July 1	2,920,288	2,888,126	3,397,105	3,724,575	3,870,648	13.9%
Fund Balance - June 30	**$2,888,126**	**$3,724,575**	**$3,271,985**	**$3,870,648**	**$3,644,331**	**11.4%**
DEBT SERVICE FUND						
REVENUES						
Tax Revenue	$528,119	$0	$0	$0	$0	#DIV/0!
Interest Income	1,051	0	0	0	0	#DIV/0!
Total Revenues	**$529,170**	**$0**	**$0**	**$0**	**$0**	**#DIV/0!**
EXPENDITURES						
Bond Principal	$1,150,000	$0	$0	$0	$0	#DIV/0!
Bond Interest	8,050	0	0	0	0	#DIV/0!
Total Expenditures	**$1,158,050**	**$0**	**$0**	**$0**	**$0**	**#DIV/0!**
Revenues Over (Under) Expenditures Before Transfers	**($628,880)**	**$0**	**$0**	**$0**	**$0**	**#DIV/0!**
Transfer to Bldg & Equipt Reserve	0	(52,547)	0	0	0	#DIV/0!
Fund Balance - July 1	681,427	52,547	0	0	0	#DIV/0!
Fund Balance - June 30	**$52,547**	**$0**	**$0**	**$0**	**$0**	**#DIV/0!**
BUILDING & EQUIPMENT SPECIAL RESERVE FUND						
REVENUES						
Investment Income	($128,937)	$50,900	$0	$0	$0	#DIV/0!
Transfer from Debt Service Fund	0	52,547	0	0	0	#DIV/0!
Total Revenues	**($128,937)**	**$103,447**	**$0**	**$0**	**$0**	**#DIV/0!**
EXPENDITURES						
Furniture & Equipment	0	0	66,185	19,185	55,703	-15.8%
Special Projects	0	0	107,268	40,952	68,500	-36.1%
Building Improvements	0	0	1,123,296	558,160	437,580	-61.0%
Transfer to General Fund	0	381,633	0	0	0	#DIV/0!
Total Expenditures	**0**	**381,633**	**1,296,749**	**618,297**	**561,783**	**-56.7%**
Revenues Over (Under) Expenditures	**($128,937)**	**($278,186)**	**($1,296,749)**	**($618,297)**	**($561,783)**	**-56.7%**

EXHIBIT 5.3: Budget Format for a Library Special Exhibition

EXHIBITION TITLE: _____ CURRENT DATE: _____

Exhibition Expenses	Amount
Assembly and Dispersal	
Insurance	
Installation	
Materials	
Signage	
Wall texts	
Conservation	
Educational Programs	
Visitors' information sheet	
Lectures	
Concerts	
Audiovisual production	
Gallery talks	
Special Fundraising Events	
Opening for sponsors	
Opening for supporters	
Reception	
Publicity and Advertising	
Paid advertising	
Photography	
Press kits	
Banners	
Brochure	
Outdoor signage	
Posters	
Catalogue	
Artist's fee and expenses	
Printing/design	
Per Diem and Travel to Openings for artist	
Honorarium for Lecturers	
Contingency	
Total Exhibition Expenses	

Exhibition income	Amount
Grants	
Sponsorships	
Admission Fees	
Catalogue Sales	
Poster Sales	
Special Fundraising Events	
Major Donor's opening	
Friends' opening	
Fund raising reception	
Educational Program Fees	
Lectures (three)	
Concerts	
Rental of equipment	
Sale of products	
Gallery talks	
Total Exhibition Income	
Exhibition Surplus/(Deficit)	

XYZ Department

Click buttons below to access budget tabs

Account	Name	Jul	Aug	Sep	Oct	Nov	Dec	Jan	Feb	Mar	Apr	May	Jun	Total	2015	2014	2013
Personnel Services																	
5000-1-1-09-01	Salaries	20,000	20,000	20,000	20,000	20,000	20,000	20,000	20,000	20,000	20,000	20,000	20,000	240,000	239,242	235,000	234,000
5000-1-1-09-04	Salaries ILL	5,100	5,100	5,100	5,100	5,100	5,100	5,100	5,100	5,100	5,100	5,100	5,100	61,200	61,340	61,240	61,100
	Total Salaries	25,100	25,100	25,100	25,100	25,100	25,100	25,100	25,100	25,100	25,100	25,100	25,100	301,200	300,582	296,240	295,100
Other																	
4100-1-1-09-01	ILL Replacements	250	250	250	250	250	250	250	250	250	250	250	250	3,000	2,575	2,435	2,345
6300-1-1-09-01	Small Furniture and Equi	0	0	0	0	500	0	0	750	0	0	0	0	1,250	1,112	1,010	1,110
6408-1-1-09-01	Supplies	1,000	1,000	1,000	1,000	1,000	1,000	1,000	1,000	1,000	1,000	1,000	1,000	12,000	12,575	15,260	13,350
6600-1-1-09-01	Staff Dev.	0	0	0	0	0	0	0	0	0	0	0	0	0	1,475	1,350	1,200
6900-1-1-09-01	Repairs	0	0	0	500	0	0	0	500	0	0	0	0	1,000	750	700	720
7003-1-1-09-01	Hardware & Peripherals	0	600	0	0	0	600	0	0	600	0	0	0	1,800	1,200	1,200	1,200
7004-1-1-09-01	Software Subscriptions	0	0	0	0	500	0	0	0	0	0	0	600	1,100	1,025	1,015	1,020
7005-1-1-09-01	Technology Consulting	0	0	0	0	0	0	0	0	0	0	0	0	0	0	0	0
	Total Other	1,250	1,850	1,250	1,750	2,250	1,850	1,250	2,500	1,850	1,250	1,250	1,850	20,150	20,712	20,535	20,945
Total Other		26,350	26,950	26,350	26,850	27,350	26,950	26,350	27,600	26,950	26,350	26,350	26,950	321,350	321,294	316,775	316,045
Grand Total XYZ Department		26,350	26,950	26,350	26,850	27,350	26,950	26,350	27,600	26,950	26,350	26,350	26,950	321,350	321,294	316,775	316,045

Buttons: Salaries | Salaries ILL | Materials | Furniture and Equipment | Supplies | Staff Development | Repairs | Hardware & Peripherals | Software | Technology Consulting

Narrative | 2015 Budget | Personnel Req Form

Schaumburg Township District Library
2015/2016 Operating Budget
Community Engagement Department

Account Number	Account Description	2012/2013 Actual	2013/2014 Actual	2014/2015 Budget	2014/2015 Projected	2015/2016 Budget	Percent Change
1104-01	**Programming & Outreach**						
	Personnel Services						
5000-1-1-04-00	Salaries	$253,895	$163,499	$174,896	$174,896	$251,271	43.7%
5001-1-1-04-00	Sunday Hours	1,297	1,870	2,125	2,125	3,006	41.5%
5003-1-1-04-00	Special Projects	0	172	1,272	1,272	0	-100.0%
		255,192	165,541	178,293	178,293	254,277	42.6%
	Other						
4300-1-1-04	Extension Materials	4,245	21,729	35,250	30,250	33,250	-5.7%
4350-1-1-04	Literacy Materials	14,396	11,725	18,653	15,653	15,653	-16.1%
6300-1-1-04	Furniture & Equipment	2,830	0	0	0	1,850	#DIV/0!
6600-1-1-04	Staff Development	1,729	152	2,500	700	5,000	100.0%
6802-1-1-04	Programs-Literacy	4,166	4,189	4,600	4,600	5,250	14.1%
6803-1-1-04	Programs-Outreach	9,231	7,369	9,000	9,000	7,800	-13.3%
6804-1-1-04	Programs-Adult	158,332	139,647	133,225	135,000	162,400	21.9%
7003-1-1-04	Computer Hardware	0	0	1,100	206	3,400	209.1%
7004-1-1-04	Service Contracts	0	0	1,550	1,550	2,000	29.0%
7006-1-1-04	Software	0	0	0	0	472	#DIV/0!
	Total Programming & Outreach	450,121	350,352	384,171	375,252	491,002	27.8%
12	**Hoffman Estates Branch**						
	Personnel Services						
5000-1-2-04-00	Salaries	$326,266	$302,118	$307,915	$307,915	$311,449	1.1%
5001-1-2-04-00	Sunday Hours	2,430	1,553	1,918	1,918	1,957	2.0%
5003-1-2-04-00	Special Projects	0	0	1,272	1,272	1,080	-15.1%
	Total Salaries	328,696	303,671	311,105	311,105	314,486	1.1%
	Other						
4300-1-2	Materials	67,908	81,079	89,500	89,500	89,500	0.0%
6000-1-2	Utilities	31,220	36,579	37,848	36,793	38,602	2.0%
6300-1-2	Furniture & Equipment	10,345	11,036	14,900	13,950	1,350	-90.9%
6500-1-2	Maintenance Services	42,453	35,898	79,321	73,731	78,081	-1.6%
6600-1-2	Staff Development	912	674	3,000	1,800	2,800	-6.7%
6900-1-2	Repairs/Service Contracts	0	0	0	0	15,000	#DIV/0!
7003-1-2	Computer Hardware	0	16,737	7,540	4,040	29,104	286.0%
7004-1-2	Service Contracts	0	3,750	7,646	7,646	9,345	22.2%
8305-1-2	Building Improvements	0	7,394	0	0	18,300	#DIV/0!
	Total Hoffman Estates Branch	481,534	496,818	550,860	538,565	596,759	8.3%

6

Revenue Sources

Learning Objectives of This Chapter Are to:

☐ Identify the alternative sources of library revenue.

☐ Recognize that tax funding is the primary source of funding for all types of libraries.

☐ Review the process that is used in different types of libraries to distribute tax revenue from the parent organization to the library.

☐ Examine some alternative sources of revenue including philanthropy, fines and fees, rental of space, and sale of library items.

☐ Understand that most of the populace supports libraries because they are a public good that enhance the education and enjoyment of society.

Chapter 5 discussed alternative budget strategies. This chapter reviews the revenue side of the budget equation. Although revenues were mentioned in the previous chapter, they were viewed as part of the budget equation where revenues = expenditures. According to the *Business Dictionary*, "revenues are the income generated from sale of goods or services, or any other use of capital or assets, associated with the main operations of an organization before any costs or expenses are deducted. Revenue is shown usually as the top item in an income (profit and loss) statement from which all charges, costs, and expenses are subtracted to arrive at net income" (Business Dictionary 2016).

For almost all libraries, whether academic, public, or school, revenues come from the parent institution. Special library expenditures are part of the overall organizational budget. Consider a special library that is part of an advertising agency. Library expenditures in the ad agency are balanced against the funding requirements of the other parts of the agency, and the needs and priority of the ad agency determine revenue. Although most libraries are part of a larger organization, be it a university, city, or school district, their revenues often meander from the parent organization to the library. This is the case with San Diego State University (SDSU), where the amount allocated by the California Legislature to the California State University System determines the amount received by the provost's office at SDSU. The provost decides what revenue the SDSU Library will receive. A few libraries have their own taxing authority, as is the case with the Schaumburg Township District Library; the revenues flow from the taxpayers, to the county clerk, to the special district.

No matter what other revenue sources are employed, most revenue for all types of libraries is generated by the parent organization.

Tax-Supported Academic Libraries

Although tight budgets and downsizing have impacted organizations of all kinds, public and some private universities must deal with the expectations of stakeholders (who could include the entire population of a state). Stakeholders have reasonable demands, such as transparency about how tax dollars are spent, and perhaps less reasonable demands, such as unfettered access to university property.

For some academic libraries, tuition and fees generate a significant portion of revenue. A public university, for example, is in great part supported by the taxpayers of its state, but the university also charges tuition and fees and sells products through its bookstore and tickets to artistic and athletic venues. Some of that income indirectly helps support the library.

From the 1960s through early 1990s, the California State University System "was largely funded by the State's General Fund. This enabled the university to keep tuition fees at a very low amount because most of the system's operating costs were covered by the state. In the 1990s, the state's investment in the CSU began to lag behind the amount needed to fund enrollment growth, operating costs and capital improvements. Today, the system's funding is a partnership between the state, students and their families" (CSU 2016).

Because universities are public institutions, they operate under a decentralized management structure as revenues and expenses for each division are assigned to the respective units or cost center. The costs that can't be directly assigned in a division, such as central administration, operations, student services, libraries, and auxiliary operations, are distributed to cost centers on an allocation basis. Allocation bases are created from a variety of metrics using statistical information or effort studies (Hofmann 2010).

The total allocation for libraries is the annual operating budget that includes salaries, materials, and everything else, which we will categorize as administration. Capital budgets will be reviewed later in this chapter and in chapter 7.

The process may work this way. During the annual budget process, the university's central budget office requests the library to submit a line-item budget for annual operation. The operating budget seldom sets out long-range strategies; it usually deals with the quantitative allocation of people and resources. The budget coordinates the various activities of the library, with a formula mostly guided from the university's central budget office. Most of the line items in the budget are decided on an incremental basis from prior years' actual spending, keeping in mind inflationary increases. In some cases, zero-based budgeting requires department heads to start from ground zero and redefine activities in terms of library goals. The major appeal of zero-based budgeting is that it questions each activity and determines whether it should be increased, maintained, reduced, or eliminated. Alternative budget strategies were discussed in the previous chapter.

Changes in demographics and technology will set new directions for the library over the next few decades. The digitization of unique library collections and the growth of mobile internet devices will require a larger share of resources. Budget resources will shift to user-driven collections and electronic subscription renewals, and libraries will continue expanding their virtual resources. Libraries will move more collections online and get deeply involved in social networks and course-management systems. Physical library buildings will be redesigned as student workspaces. Some libraries have already begun the process by devoting space to academic support services such as writing and media centers. However, achieving a balanced budget that serves all clientele continues to be a challenge for the library administration. Nevertheless, creating a positive climate by expressing real needs and benefits associated with university goals could be a winning argument.

An example of the changes taking place may be illustrated by the author's experience in researching topics for this book. I rarely went into the physical library, but rather accessed collections and resources on an almost daily basis from my home or office using the SDSU library's excellent and easy to use electronic resources. Materials that were not available in the SDSU Library collection were quickly acquired through electronic interlibrary loan and delivered to me via e-mail.

Another trend in university library budgets is to consider outsourcing of services and facilities. A sizable university fund can be used efficiently with an effective spending plan. Libraries today are outsourcing services, negotiating rates with technology vendors, entering service level agreements (SLAs) for things like computer maintenance, software updates, and server maintenance. Operating lease agreements are used to rent buildings or property somewhere nearby for short or long periods of time, for uses such as a library annex, which include infrequently used materials. During the lease period, libraries make monthly rent payments and pay other expenses such as heat, utilities, and security. The landlord is usually responsible for regular wear and tear, snow removal, and landscaping. Libraries have an opportunity to sublease vacant sections of the building (if expressed in the contract) to other local libraries, which can offset some portion of the leasing cost. Capital leasing is somewhat more complex because the risk of ownership is transferable to the lessee, that is, the library may be required to purchase equipment at the end of the lease period either at the regular price, a discounted price, or below the fair market value of the asset. Another arrangement could be to transfer the ownership of an asset on a minimum $1 payment after the end of the lease period. The asset sale and leaseback decisions are decided prior to finalizing a leasing agreement. Lease payments are typically taken from operating budgets. It is also important to determine the present value of the payment schedule to decide whether to purchase the assets after the leasing period, and to determine annual depreciation on the assets. (Rauf 2011)

Another example to illustrate this budget process is the University of Hawaii at Hilo.

> The University Librarian and staff meet to discuss budget priorities. The Director confers with the Head of Technical Services and the Library Secretary before finalizing the budget. The Director confers with the Vice Chancellor for Academic Affairs to request funding. Funding is received in one lump sum.
>
> Funds for student workers are negotiated with the Vice Chancellor for Student Affairs. Student workers are used to support every functional and service area of the Library, including weekend and evening hours.
>
> The addition of new programs requires the library to acquire additional resources (e.g., journals and books) to support these programs. Historically, the library has not received additional funds when new academic programs are added. For the first time, two years ago, the library received a one-time $14,000 budget to support the master's program in Education. The Library receives no system wide funds. It both lends and borrows books and resource materials within the system campuses for students, faculty, and staff. (UH Hilo Faculty Congress 2016)

The budget process at SDSU closely follows the processes described above, with budgeted funds proceeding from the California Legislature to the CSU System to the SDSU provost. who allocates funding for the library. As discussed earlier, The SDSU Library seems to be always moving spaces, adjusting seating, and adding and enhancing technology to meet the ever-changing needs of students (CSU 2016).

Privately Supported Academic Libraries

Oberlin College is a four-year, highly selective liberal arts college and conservatory of music in Ohio. Founded in 1833 by a Presbyterian minister and a missionary, it holds a distinguished place among American colleges and universities. The college has an annual operating budget (FY 2015) of $155.4 million and an annual capital budget of $14.6 million. Oberlin is heavily dependent on tuition and fees as a percent of total revenues (Oberlin College and Conservatory 2014).

The Oberlin College Libraries held 2,481,513 items in 2013. The total library budget in 2013 was $6,823,398, with materials totaling $2,618,328 of the budget to serve its 2,900 students. This budget is approximately four percent of the college's total operating budget (Oberlin College and Conservatory 2016).

The Oberlin libraries' budget is determined by the college because the libraries are part of the operating expenses of the institution. Funds are derived through different forms of gifts and giving from a variety of donors. The libraries' associate director operates as the unit budget manager and partners with the library director and other department heads to determine the appropriate allocations of the budget within the libraries. At this point, the internal control mechanisms for the libraries' budget process are under review and evolving. The collection development librarian, associate director and director continuously monitor the materials portion of the budget. Salaries are addressed on an annualized basis in partnership with the institution.

It is the goal of the director, Alexia Hudson-Ward, "to empower her staff to take 'ownership' of certain portions of the budget for things such as professional development, programming, and outreach." In order to accomplish this, she is providing additional training and support for staff to manage their budgetary allocations (Hudson-Ward 2016).

Tax-Supported Public Libraries

The first tax-supported public library in the United States is the Peterborough Town Library in New Hampshire, which was founded at a town meeting on April 9, 1833. No real answer has ever answered the question of why the citizens of Peterborough would tax themselves to pay for library service.

> In January of 1833 a group of farmers and small manufacturers under the leadership of the Rev. Abiel Abbot formed a social library whose shares sold at two dollars and whose annual membership fee was fifty cents. On April 9 of the same year, the town, apparently under the inspiration of the same Rev. Abbot, voted to set aside for the purchase of books a portion of the state bank tax, which was distributed among New Hampshire towns for library purposes. This was the way the first American town library to be continuously supported over a period of years was begun. (Nix 2008)

There are over 9,000 public libraries in the USA, almost all of which are financed through taxes (ALA 2016). Most libraries receive their share of tax support through their parent organization, whether it is a city, town, or county. This is the case of the Chula Vista Public Library (CVPL), which is a department of the city of Chula Vista.

Taxes are the way that governments finance the services that citizens want and need, and for most people libraries are a desirable public service. "Taxes come in a variety of types including income taxes, payroll taxes, property taxes, sales taxes, user fees and gambling revenue. However, the major revenue sources used by governments—income taxes, property taxes, and sales taxes—are used in large part because the number and value of taxable events or the value of the base are so large, and therefore have the potential to generate so much income" (Lee, Johnson, and Joyce 2013, 233). The library's parent institution receives taxes from at least one and usually a combination of these taxes.

One of the questions that citizens have about taxes is whether they provide vertical equity, (i.e., treating taxpayers differently). Vertical equity is measured by computing the effective tax rate, which is computed by dividing the tax paid by a given individual by some measure of wealth or income. There are three possible outcomes; a given tax may be:

- progressive, if effective tax rates are higher for higher-income taxpayers than for lower-income taxpayers
- proportional, if effective tax rates are essentially the same across different income categories
- regressive, if lower-income taxpayers experience higher effective tax rates than higher-income taxpayers (Lee, Johnson, and Joyce 2013, 136–37)

Of the three main sources of governmental revenues used to finance libraries, income taxes are generally viewed as progressive, because the tax increases as income rises. Property taxes may be considered proportional, or maybe progressive, because generally higher income people will own and pay taxes on more expensive properties. Sales taxes are regressive because both higher and lower income tax payers pay the same amount per dollar spent. Sales tax rates are established at the local or state level. They are easy to calculate—if the local rate is 6 percent for every dollar spent, the tax on a $100 purchase is $6. Some states exempt certain purchases such as food or medicine from taxation. Local income tax rates (state or municipality) are set by the local governmental jurisdiction and follow a sliding schedule with the tax rate increasing as income rises.

Of the three major sources of revenue, the one that is most difficult to understand is property tax. Property tax is difficult to understand because the process varies from county to county across the USA, and difficult to calculate because the calculation requires some arithmetic. An example from the assessor in Douglas County, Colorado, explains the property tax process in that county.

Statute provides that the actual value of property is not the taxable value. Rather, the taxable value is a percentage of the actual value. The percentage is called an "assessment rate," and the resulting value is called the "assessed value." The assessment rate is 29 percent for all properties except residential. The residential assessment rate is established by the legislature every odd-numbered year. It has remained at 7.96 percent since 2007. The intent of having the ability to change the residential assessment rate is to maintain the tax burden balance between residential properties and all other property types.

Property taxes are calculated by multiplying the mill levy or tax rate by the assessed or taxable value of an individual's property. Keep in mind that tax rates are not finalized until December of each year and are subject to change. An example for a residential property illustrates the process:

The actual value of Mr. Brown's home is $300,000. The Notice of Valuation shows the current assessment percentage is 7.96 percent.

Actual Value × Assessment Percentage = Assessed Value $ 300,000.
Actual Value x 7.96 percent Assessment Percentage = $ 23,880 Assessed Value

To determine the property tax, multiply the assessed value times the decimal equivalent of the total mill levy. A mill is equal to 1/1000 of a dollar. A tax rate is the mill levy expressed as a percentage. Thus 98.42 mills = 9.842 percent or .09842 as the decimal equivalent.

If Mr. Brown's assessed value is $23,880, his taxes will be:

Assessed Value x Mill Levy = Taxes $ 23,880
Assessed Value x .09842 Mill Levy = $ 2,350.27 Taxes

(Douglas County Assessor 2016)

In addition to property, income, and sales taxes, there are some more unusual taxes that help finance public libraries. Since 1835 penal fine income in Michigan has been reserved for the support of public libraries, which is distributed to public libraries by county treasurers. The amount is determined yearly based on population and local laws. In the past problems have arisen because funds have been retained to cover "court costs," with only the remaining funds being considered penal fine income. In certain areas of the state, 100 percent of court receipts have gone to court costs, leaving no penal fine income for libraries. Another problem with the system is that each county has its own policy on court costs and fines collected and distributed by county. Counties are required by law to distribute penal fines before August 1 of each year. Most counties make annual payments, although there are a few counties that distribute monthly, quarterly, or semiannually (Library of Michigan 2016).

Why do American citizens support public libraries with their tax dollars, volunteer hours, and gifts? In 2008, OCLC issued a report trying to explain the phenomena of citizen library support, and provide suggestions for successfully winning a library campaign to increase support for the library.

Library funding behavior is driven by attitudes and beliefs, not by demographics. Voters' perceptions of the role the library plays in their lives and in their communities are more important determinants of their willingness to increase funding than their age, gender, race, political affiliation, life stage or income level. The more that can be learned about library perceptions, the better the chances of constructing a successful library support campaign to improve library funding.

Eight key insights that try to explain citizen voter support are:

1. Most people claim they would support the library at the ballot box—fewer are firmly committed to it.

2. There is a lot that people don't know about their public libraries.

3. Library support is only marginally related to visitation. Advocating for library support to library users focuses effort and energy on the wrong target group.

4. Perceptions of the librarian are highly related to support. Passionate librarians involved in the community make a difference.

5. The library occupies a very clear position in people's minds as a provider of practical answers and information. This is a very crowded space, and to remain relevant in today's information landscape, repositioning will be required.

6. Belief that the library is a transformational force in people's lives is directly related to their level of funding support.

7. Increasing support for libraries may not necessarily mean a trade-off with financial support for other public services.

8. Elected officials are supportive of the library—but not fully committed to increasing funding. Engaging Super Supporters and Probable Supporters to help elevate library funding needs is required. (De-Rosa and Johnson 2008, 4-1).

Tax-supported public libraries, whether special districts or part of a larger governmental authority, occasionally may decide to place a taxation measure before voters to increase support for their libraries.

John Chrastka, Executive Director of EveryLibrary, explores a range of innovative options to energize, focus, and improve library advocacy efforts while learning how to put proven techniques that political campaigns use to reach voters to work (Chrastka 2016).

District Libraries

District public libraries are also tax supported, but they are their own taxing authority (as is the case with the Schaumburg Township District Library, as was discussed earlier).

New York State has allowed the creation of independent public library districts since 1835. By 1999, 154 such districts had been created in the state, representing approximately 20 percent of all of New York's public libraries. New York's public libraries are heavily dependent on local tax support; in 2010, more than two-thirds of the state's public libraries received more than 75 percent of their funding from local taxes according to a study by Elliott, which found that libraries that submit their budgets to the voters do indeed have more predict-able budgets. Throughout the course of the ten-year study, district libraries in New York were much less likely to have either a year in which their budgets were cut or a year in which they saw no increase at all. Although overall increase in local public funding did not grow more dramatically for the district libraries than it did for other types, the rela-tive stability in budget numbers is an advantage to library boards and directors working to plan future projects. The frequent fluctuations in public funds experienced by pub-lic and association libraries inhibit multiyear planning and are a source of considerable stress. In this area the district library model shows a clear advantage. District libraries did not, however, show higher per capita funding. Overall growth in funding during the ten-year period was just below the average for all types combined. District libraries appear to be no more likely than the average library to increase funding over the long term, despite their less frequent budget cuts. While a gain in budget stability may be sufficient to con-vince a library to pursue conversion to the public library district model, an anticipated growth in annual public funding should not be a major consideration. (Elliott 2013, 135).

New York State has three types of public library districts, which the State Library describes each as follows:

1. *School District Public Library*

   A School District Public Library is created by passage of a referendum placed on the school district ballot. A petition signed by 25 qualified voters within the school district is necessary to put up the proposition for a vote. School Dis-trict Public Libraries have service areas that coincide with the school districts in which they are located, and voters within the school district determine the library's budget and trustees.

   School District Public Libraries are totally independent of the school district. Once the library has been established, the library board has the authority to sched-ule a vote on a library budget each year. If the proposition to fund a school dis-trict public library passes, the school district must collect the tax money and pay the funds to the library. Because they are public entities, School District Public Libraries are subject to civil service and public procurement laws and regulations.

2. *Special Legislative District Public Library*

   The vote to create a Special Legislative District Public Library is authorized by state legislation. A state legislator introduces a bill specifying the service area of the library and authorizing a public vote to create the library, elect trustees, and establish a budget. Once the state legislation is passed, an election is scheduled within the municipality to select trustees and approve the initial library budget. ...The municipality collects taxes on behalf of the library and turns the funds over to the library board, which is completely autonomous. If the new special Legislative District Public Library is replacing an existing library, the existing library transfers assets to the new library and surrenders its charter to the Board of Regents.

3. *Association Library District*

This model is available to libraries currently chartered as association libraries that do not want to relinquish their "private" status by re-chartering as a school district public library or a special legislative district public library.

Although an association library district is not a public entity, the library can emulate the basic characteristics of a public library district by providing a process for

a. public election of its trustees;
b. the library to secure 60 percent or more of its operating revenue through a public budget vote; and
c. the library to ensure financial accountability by presenting annually to appropriate funding agencies, and the public, a written budget that would enable the library to meet or exceed the minimum standards and to carry out its long-range plan of service (New York State Library 2016).

Fines and Fees

Most public and college libraries collect fines, which is usually part of their circulation policies toward maintaining collections by getting materials back on time. When one library customer keeps a book beyond the due date, there may be another customer who is inconvenienced by waiting longer for it. The rationale for fines is that they allow materials to be readily available for borrowers by encouraging the greatest possible access for the most people. The threat of paying a fee discourages a person for keeping materials for an "unreasonable" amount of time. However, fines for overdue materials have been controversial in libraries. Many libraries have eliminated overdue fees (especially for children), and some libraries hold amnesty periods where all fees are forgiven if the materials are returned. Library literature is full of examples of libraries that have eliminated fees or forgiven them. Librarians have debated fines for overdue materials without reaching a conclusion as to whether they are beneficial or harmful in the long run (Gres and Hicklin 1999).

For most libraries, fines and fees do not generate a significant amount of revenue. For example, fines in the Schaumburg Township District Library (STDL) total $104,000 in a $15- million-dollar budget. The reason for overdue fines is to get materials back.

Some libraries hold an "amnesty period" where people can return materials and have part or all of their fines forgiven. Most libraries schedule this around National Library Week, or during a special local event like the opening of a new library or start of a new service. Taking the opposite approach, some libraries employ collection agencies to encourage scofflaws to return their materials and pay their fines.

Many libraries charge fees for the rental of spaces within the library building. The San Diego Public Library (SDPL) charges fees for the use of its 350-seat (5,000 square feet) Neil Morgan Auditorium. The room is a state-of-the-art theater and performance space with floor-to-ceiling folding glass doors expanding into the outdoor courtyard. Eight-hour rentals of the space for commercial groups are $3,600 a day and $2,800 for nonprofit organizations. The SDPL has six meeting rooms in its new main library, many of which are booked a year in advance for weddings and other special events (City of San Diego 2016).

Many fees collected by colleges and universities trickle down to the library as part of their budget grants from the parent institution.

Philanthropy

Charitable contributions are becoming a major source of revenue for many nonprofit organizations including libraries. According to Giving USA, total charitable giving in the United States reached more than $373.25 billion in 2015, the highest in history. Of that amount, 71 percent came from individuals. The rest of the philanthropic pie consisted of foundation grants (16 percent), bequests (9 percent), and corporate philanthropy (5 percent) (Giving USA 2016).

Libraries have enthusiastically endorsed philanthropy as a revenue source to offset sometimes declining budgets. In general, a number of different approaches may be taken. In addition to seeking support from a variety of sources, a library fund-raising program should find both ongoing financial support and episodic support. Libraries also enter into capital campaigns.

Ongoing Support

Ongoing support usually comes via:

- *An Annual Fund.* Funds from annual (or more frequent) appeals to a core group of constituents are usually unrestricted and may represent a significant percentage of annual income. Their unrestricted nature makes them attractive because of their flexibility of use.
- *Sales of Products and Services.* Some nonprofits own stores or provide services that generate a substantial income stream. Earned income must be related to the mission of the organization or it can be taxed as unrelated business income. Gift shops that sell products associated with the library are found in many public and academic libraries. The Salt Lake City Public Library, as well as a number of others, have rented out space in their buildings as an income source. Another library that has leased space is the Nampa (Idaho) Library. Library Square is a mixed-use project in the heart of historic downtown Nampa that features the three-story, 62,000-square-foot Nampa Public Library, 13,267 square feet of Class A office and retail space, a 300 parking-stall garage, and a scenic public plaza with a water feature and park (Gardner Company 2016).
- *Multiyear Grants.* A grant-giving organization such as a foundation may provide restricted funding for a particular project or program, or for unrestricted funding to help cover the overhead costs of running the organization.

- *Endowment Income.* Many libraries build up large endowment funds that produce interest that is used to support their programs.
- *Planned Giving.* Many libraries now have planned giving programs that help donors to include the library in their wills and estate planning. The charitable gift annuity has become popular among donors because it allows many tax advantages while providing income during the donor's lifetime.
- *Episodic Funding.* This can come from foundation or corporate grants, special events, or bequests. These funds may be restricted to one purpose or devoted to unrestricted use by the nonprofit (National Resource Center and Paul Edwards 2010).

Capital Campaigns

A capital campaign is a time-limited effort by a nonprofit organization to raise significant dollars for a particular project, such as

- funding a new building
- raising funds for a specific project, such as a book endowment or a new automation system
- increasing a particular asset, such as an endowment

Capital campaigns have defined beginning and end dates, and often span several years. A capital campaign employs all the usual means of raising funds, including as direct mail and direct solicitation. Capital campaigns require extraordinary preparation and skillful execution, and will be covered in more detail in chapter 7.

College and Research Library Philanthropy

Latour conducted a survey of college and research library philanthropy for the Association of College & Research Libraries. Library directors were surveyed at 600 randomly selected colleges and universities, proportionally stratified by Carnegie Foundation research level, and classified as being baccalaureate-granting colleges or above. Usable responses were received from 517 institutions, or 86.1 percent of the libraries in the sample.

> Fund-raising is engaged in by approximately two-thirds of all academic libraries. They do so primarily because of a desire to supplement their budgets in order to deal with the increased costs of materials and equipment. Fund-raising requires a significant commitment of staff time and resources. In about 70 percent of the cases the efforts are successful, but that also leaves approximately 30 percent of the cases that are not successful. Libraries pursue fund-raising because of a shortage of resources, yet they must make a substantial commitment of resources to fund-raising efforts in order to be successful.
>
> There are no magic formulas for fund-raising success. Local conditions are a major determinant of what may or may not be the most appropriate fund-raising techniques and methods to employ. The data collected in this research makes it abundantly clear that research level institutions are significantly different in their fund-raising efforts (and

many of their other operations) than most other types of academic libraries. Yet, the fund-raising literature pertaining to academic libraries often describes the experiences of major research libraries. There is a dearth of literature that pertains to fund-raising activities at other types of academic libraries. The data contained in the comprehensive report of this research is of particular value to these other types of libraries. (Latour 2016)

Whitchurch and Comer published a case study of philanthropy at the University of Utah, Salt Lake City. When the library's external relations director retired in 2014, the Marriott Library's new dean used this opportunity to move library fund-raising in a new direction. The dean changed the position's duties when hiring a new development director to change the culture of development at the Marriott Library by not only working closely with library faculty and staff but also through making them partners in all aspects of development work. Although the new program has only been in place for a little more than a year, positive outcomes are emerging, including a more engaged staff, better served donors, and an increase in donations to the library including a multimillion-dollar gift for a major renovation as well as a $3.5 million gift of rare materials (Whitchurch and Comer 2016).

Public Library Philanthropy

Peet wrote of the changing nature of funding for public libraries,

> State and even federal funding are also subject to the inconsistencies of a shifting political landscape, and libraries have yet to secure a permanent place at the table when it comes to budget-making decisions at either level. Grants from private organizations interested in promoting libraries and cultural institutions—or the positive impact libraries can deliver—can be a great source of money for pilot programs, but these funds are finite in scope and unlikely to be available for long-term sustainable support. Increasingly, libraries need to be their own best advocates across all sectors to put together a winning mix. (Peet 2016b, 42)

A number of foundations, including the Bill and Melinda Gates Foundation, the John S. and James L. Knight Foundation, the John D. and Catherine T. MacArthur Foundation, and the Alfred P. Sloan Foundation have supported libraries in the past, and while their support is much appreciated, it has not been a significant percentage of the public library's operation budget. Reporting from the LJ's Directors' Summit held in November 2015, Peet concluded that

> money from foundations comes with its own limitation: the challenge of sustainability. Grant periods expire, funds run out, and major players can shift their focus—for instance, after nearly two decades of supporting library capacity building worldwide, the Gates Foundation is in the process of winding down its Global Libraries program. Despite what sound like impressive numbers, philanthropic organizations still account for a relatively small percentage of total library funding—IMLS reports that in FY12 only 8.2 percent of

revenue came from sources other than local, state, and federal government, including donations. (Peet 2016b, 43–44)

Local Public Library Philanthropy

Many public libraries raise money through a number of sources. According to Peet,

> fundraising efforts are commonly distributed among Friends of the library, the foundation, and the development office. Not all libraries have all three, however, and the distribution of responsibilities varies. Usually the Friends is an all-volunteer group that takes charge of used book sales and other events, while the foundation is a nonprofit with its own board. An in-house development office can take on other roles, or coordinate the efforts of all three entities. There are as many variations as there are libraries. Sharing the labor can be efficient, but efforts must be made to ensure that tasks are distributed appropriately and not duplicated. (Peet 2016a)

Foundations and Grants

IMLS conducted a survey in 2015 that highlights the contributions that State Library Administrative Agencies (SLAAs) make in the development of library services across the country. One of the most substantial findings of this report is

> The continued decline in total revenues to SLAAs. This decline coincides with the Great Recession and has continued through FY 2014. In FY 2014, total SLAA revenues equaled $1.1 billion, coming from federal, state, and other revenue sources; this total represents a 17 percent decrease in federal revenue, an 11 percent increase in state revenue, and a 13 percent decrease in other revenues when compared with FY 2004. Yet, the pattern may be changing, as total revenues increased by 5 percent from FY 2012 to FY 2014. Total expenditures across the fifty states and the District of Columbia equaled approximately $1 billion in FY 2014. These included $688 million for financial assistance to libraries and $345 million for operating expenditures. Expenditures closely followed the trend of declining total revenues between FY 2004 and FY 2014. (IMLS 2016).

Public libraries of all sizes have asked their communities to support them in their roles as institutions that are universally loved and admired, an effort at which most libraries succeed. Self-advocacy to the community needs to be ongoing.

Other Revenue Opportunities

Some libraries provide revenue-generating services to their communities that are a potential source of growth in the future. Identifying how to adapt and package the resources of the library, both human and materials, has the potential to be an attractive and lucrative source of revenue.

Summary

Revenue to support academic, public, and special libraries comes primarily from their parent institutions. In the case of public and publicly supported academic libraries, most revenue is tax-generated and delivered through the parent institution.

Although other revenue opportunities including philanthropy, fees, rental space, and other sources contribute, in the end it is tax dollars that support libraries because the vast majority of citizens believe they are a public good that requires public support. Funding through tax dollars will most likely continue into the future, although some of the alternative revenue alternative may grow in importance.

EXERCISES

1. Select a library you know and construct a diagram tracking the flow of revenue from the tax authority to the library.

2. Find a library that is adept at philanthropy, describe its program, and explain why it succeeds.

3. Interview the director of a library foundation and find out what is included in her job duties, the successes and challenges that the foundation faces, and how the foundation interacts with library administration. Are there conflicts between the foundation and the library?

4. Identify a library that had a referendum to increase its operating (not capital) income pass. Why was the referendum successful?

5. Find information on a library that had a referendum to increase its operating (not capital) income fail. Why didn't the referendum pass?

6. Visit a "library store" and list the categories of products and services it sells. Is operation of the store outsourced or does the library manage it? What revenue does the store generate for the library and what percentage of the library's income come from store revenue?

7. Consider opportunities to develop library-based revenue-generating consulting services that might be sold to local governments, businesses, or individuals? Identify what those programs might be, and identify libraries that have such programs and review their success.

References

American Library Association. 2016. "ALA Library Fact Sheet 1." www.ala.org/tools/libfactsheets/alalibraryfactsheet01.

Business Dictionary. 2016. "Revenue." www.businessdictionary.com/definition/revenue.html.

California State University. 2016. "CSU Budget Central." http://blogs.calstate.edu/budgetcentral/.

Chrastka, John. 2016. "EveryLibrary." http://everylibrary.org/.

City of San Diego. 2016. "Special Event Space Rentals." https://www.sandiego.gov/public-library/specialevents/auditorium.

De-Rosa, Cathy, and Jenny Johnson. 2008. *From Awareness to Funding: A Study of Library Support in America*. Dublin, OH: OCLC.

Douglas County [Colorado] Assessor. 2016. "Property Tax Calculations." www.douglas.co.us/assessor/property-taxes/property-tax-calculations/.

Elliott, Mara. 2013. " Impact of the Public Library District Model on Local Funding of Public Libraries in New York State." *Public Library Quarterly* 32 (2): 124–37. doi: 10.1080/01616846.2013.788940.

Gardner Company. 2016. Library Square. http://gardnercompany.net/portfolio-item/library -square/.

Giving USA. 2016. "See the Numbers—'Giving USA 2016' Infographic." https://givingusa.org/see-the-numbers-giving-usa-2016-infographic/.

Gres, Dusty, and Karen Hicklin. 1999. "To Fine or Not to Fine." *American Libraries* 30 (8): 75.

Hofmann, Mark A. 2010. "Public Universities Cope with Budget Demands." *Business Insurance* 44 (23): 14.

Hudson-Ward, Alexia. 2016. Oberlin College and Conservatory Budget.

Institute of Museum and Library Services. 2016. State Library Administrative Agencies Survey Fiscal Year 2014. Washington, DC: The Institute of Museum and Library Services. https://www.imls.gov/publications/state-library-administrative-agencies-survey-fiscal-year-2014.

Latour, Terry S. 2016. "Fund Raising Activities at Colleges and Universities in the United States." Association of College & Research Libraries. www.ala.org/acrl/publications/whitepapers/nashville/latour.

Lee, Robert D., Ronald W. Johnson, and Philip G. Joyce. 2013. *Public Budgeting Systems*. 9th ed.: Jones and Bartlett Learning.

Library of Michigan. 2016. "Penal Fines." www.michigan.gov/documents/mde/lm_2010_Penal FinesandPublicLibrariesfinal_348778_7.pdf.

National Resource Center. 2010. Building Multiple Revenue Sources. Washington, DC: US Department of Health and Human Services. http://strengtheningnonprofits.org/resources/guidebooks/BuildingMultipleRevenueSources.pdf.

New York State Library. 2016. "Public Library Districts: An Introduction." www.nysl.nysed.gov/libdev/libs/pldtools/.

Nix, Larry T. 2008. "The Peterborough Town Library: The Oldest Free Public Library in the World Supported by Taxation." www.libraryhistorybuff.org/peterborough.htm.

Oberlin College and Conservatory. 2014. "Strategic Planning Student Session." https://docs .google.com/viewer?a=v&pid=sites&srcid=b2Jlcmxpbi51ZHV8c3R1ZGVudHNlbm FoZXxneDozN2Q1ZjRlYmQzYjdkNGM3.

———. 2016. "Selected Library Statistics." www.oberlin.edu/library/statistics.html.

Peet, Lisa. 2016a. "360° Fund Raising." *Libary Journal* 141 (8): 32–34.

———. 2016b. "The New Fundraising Landscape." *Libary Journal* 141 (1): 42–45.

Rauf, Tahir. 2011. "The Art and Science of Managing a University Library Budget." *University Business* (October). https://www.universitybusiness.com/article/art-and-science-managing -university-library-budget.

University of Hawaii, Hilo Faculty Congress. 2016. "Library Budget Preparation Process." https://hilo.hawaii.edu/uhh/congress/committee_budgetproc_lib.php.

Whitchurch, Jesse, and Alberta Comer. 2016. "Creating a Culture of Philanthropy." *Bottom Line: Managing Library Finances* 29 (2): 114–22. doi: 10.1108/BL-02-2016-0012.

7

Capital Budgets

Learning Objectives of This Chapter Are to:

☐ Understand the differences between an operating and a capital budget.

☐ Recognize the reasons for undertaking a capital improvement project.

☐ Review four different investment analysis techniques relating to the time value of money that could be used to evaluate a capital project.

☐ List the steps in planning a capital project.

☐ Identify the alternative financing mechanisms available to fund a capital project.

☐ Apply capital budgeting techniques to the planning of a new university library branch.

Capital Budgeting

Capital budgeting describes how organizations and their managers plan significant investments in projects that have long-term implications, such as the purchase of a new library computer system, a multiyear digitalization of a special collection requiring additional staff and equipment, an addition to an existing building, or the construction of a new library building. The difference between a library's operating budget and the capital budget is time determined. Most library operating budgets are tied to either a calendar or fiscal year, and in many cases the fiscal year and the calendar year may be the same. Capital budgets, on the other hand, are used to acquire assets that last longer than one year, and usually involve the expenditure of significant funds (Shapiro 2005, 2). For example, a library may have an operating budget of $10 million a year, and a one-time capital budget to plan and build a new library building that may exceed $100 million.

There are several reasons to use a separate capital budget.

- The budget expenditure will be enjoyed by the library for a long time. Some capital projects may last for more than twenty years. For example, a well-planned library building that is designed to be flexible and expandable can last for fifty years or longer.
- The initial cost is high and may exceed many years of spending for the library's operating budget.
- Justifying the expenditure requires examining the benefits of the outlay over the entire life of the asset acquired.

Capital Budgeting Decisions

Because a capital project requires the expenditure of a significant amount of resources, several decisions must be made before a library can proceed. The first question that should be asked is why the library is considering a major expenditure. Capital budgeting decisions can be either screening or preference decisions. Screening decisions relate to whether a proposed project is acceptable: does it meet the needs that the library has identified? For example, the library may consider purchasing a materials-handling system if it results in the elimination of four positions, which is the payback criteria set for purchasing the system. Preference decisions involve selecting from several acceptable alternatives. Preferences may be determined by which vendors provide the features that the library desires in its materials-handling decision (Noreen, Brewer, and Garrison 2008, 548).

Some of the issues to consider before financing a capital expenditure may include:

- Should the library undertake the capital project? Is there any reason that the existing building, circulation system, or other capital project being considered should not be replaced at this time? Reasons for not moving forward may be a lack of resources or a poor political climate.

- Will the project reduce operating costs? Examples of this include a new automated bibliographic control system to reduce staff personnel costs, or a materials handling system to reduce costs of returning books and media to their storage locations.
- Is there need for physical expansion? For example, a university library may undertake expansion to service a new or increased customer base. San Diego State University (SDSU) may build new facilities approximately five miles away from the existing campus on land once occupied by the San Diego Charger's stadium, and the remote academic facilities may require space for an on-site library service. Or perhaps a public library in a growing community may need another branch to serve the population in the new community areas.
- What type of financial model should be used to acquire the new capital facility or equipment? Should it be purchased or leased? Leasing does not require an immediate capital investment, but it adds significantly to the library's annual budget expenditure. Leasing may be the only alternative if the need for the capital good is high and the prospects for funding the expenditure are low. Sometimes a contract may be created that results in a lease arrangement that turns to ownership after several years.

Capital Budgeting in the Profit and Nonprofit Sectors

In the private sector, capital budgeting decisions are based on expending resources today in the hope of realizing future profits. Examples may include opening a new retail store, building a new manufacturing plant, or launching a new product. Hopefully, all these current expenditures will create cash flows in the future when the capital project comes online. Capital budgeting compares current cash outflows against future cash inflows. A discount rate is the interest rate that is used to convert future dollars to their present values. Although libraries are nonprofit organizations, there may be reasons to borrow some of the financing techniques used in private sector capital budgeting. A short review of some of the concepts follows.

Investment decisions in capital projects recognize the time value of money when evaluating where to make capital expenditures. The time value of money means that a dollar today is worth a dollar tomorrow, because that dollar can be placed in a bank and return more than its current value (excluding inflation or deflation). The further in the future an amount is paid, the less value it has today. Capital budgeting techniques recognize the time value of money through analysis that uses discounted cash flows. Discounted cash flow shows comparisons of amounts of money paid at different points of time by discounting all amounts to the present—the time value of money. To determine whether a capital project will produce the desired cash flows, net present value is calculated to determine whether the capital project is an acceptable investment.

Four different investment analysis techniques may be used to evaluate a capital project, all of which relate to the time value of money (Finkler, Smith, Calabrese, and Purtell 2017).

Net Present Value (NPV)

The present value of a series of receipts less the present value of a series of payments. The present value of a project's cash inflows is compared to the present value of the project's cash outflows. The difference between the present value of these cash values is the net present value.

Internal Rate of Return (IRR)

A discounted cash-flow technique that calculates the rate of return earned on a specific project or program.

Net Present Cost

The aggregate present value of a series of payments to be made in the future.

Annualized Cost

An approach used to compare capital assets with different lifetimes. The net present cost for each alternative is determined and then translated into a periodic payment for each year of the asset's life to find the cost per year.

Microsoft Excel has two functions that can be extremely valuable in capital budgeting and make the financial calculations easier. One is the NPV function, the other is the IRR function. The NPV function, which Excel refers to as the "Net Present Value" function, computes the present value of a series of periodic cash flows that are not necessarily the same amount each period. The IRR function computes the internal rate of return of an investment project (Mason 2011)

Estimating Capital Needs

For libraries, the largest capital project is usually the construction, expansion, or major renovation of a library building. If their useful life and cost extend beyond the current fiscal year, acquisitions of automated library or materials handling systems, or digitization conversion projects, would also qualify as capital projects.

In planning any type of capital project, libraries should:

1. Identify needs by inventorying existing facilities and services to determine if a capital project may be required. Are existing library services and facilities inadequate to meet existing needs or inefficient? Have there been changes to

the environment, such as population changes, regulatory requirements, economic changes, service goals? Any of these factors may require a new capital project.

2. Recognize changes to the library's service goals. These may require a capital project to meet the new service goals.

3. Determine the financial resources required to finance the capital project. Sources of financing may include the parent institution, a ballot measure, a loan, a foundation grant, gift, development fees.

4. Develop a multiyear capital investment plan to fund the capital projects.

5. Identify future recurrent costs that will result from the capital project and their impact on operating budget.

Financing Capital Projects

Chapter 6 was a review of revenue sources required to finance library operations, some of which may also be used to finance a capital project. However, the cost of capital projects is so large that as rule, a special source of money must be identified to pay for capital projects.

Bond Issues

Most public library capital projects are financed through bond measure elections. The National Conference of State Legislatures publishes a database of elections from 1892 to the present that may be searched by year and state. It is a good idea to obtain a summary of recent and past ballot measures that have passed or failed.

For example, this is an entry for New Mexico for 2016:

> Bond Issue—Libraries   Bond Question B
> Election: General—2016
>   Type: Legislative Referendum
>   Status: Pass (Yes votes: 64.8 percent unofficial)
>   Topic Areas: Bond Measures | Education: Higher Ed | Education: PreK-12....

The 2016 Capital Projects General Obligation Bond Act authorizes the issuance and sale of library acquisition bonds. Shall the state be authorized to issue general obligation bonds in an amount not to exceed ten million one hundred sixty-seven thousand dollars ($10,167,000) to make capital expenditures for academic, public school, tribal, and public library resource acquisitions and provide for a general property tax imposition and levy for the payment of principal of, interest on and expenses incurred in connection with the issuance of the bonds and the collection of the tax as permitted by law? (Underhill 2015)

The nonprofit organization EveryLibrary has had success acting as a campaign strategist and consultant to public, school, and academic libraries planning ballot measures. Every-Library describes its role as follows:

> [EveryLibrary] is the first and only national organization dedicated to building voter support for libraries. We are chartered "to promote public, school, and college librar-ies, including by advocating in support of public funding for libraries and building pub-lic awareness of public funding initiatives." Our primary work is to support local public libraries when they have a referendum or measure on the ballot. We do this in three ways: by training library staff, trustees, and volunteers to plan and run effective Information Only campaigns; by assisting local Vote Yes committees on planning and executing Get Out the Vote work for their library's measure; and by speaking directly to the public about the value and relevance of libraries and librarians. Our focus on activating voters on Election Day is unique in the library advocacy ecosystem. This is reflected in the train-ing and coaching we do for campaigns.
>
> In each election cycle, tens of millions of dollars are at stake for libraries. From bond-ing for new or remodeled building projects to changing millages, levies, or taxes that impact staffing, collections, programs, and services, libraries are on the ballot. Every-Library helps libraries:
>
> - Assist libraries in both the pre-filing and campaign stages of an initiative.
> - Provide strategic consulting services, voter segmentation advice, and assistance in developing ballot language.
> - Conduct feasibility studies and assist in setting up a local committee PAC.
> - Develop a fund-raising strategy for your local committee or PAC.
> - Train volunteers in voter education and get-out-the-vote techniques.
>
> During the run of a campaign, EveryLibrary
>
> - Continues technical and capacity-building consultancy.
> - Provides direct financial support to the local committee or PAC in seed-stage or sustaining levels of support.
> - Conducts direct voter education and get-out-the-vote efforts. (Chrastka 2016)

Not all agree that a new building is the best path to excellence in library service. Coff-man has suggested that libraries consider doing away with the physical library building and create an Amazon-type model where the library would deliver information online directly to the user. He points out industries where buildings have been replaced by online delivery of services, including banking and travel, and have thrived, and he asks, why not libraries? In such a case the capital project would be the acquisition of a robust information technology system for the library and databases to serve the target popula-tion (Coffman 2006, 30).

Funding from the Parent Institution

Many academic libraries are funded by their parent institutions. That was the case with the original construction and expansion of San Diego State University's Love Library and the original University of California San Diego Geisel Library, both of which were built with state funds. However, many academic libraries also have been the beneficiaries of donations to build the entire library or a significant portion of it. La Jolla resident Audrey Geisel donated $20 million to the UCSD library, in addition to her 1991 donation of $2.3 million worth of her husband Theodor Seuss Geisel's original works. In exchange, the library was renamed Geisel Library (Perry 1995).

Foundation Grants

Foundation grants may also be used to fund a portion of the costs of a capital project. The Foundation Center offers Foundation Maps, an interactive tool that displays library grant information. The Center's Visualizing Funding for Libraries data tool shows information on funders, grant recipients, and grants through a variety of filters. With millions of grants from 2006 to the present, innovative ways to visualize funding data, and the flexibility and precision to tailor research, these resources help funders and nonprofits access the knowledge they need to make strategic decisions and strengthen their impact.

For example, the map tool shows that the Greater Kansas City Community Foundation made a grant of $33,263,457 to the Kansas City Public Library in 2009. Using the interactive map, searches may be made using the following filters:

- *Map View* displays yellow bubbles for grant recipients and magenta bubbles for funders. Click a bubble for more details.
- *List View* lets you see and sort funders, grant recipients, and grants in a table format. Click on an organization name or details icon for more information.
- *Advanced Search* allows you to apply more filters to your search criteria.
- *Charts* analyzes aggregate funding data by library type. Click on a point in the trend line to view a grants list for that year.
- *Pathways* reveals direct links between funders and their grant recipients. Click on the pathways link between two organizations to see grants between the Kansas City Community Foundation and the Kansas City Public Library. Double-click on an organization bar to see funding flows that start with that organization.
- *Constellations* demonstrates a broader view of organization networks. The names of the top ten organizations most central or closest to your organization appear by default. Hover over the bubbles to see the names of other organizations. Click on a bubble for more details. Drag any of the bubbles to reposition them on your screen. Click on the curved lines to reveal a grants list between two connected organizations.

- *US Demographics* add a rich dimension to the maps, demonstrating the need for funding in a region or subject area. Select a location in the United States and click on the tab in the lower right corner of the map to select a demographic. For custom locations, select the polygon in the lower right corner and draw a shape of the area for which you'd like to see demographic data (Foundation Center 2017).

The Foundation Center offers extensive training in how to use the interactive map through regional workshops, webinars, and self-paced e-learning courses.

Developer Fees

As part of the requirements for developing a new area or community, local governments sometimes require developers to pay a development fee to pay for infrastructure needed to service the new development. Infrastructure may include roads, utilities, parks, and so on.

An example of a public library project funded through development fees is the City of San Diego's new 18,000-square-foot Pacific Highlands Ranch branch library facility, located on a three-acre site in Pacific Highlands Ranch. It will serve the entire North City Future Urbanizing Area (NCFUA). This project will provide branch library service to the NCFUA for future development and population and will serve four City of San Diego communities. Construction is scheduled to begin in FY 2020 and be completed in FY 2021.The capital project cost is $18,500,000. It is recognized that the new branch will have a future cost on the operating budget and will require an ongoing operational budget for personnel and non-personnel expenses. Estimates of the operating budget impact will be developed as the project progresses (City of San Diego 2016, 164).

Most capital projects are financed through a combination of options, including allocations from the parent organization, philanthropy, grants, bond measures, and developer fees.

Estimating Capital Budgets for Library Buildings

Using buildings as an example, budgets for capital projects include several subcategories including (Leighton and Weber 2000, 335):

1. The basic structure itself, including finishes and fixed equipment.
2. Electrical, mechanical, and data installations, including elevators, fire protection, security system; heating, ventilation, and air conditioning; and telecommunications.
3. Furniture and movable equipment.
4. Site development, including utility connections, grading, parking lots, landscape work, and any necessary site remediation.
5. Architectural, construction management, and other fees of consultants.
6. Administrative costs.

Case Study—New Library Branch for San Diego State University

For purpose of this exercise, the assumption is that the capital project under consideration is a new library building for a branch library for SDSU at a new campus in Mission Valley. This case study is now hypothetical, but the need may arise in the future because SDSU's existing campus has reached its maximum capacity. With the departure of the San Diego Chargers, there has been a movement to open an auxiliary campus at the Chargers' former Qualcomm site. The assumptions made in the analysis are the author's alone. The case below is pure conjecture, based on the possibility of what might happen, and why. The same analysis procedures used for SDSU could apply to other projects as well.

What Factors Drive the Need for a New Library Building?

Many factors drive the need for a new building. For example, the population served by the library may have increased, resulting in a need for more space to service the new users. Or the population may have shifted, and the existing library is not in the best location to service the new geographic areas. Perhaps the building cannot accommodate the technology required to serve users. Maybe the building has some structural or environmental conditions that make moving to a new building a necessity. These are just a few of the countless reasons why a new building may be necessary. For SDSU, the reason for a new library building is to accommodate an additional 10,000-student population at the proposed Qualcomm satellite campus:

> Breaking a long silence, San Diego State President Elliot Hirshman on Tuesday endorsed turning the Qualcomm Stadium property into a new 166-acre campus. "Let's dream as a community, knowing that the opportunity to advance the future of our university is before us," Hirshman said in a blog post issued by his office. Hirshman said SDSU can't support its current programs on 225-acre Montezuma, where the university has been located since the 1930s. (Showley 2016)

The tentative plans for the Qualcomm site include:

- 3,900 student apartments
- 400 faculty housing units
- A 200-room hotel
- 630,000 square feet of academic and campus space
- 200,000 square feet of commercial office space (which might be marketed to high-tech companies linked to campus research)
- 40 acres of open space including the San Diego River Park

The existing SDSU Library Malcolm A. Love Library, opened in 1971 and was expanded in 1996 through state funding, and is the primary academic library building on the campus.

The Library is in a central position on the SDSU campus, occupies more than 500,000 square feet, seats more than 3,000 people, and circulates more than 500,000 books yearly. It has more than 2.2 million volumes, 4.6 million microform items, and 140,000 maps. The operating budget for FY 2015/16 was $11.5 million (SDSU Library 2016).

If the proposed Qualcomm site is developed, SDSU will require a library branch at the new site to service the academic departments and students who will be located at the site. The assumption is that the existing library will not be able to serve the new academic space effectively and efficiently due to the increased student and faculty population and because the two campuses will be three miles apart.

Student enrollment today is approximately 35,000 students. With the new campus, student population will grow to 45,000 students.

Who Will Be Served?

Because a library building can last for approximately fifty years, it must be planned to accommodate changes in technology, products and services offered, customer needs and wants, and potential growth or shrinkage of the population served. Estimating all these factors requires good information—and sometimes a lively imagination.

For SDSU, the following assumptions are made on the needs of the population that will use the Qualcomm site.

- The student and faculty population will be 10,000. Although many of these people will reside on the site, many others will travel there from the main campus or from other areas of San Diego, because the site is served by a light rail system that is two stops away from the main campus; there is also excellent freeway access.
- Two colleges will move to the new campus: the Fowler College of Business Administration and the College of Sciences. These colleges will serve the mission of the auxiliary campus as sites for high-tech companies and research.
- Based on the ratio of number of students to square feet of the existing library space (500,000/35,000 = 14.29 square feet per student), the new facility is planned to be approximately 125,000 to 150,000 square feet (10,000 students × 14.29 square feet per student = 142,999 square feet). This calculation is simplistic for several reasons, among which are that it is projecting existing square feet of a main library for a branch, and the two colleges selected for the site may not use library facilities in the same way as do other colleges. ACRL does not provide metrics on square footage per student, nor any quantitative measures for estimating the size of library buildings. The movement has been away from these types of standards and towards service needs. But the quantitative measure calculated above is the key number in planning a budget for the proposed library building at the Qualcomm site. It is only an estimate, but an estimate needed to complete the analysis. The square footage of the building determines most of the costs required to build the library.

- Another method for calculating the size of the proposed building is to "program" the needs of all the potential users, calculate space requirements based on those needs, and total the results. For example, the library will need space for a certain number of readers and 25 square feet is required for each reading space, and for books, media, and other aspects of library space.
- Once a general size is determined, it is helpful to establish a benchmarking set of similarly sized libraries to compare costs and library characteristics. A set consisting of five to ten similar libraries is optimum. However, for the sake of simplicity, only one library will be in the benchmarking set: the Tidewater Community College/City of Virginia Beach Joint Use Library, which is 125,000 gross square feet.

The financing of the SDSU branch library may be complex. Usually a California State University library building is funded by the State of California. Because the Qualcomm site is a development project, funding may come from a variety of sources, including private donations, developer funds, and the state. All the funding options will develop over the next few years if the project proceeds.

The Tidewater Community College/City of Virginia Beach Public Library (TCC/VBPL), which is being benchmarked against the proposed SDSU branch, had a total project budget of $41,756,598 for its 125,000-square-foot building. The construction cost per square foot for the library was $202.23, and the land cost was $3,264,959. Furniture, fixtures, and equipment cost was $9,400,000 (Tidewater CC 2014). Construction costs vary considerably around the United States as well as on the state of the economy and regional labor conditions. If there are many construction projects, prices will be higher because construction companies become a scarce resource.

Table 7.1 shows the assumptions on the costs to build a 150,000-square-foot branch library for SDSU at the Qualcomm site. The costs are estimates based on the author's experience.

The estimates given in table 7.1, a best guess of what will be required to build the new SDSU branch, are based on several assumptions that may not hold. But because it is a planning tool, this type of estimate does not require complete accuracy. The estimate is the information that staff would present to decision-makers when they ask how much will it cost to provide library facilities to the new campus. It uses the best information currently available, and may be refined as the project evolves. One reality check is to look at costs for the TCC/VBPL library that was completed a few years ago. Although the TCC/VBPL totaled almost $42 million as opposed to the $62 million for the SDSU branch, the SDSU branch library has 25,000 more square feet, is on much more expensive land, has higher construction costs per square foot based on local labor conditions, and includes $5 million for a startup collection. Altogether, it seems that the estimate is the best that can be made now and will provide the information decision-makers need to estimate the cost for building the branch.

TABLE 7.1

Cost Assumptions for Branch Library

FACTOR	MEASURE	COST	COMMENTS
Design Fees	Fee to architect and architect's sub-consultants	$500,000	Related to the size of project to some extent but it is a negotiated fee
Engineering, Design & Construction Fees	Project management fee paid to a construction manager	$750,000	Work may be done by a project management company or SDSU staff. Most likely an outside company for a project this size, and fee is negotiable.
Land	5 acre site	$5,400,000	Total site size is 166 acres and estimated land value is $180,000,000 or $1,080,000/acre (National University System Institute for Policy Research 2015, 2)
Construction Cost per Square Foot	$225/square foot	$33,750,000	Includes site improvements and construction. Based on conversations with San Diego contractors
Furniture, Fixtures and Equipment	Estimated at $80/square foot	$12,000,000	Based on comparison to costs paid by TCC/VBPL. Should not be influenced greatly by regional factors
Telecommunications and Data Processing	Based to some extent by the size of the building	$500,000	Estimate made by reviewing costs of other libraries.
Public Art	Required as part of public buildings in California	$250,000	May sometimes be based on a percentage of construction costs
Books & Media	Library will have no materials to transfer from the existing library	$5,000,000	Startup collection for new library
Contingency	Requires tight control during design and construction	$4,000,000	Approximately 10% of construction costs
Total		$62,150,000	

Few construction projects go from start to finish without a change order being issued, and while often necessary, they are the fastest way to increase the costs of a new library building. Funding for change orders and additions is part of the contingency item in the budget above. According to Glazov (2011)

> A Change Order is a technical term for an amendment to a construction contract. When you hear Change Order, think contract amendment. Why? Because a Change Order is a bilateral agreement between parties to the contract—an owner and prime contractor, prime contractor and subcontractor, two or more subcontractors—to change the contract. A Change Order represents the mutual consensus between the parties on a change to the work, the price, the schedule, or some other term of the contract. And, because it represents a mutual consensus, a Change Order is usually the best, and least controversial, way to make changes.

It is recommended that during their interviews, both the architect and the construction manager candidates are asked about their history of change orders. Often a change order results from construction documents that are poorly designed, and although change orders are necessary because conditions change, excessive change orders may greatly increase building project costs. Usually a contingency of 10 percent of construction costs will cover any required or desired changes in a project.

Selection of the architect and construction manager should not be based primarily on price. The best architects have the skills and temperament of an artist and the analytic ability of a scientist. If your library will require working with the architect during the three or four years of design and construction, and the facility will last for up to fifty years, selection should be based on who is the best, most creative person for the job. The fees of the most talented architects are not that much higher than what is charged by an average performer. The same holds for selecting construction managers.

A capital acquisition may have an impact on the library's operating budget. If the capital project is a new library building, or a significant addition to an existing building, additional staff may be needed to staff the increased space. A library may reduce the number of staff required by carefully planning the proposed expansion. For example, the 150,000-square-foot SDSU branch would probably require more staff if the floor sizes were either excessively small or large. A two-story building of 75,000 square feet would require as many staff service points as would a ten-story building of 15,000 square feet. The optimum size for a building with the fewest service points might be four or five-stories. At that size, only one or at the most two service points would be required to service and supervise an entire floor. Minimizing the number of service points to reduce the need for additional staff requires careful planning on the part of the library staff and an accomplished architect to translate service needs into space.

Summary

Capital budgeting is different than the library's operating budget. A library's operating budget may be considered a tactical decision because, if it needs adjusting, it may often be changed during the budget cycle and if needed during the next budget year. Capital expenditures are strategic decisions insofar as they will last a long time, and once the capital acquisition is made a library will use the asset for up to fifty years.

Funding for capital expenditures usually comes out of a separate fund rather than the library's operating budget. Just as in a household budget, the ongoing expenditures for food, clothing, and medicine are budgeted out of current income. But if an expensive item like a house or car is needed and cannot be afforded from current income, the desired asset is usually financed through long-term financing or debt.

The sources of capital funding also vary. The expenditure may be financed through a ballot measure, an allocation from the legislature, grants, philanthropy, development fees, and sometimes a combination of these sources.

EXERCISES

1. Select a library you are familiar with and identify a capital project that you believe the library will need completed during the next five years.

2. Justify the reasons for the capital budget. What impact will it have on improving library services.

3. For the library selected, list at least three possible sources of revenue to finance the capital project. List the advantages and disadvantages of each alternative revenue source.

4. Create a budget for the capital project you selected, and list all the major costs and how the cost estimates were determined.

5. List the approvals that will be required for your capital project to be approved.

6. Estimate any increases or decreases in the library's operating budget resulting from the new capital project.

7. Select three different libraries that have launched capital projects in the last five years, and find an example of capital funding from:

    a. The parent institution, as was the case for SDSU.

    b. A bond measure, information about which can be found by searching the National Conference of State Legislatures' database of elections from 1892 to the present.

    c. Grant funding using the Foundation Center's Visualizing Funding for Libraries data tool.

    d. Developer fees to finance a library as part of a development agreement with a local government entity.

References

Chrastka, John. 2016. "EveryLibrary." http://everylibrary.org/.

City of San Diego. 2016. Fiscal Year 2017 Adopted Budget. San Diego, CA: City of San Diego.

Coffman, Steve. 2006. "Building a New Foundation: Library Funding." *Searcher* 14 (1): 26–34.

Finkler, Steven A., Daniel L. Smith, Thad D. Calabrese, and Roberty M. Purtell. 2017. *Financial Management for Public, Health, and Not-for-Profit Organizations.* Thousand Oaks, CA: Sage.

Foundation Center. 2017. "Visualizing Funding for Libraries." http://libraries.foundationcenter .org/training/.

Glazov, Joshua. 2011. "Construction Contracts: Top 10 Terms—Changes (Change Orders)." www.constructionlawtoday.com/2011/01/construction-contracts-top-10-terms-changes -change-orders/.

Leighton, Philip D., and David C. Weber. 2000. *Planning Academic and Research Library Facilities.* 3rd ed. Chicago: American Library Association.

Mason, John O., Jr. 2011. "Using the NPV and IRR Functions as Capital Budgeting Techniques with Microsoft Excel." *International Research Journal of Applied Finance* 2 (3): 326–36.

National University System Institute for Policy Research. 2015. Analysis of Citizens' Stadium Advisory Group's (CSAG) Recommendations. www.nusinstitute.org/assets/resources/ pageResources/NUSIPR_CSAG_Analysis.pdf.

Noreen, Eric W., Peter Brewer, and Ray H. Garrison. 2008. *Managerial Accounting.* Boston: McGraw-Hill Irwin.

Perry, Tony. 1995. "Dr. Seuss' Widow Gives Over $10 Million to UCSD." *Los Angeles Times,* September 26.

San Diego State University Library. 2016. "SDSU Library." http://library.sdsu.edu/about-us.

Shapiro, Alan C. 2005. *Capital Budgeting and Investment Analysis.* Upper Saddle River, NJ: Pearson Prentice Hall.

Showley, Roger. 2016. "SDSU Endorses 'West Campus' Concept for Qualcomm Stadium Site." *San Diego Union-Tribune* (April 5). www.sandiegouniontribune.com/business/growth -development/sdut-sdsu-qualcomm-redevelopment-2016apr05-htmlstory.html.

Tidewater Community College/City of Virginia Beach. 2014. News Release. "Academic Form for *Library Journal*'s 2014 Architectural Issue."

Underhill, Wendy. 2015. "Ballot Measures Database." National Conference of State Legislatures. www.ncsl.org/research/elections-and-campaigns/ballot-measures-database.aspx.

8

Budget Approval and Control

Learning Objectives of This Chapter Are to:

- [ ] Understand how a budget is submitted for approval by the library's parent organization.

- [ ] Recognize the components included in a budget submittal.

- [ ] Demonstrate how to communicate the finished budget to the parent organization, and become familiar with some questions that may be asked by the parent authority.

- [ ] Know the timing of budget approval.

- [ ] Understand what budgetary control is and the various types of control that a library may use.

- [ ] Identify some of the financial documents that help a library control its budget, the value of financial dashboards, and how budgets may be modified based on information gathered during the fiscal year.

- [ ] Appreciate the role that an auditor plays in the control process.

- [ ] Identify deviant behavior that may have a financial impact on the library.

Budget Submittal, Approval, and Communication

The final step in the budget process is to get the budget submitted, approved, and communicated to internal and external stakeholders. The steps in this process will be reviewed and applied to the three libraries that have been used as case studies.

Budget Submittal

As described in previous chapters, budget preparation is a collaborative process involving library staff and often representatives from the parent organization. For example, at a university that is part of a statewide system, the library dean brings together all the staff who have input to the budget to review all or some portion of the library's budget. One of the people involved may be the serials librarian, who reports to the assistant library dean. She will work with her staff to determine what the serials budget needs are for the next fiscal year and present the results to the assistant dean, who in turn meets with the dean and the library's fiscal officer to submit the university's proposed budget. The information from the serials librarian and other library staff is integrated into the total library budget. The budget may be reviewed and approved by the provost and sent to the chancellor's office to be reviewed and approved.

When preparing a library's budget submittal, a budget document is usually sent on to the library's approving authority. This document may be distributed to other interested parties after the parent authority has an opportunity to review it. The budget document may consist of a letter of transmittal that acts as the cover letter for the budget document that briefly summarizes major budget highlights such as new programs and changes to existing programs and services. It also should include a summary of the total income and expenses contained in the budget.

Generally, the budget submittal may be broken into sections that may include:

- A total organization-wide budget summary that addresses income by individual sources and a listing of the library's total expenses broken into broad categories.
- Detailed organization-wide, line-item expense budgets. Line expenses are specific individual expenses such as labor or materials. The line-item budget presents detailed information about what the budget contains; after the budget is approved, it gives managers an exact indication of the resources available.
- Program, unit, or activity budget (PUAB) summary budget. The PUAB might be a division or program of the library (e.g., technical services or circulation). Included for each PUAB should be a statement of the purpose of the program, goals and objectives for the budget year, a summary of income and expenses along with comparisons to the previous year, and a narrative summary of programmatic changes from the previous year.
- Line-item budgets for each PUAB. These individual budgets should highlight major fiscal and program changes to allow budget reviewers to understand the implications for the specific programs and services provided.

Other items that may be included in the budget submittal might be a glossary of terms used in the proposed budget, a summary of major financial and policy issues addressed by the budget, goals and assumptions used in developing the budget, and a schedule and description of the budgeting process. A discussion of how the budget will help the library reach its long-range goals and objectives and a table or the library's organizational structure including head count for each PUAB. Graphics and readability are key to helping the budget be understood by decision-makers and eventually be approved (Dropkin, Halpin, and La Touche 2007, 107–12)

Budget Communication

For the budget to be approved it must be communicated to the library's decision-makers, whether they be a public library administrative board, a public library's city council, the university's administration, or whoever makes the final decision for the parent organization concerning the amount of the budget and what programs and activities are included.

ALA's Advocacy University's web page recommends a six-step budget presentation process that includes laying the groundwork, preparing a budget presentation, gaining citizen support, a list of dos and don'ts for making the presentation, follow-up, and budgeting best practices. This site provides excellent information about budget communication aimed primarily at a public library audience (ALA 2017)

When communicating the budget to decision-makers, several questions should be addressed:

1. Has the budget increased or decreased over the last budget, and if so, why? This is the question that is of prime interest to a decision-making audience.
2. How does the budget fit into the library's strategic plan? The budget plan's rationale for enabling the library to achieve its goals and objectives should be positive, specific, and phrased in the future tense. This step is the recommendation and an explanation of what the budget will achieve.
3. Why is this budget plan recommended? Make the plan's rationale clear, rather than forcing decision-makers to sift through muddled details to determine the ultimate purpose of the budget and why programs and services were selected for funding.
4. Will the budget help the library achieve important goals that it has set? Explain what will happen if the budget is approved and how the budget will help meet the shared goals of all stakeholders.
5. What are the risks that must be considered? "What if" questions may include what will happen if revenues are not as robust as forecast, or what will occur if unexpected expenses occur.

If part of the process includes a live presentation to a public library board or an academic library committee, visual aids are highly recommended. Most speakers will require some sort of visual aid to hold the audience's attention and to explain a complicated concept. One problem with visual presentations is that their audiences may often experience "death by PowerPoint." To create a presentation that will help explain and sell your budget, several points should be kept in mind. First know why you are making the presentation. Is it to inform your audience or to get budget approval, or both? The visuals should be organized so that they guide the audience through the budget presentation in a logical sequence of slides. Because people can pay attention to only a few pieces of information at one time, slides should not be overloaded with a lot of hard-to-read statistics. Budgets are difficult to explain because they use figures, and most people are not as adept at understanding numbers as they are in understanding text. Finally, a dual form of presentation should be employed (e.g., such as the slides and a handout). A budget handout for the Sacramento Public Library is included as **exhibit 8.1** (Davis 2015).

In selecting a communication medium to communicate with your audience, some methods are more effective than others. One thing to consider is information richness, which is the potential information carrying capacity of a communication channel, and the extent to which it facilitates developing a common understanding between people. Usually an interactive presentation is the richest tool for communicating with an audience, whereas a numerical budget has the lowest richness. A presentation to a board or approving body should have a high degree of communication richness to allow an interactive dialogue between the staff presenting the budget and the reviewing body. A face-to-face presentation has the benefit of reading body language and nonverbal communication. Relationships and trust can be built during a convincing budget presentation to decision-makers (Baldwin, Bommmer, and Rubin 2013, 178–79).

During the budget presentation, you may be asked questions related to the budget, which presents an opportunity to explain and promote the budget. Be prepared to answer questions such as these:

- Can you help me understand what this means?
- Is this a trend or pattern that we should talk about?
- Is this unexpected?
- How did you decide to add this new program and/or service to the budget?
- What programs and/or services are not included in the budget that you believe would be beneficial to the library?
- What will the benefits to the library be if the budget is approved?
- Even though this is an annual budget, are there long-term financial commitments that we should know about that might impact future budgets?

You can be certain that if one person asks a question, she isn't the only person who wants to know the answer. Questions mean that your audience is paying attention and cares about the information you are presenting (Barr 2015).

Once the budget is approved, it is vital that the entire staff know what is contained in the budget and what it means to the operations of the library. This may take place in department meetings or an all-staff meeting. Consider an all-in-one employee engagement platform to disseminate budget information to all library staff and internal stake-holders. The library's budget may use this type of engagement platform to communicate library goals and explain how the budget will help achieve them, as well as serving as a source of ongoing information for library staff. Although this type of system may be developed internally, systems may also be purchased from companies like SmartHub (www.rewardgateway.com/smarthub-employee-engagement-platform) that can be cus-tomized to meet the communication needs of the library to internal stakeholders. It is important for library employees to be engaged in the budget process.

The approved budget can be communicated to the public served by the library using the library's website, e-mail lists, blogs, and podcasts; print materials such as posters, handouts and giveaways; events like orientation tours and workshops; and other tools such as library publications, contests, brochures, and direct mail. All these tools will not only communicate the approved budget but also promote the library's services and resources. The library's customers and other stakeholders need to understand the budget to trust and support the library.

Budget Approval

For operating budgets in both academic and public libraries, budget approval comes from the parent authority whether the regents of the state university system or the city council of a municipality. All budgets go through several reviews and steps before final approval is received.

For San Diego State University (SDSU), the state board of regents receives the budget, approves it, and sends it back to the California State University Chancellor's Office and back to San Diego State University for implementation. After the library receives the budget from the provost, it becomes the library's approved budget.

For the Schaumburg Township District Library (STDL), the budget is approved when the Board of Library Trustees votes on the budget. The resolution that the board used to approve the budget follows.:

> I do further certify that the deliberations of the members of said Board of Library Trust-ees of Schaumburg Township District Library on the adoption of said ordinance were taken openly; that said meeting was held at a specified time and place convenient to the public, that the vote on the adoption of said ordinance was taken openly; that notice of said meeting was duly given to all newspapers, radio or television stations and other news media requesting such notice; and that said meeting was called and held in strict accordance with the provisions of "An Act in Relation to Meetings," approved July 11, 1957, as amended, and that said Board of Library Trustees has complied with all of the applicable provisions of said Act and its procedural rules in the adoption of said ordi-nance. IN WITNESS THEREOF, I hereunto affix my official signature and the seal of said Schaumburg Township District Library this 21st day of the month of September in the year 2015 (STDL 2015)

In Chula Vista, the city manager is responsible for preparing the city budget, in which the Chula Vista Public Library (CVPL) is included. In FY 2016/17, the process was summarized as follows: "The City Manager sends a budget message to the city council for the council's approval and on June 7, 2016 the city council held a public hearing and adopted the fiscal year 2016–17 budget. The adopted budget includes a General Fund operating budget of $146.4 million and a Capital Improvement Program (CIP) budget of $20.8 million" (City of Chula Vista 2016). The library's budget was approved with the vote.

For most libraries, the budget approval process is some variation of the three budget models.

Control

Control is the process of monitoring activities to ensure that they are being accomplished as planned and any significant deviations are corrected.

It helps to think of the control process as consisting of measuring actual performance, comparing actual performance against a standard (in this case the library's budget), and taking managerial action to correct deviations or inadequate standards. The control process may be thought of as four separate and distinct steps: (1) establishing a standard (the budget plan); (2) measuring actual results; (3) comparing the results against the plan (financial results to date): and (4) deciding what kind of managerial action to take. If there is a deviation from the budget plan, managerial actions could include declining to take immediate action but instead monitoring the deviation, changing the budget to correct the deviation, or modifying the budget (Robbins 2000, 172). According to Garrison, Noreen, and Brewer (2015, 24)

> Internal control is an important concept for all managers to understand and, although you may not be aware of it, it also plays an important role in your personal life. Internal control is a process designed to provide reasonable assurance that objectives are being achieved. For example, one objective for your personal life may be to live to a ripe old age. Unfortunately, there are risks that we all encounter that may prohibit us from achieving this objective. For example, we may die prematurely due to a heart attack, a car accident, or a house fire. To reduce the risk of these unfortunate events occurring, we implement controls in our lives. We may exercise regularly and make nutritional food choices to reduce the likelihood of a heart attack. We always wear seat belts and instruct our friends to prohibit us from drinking alcohol and driving a vehicle to reduce the risk of a fatal car crash. We install fire detectors in our homes to reduce the risk of a fatal fire. In short, internal controls are an integral part of our daily lives. (Garrison, Noreen, and Brewer 2015, 24)

There are two basic types of control: preventive control, which deters undesirable events from occurring, and detective control, which detects undesirable events that have already occurred. Usually managers are given a maximum dollar amount they are authorized to approve, for example, a serials section manager has authorization to approve contracts up to $10,000 for each separate contract. A detective control could be a reconciliation of expenditures against budgets. Table 8.1 lists types of internal controls that may be used for financial reporting: (Garrison, Noreen, and Brewer 2015, 25).

TABLE 8.1
Internal Controls for Financial Reporting

TYPE OF CONTROL	CLASSIFICATION	DESCRIPTION
Authorizations	Preventive	Requiring management to formally approve certain types of transactions.
Reconciliations	Detective	Relating data sets to one another to identify and resolve discrepancies.
Segregation of duties	Preventive	Separating responsibilities related to authorizing transactions, recording transactions, and maintaining custody of the related assets.
Physical safeguards	Preventive	Using cameras, locks, and physical barriers to protect assets.
Performance reviews	Detective	Comparing actual performance to various benchmarks to identify unexpected results.
Maintaining records	Detective	Maintaining written and/or electronic evidence to support transactions.
Information systems security	Preventive/Detective	Using controls such as passwords and access logs to ensure appropriate data restrictions.

Control is the centerpiece of a library's attempts to accomplish its budget plans, and a management control system (MCS) is a set of policies and procedures designed to keep operations going according to the budget plan. An important part of that system is a financial reporting and monitoring system that reports information in a timely way, which means that a schedule has been established that lists all the reports that the library will issue and the dates on which they will be issued. For example, a report detailing salary costs for the month might have a report issuance date of the fifteenth of the next month.

Control is one of the four basic management functions in organizations. The control function, in turn, has four basic purposes. Properly designed control systems can fulfill each of these purposes:

- Adapting to environmental change. Change is a constant factor in today's complex and turbulent environment. If managers could establish goals and achieve them instantly, control would be unnecessary. But between the time a goal is established and the time it is reached, many things can occur in the organization and its environment to disrupt movement toward the goal—or even to change the goal itself.
- Limiting the accumulation of error. Small mistakes and errors do not often seriously damage the financial health of an organization, but over time, small errors may accumulate and become very serious indeed.
- Coping with organizational complexity. Libraries are complex systems and need a robust and sophisticated system to maintain adequate control.
- When it is practiced effectively, control can also help reduce costs and boost the library's productivity. (Griffin 2017, 616–18)

Financial Control Process

Financial control is the management of financial resources as they flow into the organization (revenues, tax dollars, grants, etc.), and are held by the library or its parent authority) and flow out of the library to pay for employee wages and salaries, operating expenses, book and media purchases, and so on. Because of their quantitative nature, budgets provide yardsticks for measuring performance and facilitate comparisons across departments, between levels in the library, and from one time period to another. Budgetary controls must allow for the immediate recognition of variances that require action or change.

For example, the research services department at SDSU has a staff of thirteen professional librarians and five paraprofessional and/or clerical staff. During the first three months of the fiscal year there is almost no deviation from the department's forecast human resources budget, but during the fourth month, several unforeseen incidents occur. One of the librarians decides to take an extended leave to stay at home with his newly born child. Two other librarians take leave because of long-term illnesses, and another staffer decides to travel to New York to help his father recover from a debilitating fall. To meet service needs, new part-time staff is immediately added to fill in for the staff on leave causing a deviation in the budget. How long this deviation may continue depends on several factors including how quickly the two librarians will return from their long-term absences, what leave time and labor conditions apply to the staff. Should the SDSU Library decide to absorb the budget increases and not take any immediate action because it is believed that this will be a short-term issue? Should the library continue to monitor the situation and try to get more information? Should the library dean ask the provost for additional funds from the university's reserve to cover this unforeseen situation? Or should the library make reductions in other areas of the budget to compensate for the unexpected expenses? The control system will report the deviance, but to manage it requires cognitive action on the part of the library staff. This hypothetical example illustrates the complexity of budgeting—because the budget is an estimate based on the best information available when it was created, conditions do change.

Control means that certain budgetary information is communicated to library managers and all others who need to know it on a timely, scheduled basis. What are some of the budgets that are monitored by the library? This may vary from library to library based on what each wants to monitor, but some general information and operating information to control might include:

- an overall operating budget to determine if the library is meeting the approved financial plan
- division or operating budgets to determine where budget variances may be occurring
- income statements showing the timing and amount of revenue that the library expects to receive
- cash budgets to determine cash flow and whether the library will have to obtain some type of allotment or loan (bridge loan) to cover expenses if revenues do not arrive in time to meet financial obligations
- a balance sheet budget, which is a forecast of the organization's assets and liabilities in the event all other budgets are met
- an expense budget, which addresses the anticipated expenses for the organization during the coming time period
- a list of bills paid, including the vendor name, vendor ID, check number, check amount, date when the check was issued and cashed, expense category, and audit trail code
- capital budgets (if there is a capital project under way)

Financial Dashboards

The dashboard concept is often used to describe various instruments used to monitor and control library operations. Usually, when these tools are used in making economic decisions, they bring to mind an image of some quadrants or geometric figures that can provide essential data for running an organization. In this context, the dashboard idea is like the mage that provides the visualization of the small lights on the control panel of each system that needs to be directed and designed to provide faster partial and approximate data (Guni 2014).

Just as a dashboard in an automobile gives operating information about the car such as speed and gas left in the tank, financial dashboards can be used to provide information about the financial status of the library. Before configuring dashboards, data from the library's financial and operating information is required. The information is displayed in a graphic and colorful way using bar charts, pie charts, trend tables, and so on to indicate key indicators for the library.

Even though dashboards and scorecards may seem relatively new, they are evolutionary developments that grew out of the critical success factors (CSFs) concept that identified and monitored what companies, business units, departments, and individuals must do well to be successful. Once identified and tracked, CSFs help organizations communicate and focus on those factors that are most important to them. As executive information systems developed in the 1980s evolved, they incorporated the CSFs and key performance indicators to the dashboards we use today.

The idea of making data—especially financial data—easily readable is important for the operation of a library. Dashboards should have two critical features:

- Action lights: When the oil pressure red warning light goes on, we know we need to do something. By adding red, yellow, and green lights, the dashboard is oriented towards alerting library managers and staff that they might want to respond to a variance in financial performance.
- Changes over time: A dashboard is useful if it shows only where things stand at the moment. It becomes far more powerful when library managers and staff can see a trend line telling them that things are getting better or worse (Bell and Masaoka 2009).

Some suggestions to develop a dashboard design are

- Study other dashboards to help you prepare to design one to reflect the information your library and its individual users need. Think of how you might watch a decorating show for inspiration for your next home renovation. Get ideas from what others have done with dashboards to identify what data is most important. Then sketch it out before it goes off to design.
- Go for the graphical. The easiest way to grasp the meaning of a large amount of data quickly is through graphs and charts. This is the most effective way to present financial and statistical information.
- Use grid design. A template that allows you to control what information shows up in each section is the standard for most dashboards. The most important information, such as key performance indicators (KPIs) and budgetary information, goes on top of the screen so it is easy to see.
- Lay out information in a logical fashion and group related items using colors, labels, and borders.
- Include interactivity where appropriate. This could be as basic as the ability to drill down into an aging report to view unpaid invoices, or to move a gauge on the dashboard to see a "what if" analysis, such as "will our budget allow the hiring of a new clerk in technical services?"
- Make your dashboards readable. Coloring in graphics can improve readability, as do highlighting and bolding. Be careful about squeezing in more than can be easily read (Kianoff 2010).

Several companies offer commercially available dashboards that can be customized for library use. Microsoft's Power BI System can monitor and analyze a broad range of live data through easy-to-use dashboards, interactive reports, and data visualizations. Microsoft Excel 2016 can publish to Power BI, making it even easier to share data and insights (Microsoft Corporation 2017a).

Most library automation vendors have dashboard capability as part of their integrated library systems. SirsiDynix's BLUEclould analytics system claims to create reports from any combination of data and library tracks—from catalog items and MARC data to bills, users, and more. The system offers drag-and-drop data capabilities to create charts and graphs on the fly. Adding these visualizations to custom dashboards enables daily activity to be tracked. Financial reports may be integrated into the system (SirsiDynix 2017)

In her *Computers in Libraries* article, Archambault provides excellent color reproductions of library dashboards as well as good advice on their design and creation, emphasizing that "dashboards should stay confined within the boundaries of one screen and not provide excessive detail, while still making sure there is enough context for the data to be understood" (Archambault 2016).

For dashboards to work, both the users of the information and the designers of the dashboard must collaborate to make sure that the finished product meets the library's needs. After the dashboard becomes operational, staff that are knowledgeable about its content and process need to be assigned.

Modifying Budgets

No budget can accurately predict all the variables that impact a library during a budgetary period, and consequently it may be necessary to modify the budget. Dashboards and periodic financial reports alert library management about deviations from the library plan that may require changes. Modification is not an indication that the budget planning was flawed, but rather a planned revision to accommodate future changes.

Some of the reasons for modifying budgets might be that a program planned for the budget year was cancelled, prices unexpectedly increased for utilities, or salary savings occurred because new reference librarians couldn't be recruited.

A library should have policies and procedures for making budget adjustments, and create a form for making the request. The budget modification form should include information about the unit making the budget request, the date submitted, the reason for the adjustment, and the impact on the budget. The completed form should go to the manager identified in the modification policy to decide whether it will be approved. After the manager decides whether or not to approve the request, the decision must be communicated to the requesting unit.

Financial Condition Analysis

Financial condition analysis is a measure of the library's economic health. It analyzes the probability that the library will meet its financial obligations to creditors, employees, taxpayers, suppliers, and others, while fulfilling its service obligations to its constituents (i.e., its patrons). Some state governments regularly publish data on the finances of individual governments within the state that is required to determine the economic health of the area served by the library.

Creating a financial condition analysis is a difficult job because it requires a large amount of data as well as skilled staff to manipulate the data. However, the process may be valuable in helping determine why some libraries enjoy a higher level of support than others (Finkler, Smith, Calabrese, and Purtell 2017)

Financial Audits

Financial audits are independent appraisals of an organization's accounting, financial, and operational systems. The two major types of financial audits are the external audit and the internal audit.

Internal audits may be conducted by library staff or representatives from the parent organization. Internal auditors will review the library's financial statement and provide library management with periodic reports on the effectiveness of the controls system and the efficiency of the library's operations. Internal control staff might be from the office of the vice president of financial affairs for a university or from the city manager's office for a public library. Some libraries are not large enough to have access to this type of internal staff.

External audits are financial appraisals conducted by experts who are not employees of the organization. External audits are typically concerned with determining that the organization's accounting procedures and financial statements are compiled in an objective and verifiable fashion. The organization contracts with a certified public accountant (CPA) for this service. The CPA's main objective is to verify to the library's parent organization, the IRS, and other interested parties that the library's financial records and reporting meet generally accepted accounting rules and standards. Because they are outsiders, the auditors provide an independent review of financial statements. In performing an audit, a CPA conducts tests and procedures designed to ascertain the accuracy of the reported financial information. Because it is too expensive to review every transaction, auditors sample transactions looking for patterns. They review not only specific transactions but systems as well. For example, is the collection of library fines and fees in compliance with the policy of the library? Upon the conclusion of the audit, the CPA firm will issue an opinion on its review of the financial statements of the library (Blazek 1996, 49–53).

A copy of the Schaumburg Township District Library financial statements may be found at www.schaumburglibrary.org/sites/default/files/2017-03/Annual-Auditors-Report-June -2014.pdf.

Deviant Financial Behavior and Fraud

Deviant behavior occurs in almost every organization, and the dark side of organizations has been receiving a lot more attention from ethicists in a variety of professional disciplines. Potential deviant behavior is a factor in library finances because often the actions will have a negative impact on the library's budget. To quote Griffin and O'Leary-Kelly (2004), "the dark side of organizations is where people hurt other people, injustices are perpetuated and magnified, and the pursuits of wealth, power, or revenge lead people to behaviors that others can only see as unethical, illegal, despicable, or reprehensible."

INAPPROPRIATE ABSENTEEISM OR TARDINESS

Everyone gets sick or has a family emergency, and there are also times when "mental health days" may be justified. This type of behavior is practiced by most employees, but in an era of declining library budgets, rising material costs, and hiring freezes, library managers must seek ways to maintain and even expand library services without incurring personnel cost increases. Various means of increasing the productivity of current employees should be investigated. One often-overlooked method of increasing productivity is the reduction of employee absenteeism and tardiness. The University of Texas Moody Medical (UTMB) Library closely monitors unexcused absences, and subjects employees with serious attendance problems to progressive disciplinary measures that could ultimately result in dismissal. UTMB recognizes that personal or family problems and alcohol or drug abuse can cause employee absenteeism, and has initiated an employee assistance program that provides counseling and help to UTMB employees with such problems (Wygant 1988).

The author was director of the *Chicago Sun-Times/Daily News* library, which provided service to the newspapers' editorial staffs twenty-four hours a day, seven days a week. Two staff members were assigned to work a shift from midnight until eight in the morning. It was rumored that the two members traded off being on duty and only one was working at any given time although both were being paid. The author had to make several early morning visits to confirm the staffing, and eventually dismiss both employees for wasting library resources by not working during a period when they were paid.

THEFT OF ORGANIZATIONAL ASSETS OR PROPERTY

Virtually every employee in an organization will occasionally use the library's copier for personal copies, use the library's telephone for personal calls, or even take paper or supplies home for personal use. In libraries, the most expensive items are usually the collections. But there have been more serious offenses.

> The widespread theft of collection materials, including rare and unique items, continues to be an issue of great concern to libraries of all types. The potential loss of such items threatens not only an institution's operations but, in many cases, global cultural heritage. Despite an increasingly open attitude among institutions regarding sharing infor-

mation about lost items and suspected perpetrators, little scholarship has examined such thefts quantitatively to draw conclusions about how such incidents occur and how best to prevent them. Theft of valuable library materials may have both an "inside" as well as "outside" occurrence. Reported cases of theft suggest a full two-thirds of the incidents of theft conducted by outsider or unknown figures, and only 10 percent of total thefts (among those by known figures) being perpetuated by professional librarians. As such, it may be in the best interest of public service librarians and security personnel to reconsider the procedures their institutions have established for the prevention and prosecution of library thefts. (Samuelson, Sare, and Coker 2012)

Klas Linderfelt, ALA's president from 1891 to 1892, was forced to resign as both ALA president and director of the Milwaukee Public Library after it was discovered that he had embezzled over $9,000 from the library during a nine-year period (Snyder and Hersberger 1997).

In 1993, Dr. Hardy Franklin was elected president of the 52,000-member American Library Association.

In 1995, one year after the trustees of the DC library presented Dr. Franklin with the Martin Luther King Leadership Award, an audit revealed that the library had spent $45,000 in the preceding three years on a no-bid photography contract that went to a friend of Dr. Franklin's....

Finally, in 1998, he was indicted on charges of theft and mail fraud for allegedly defrauding the city of $24,000 in expense reimbursements. By then, the embattled Dr. Franklin had had a severe stroke and a heart attack, compounded by the diabetes he had endured for many years.

In September of that year, he pleaded guilty to a charge of conflict of interest and was ordered to pay back the money and serve five months of home detention. Leaning on a cane in court and fighting back tears, he said, "I accept full responsibility." (Schudel 2004)

DESTRUCTION OF ORGANIZATION ASSETS OR PROPERTY

Although it occurs infrequently, some employees engage in dark-side behaviors intended to damage or destroy assets. Library information systems and computers are at greatest risk for employee vandalism.

Insiders are likely to have specific goals and objectives and have legitimate access to the system. Employees are the group most familiar with their employer's computers and applications, and often know what actions might cause the most damage. Insiders can plant viruses, Trojan horses, or worms, or browse through the library's information systems. This type of attack can be extremely difficult to detect or protect against. An insider attack can affect all components of computer security. By browsing through a system, an insider can learn confidential information. Trojan horses are a threat to both the integrity and confidentiality of information in the system. Insiders can affect availability by overloading the system's processing or storage capacity, or by causing the system to crash.

Disgruntled employees can both create mischief and sabotage a computer system. Organizational downsizing has created a group of former employees with organizational knowledge who may retain potential system access. System managers can limit this threat by invalidating passwords and deleting system accounts in a timely manner. However, disgruntled current employees cause more damage than former employees. Common examples of computer-related employee sabotage include:

- altering data
- deleting data
- destroying data or programs with logic bombs
- crashing systems
- holding data hostage
- destroying hardware or facilities
- entering data incorrectly (Microsoft Corporation 2017b)

Good control systems and procedures protect the library against a variety of dark-side behaviors that cause financial and/or physical damage. This can also damage the library's image, which takes a long time to build but can be destroyed overnight.

Summary

The budgetary process is an ongoing activity that involves an interaction between library staff and its parent organization. The components of a completed budget include an overall organizational budget as well as budgets for departments and programs. Communicating the budget to the parent authority requires a good communication plan and flexibility to respond to questions.

Control is the process that is implemented to make sure the library is meeting its financial targets. Periodic financial reports and financial performance dashboards allow library managers to monitor budget process during the fiscal year. Control is also required to protect the library from fraud and deviant behavior. An auditor's report by a certified public account (CPA) verifies that the library's financial records are accurate and complete.

EXERCISES

1. Using the Sacramento budget handout (exhibit 8.1), create a PowerPoint presentation for the Sacramento Public Library Authority that might be presented to receive budget approval from the library's parent organization for the budget.

2. Select a budget from a library that interests you, and assume that you are a representative of the library's parent authority. Create a list of questions that you would ask the library about its budget.

3. For the library you selected in exercise 2, assume that the budget is going to be cut by 10 percent. How would you make the 10 percent cut and how would you defend your recommendation?

4. Select four or five financial operating measures that you would include in monitoring your library's budget. How could you adapt those measures to a financial dashboard?

5. For the library you selected in exercise 2, determine if the library staff do an internal audit and if so, how it relates to the audit conducted by the CPA.

6. List policies and procedures you would implement to limit theft of valuable library resources.

References

American Library Association. 2017. "Making Budget Presentations." www.ala.org/advocacy/advleg/advocacyuniversity/budgetpresentation.

Archambault, Susan Gardner. 2016. "Telling Your Story: Using Dashboards and Infographics for Data Visualization." *Computers in Libraries* 36 (3): 4–7.

Baldwin, Timothy T., William H. Bommmer, and Robert S. Rubin. 2013. *Managing Organizational Behavior: What Great Managers Know and Do.* 2nd ed. Boston: McGraw-Hill Irwin.

Barr, Kate. 2015. "How Board Members Can Learn to Spot Red Flags." *Balancing the Mission Checkbook,* January 8. https://nonprofitsassistancefund.org/blog.

Bell, Jeanne, and Jan Masaoka. 2009. *A Nonprofit Dashboard and Signal Light for Boards.* Blue Avocado. www.blueavocado.org/content/nonprofit-dashboard-and-signal-light-boards.

Blazek, Jody. 1996. *Financial Planning for Nonprofit Organizations,* Wiley Nonprofit Law, Finance and Management series. New York: Wiley.

City of Chula Vista. 2016. "Fiscal Year 2016–17 City Council Adopted Budget." www.chulavistaca.gov/departments/finance/budget-information.

Davis, Denise M. 2015. Sacramento Public Library Authority. Sacramento, California: Sacramento Public Library. https://www.saclibrary.org/About-Us/Budget-Documents/2015-2016/FY-15-16-Final-Budget.

Dropkin, Murray, Jim Halpin, and Bill La Touche. 2007. *The Budget-Bulding Book for Nonprofits: A Step-by-Step Guide for Managers and Boards.* 2nd ed., Guidebook series: New York: John Wiley and Sons, Inc.

Finkler, Steven A., Daniel L. Smith, Thad D. Calabrese, and Roberty M. Purtell. 2017. *Financial Management for Public, Health, and Not-for-Profit Organizations*. Thousand Oaks, CA: Sage.

Garrison, Ray H., Eric W. Noreen, and Peter C. Brewer. 2015. Managerial Accounting. 15th ed. Boston: Irwin/McGraw-Hill.

Griffin, Ricky. 2017. *Management*. 12th ed: Cengage.

Griffin, Ricky W., and Anne M. O'Leary-Kelly. 2004. *The Dark Side of Organizational Behavior*. Edited by Robert D. Pritchard, Organiational Frontiers series. San Francisco: Jossey-Bass.

Guni, Claudia Nicoleta. 2014. "The Dashboard: Conceptual Dimensions and Evolutions." *Economics, Management and Financial Markets* 9 (1): 448–56.

Kianoff, Lisa. 2010. "Dashboards: Business Intelligence at a Glance." *CPA Technology Advisor* 20 (7): 17.

Microsoft Corporation. 2017a. "Office 365: Personal and Organizational Insights." https://products .office.com/en-us/business/office-365-enterprise-analytics.

———. 2017b. "Security Threats." https://msdn.microsoft.com/en-us/library/cc723507.aspx.

Robbins, Stephen P. 2000. *Managing Today*. 2nd ed. Upper Saddle River, NJ: Prentice-Hall.

Samuelson, Todd, Laura Sare, and Catherine Coker. 2012. "Unusual Suspects: The Case of Insider Theft in Research Libraries and Special Collections." *College and Research Libraries* 73 (6): 556–68.

Schaumburg Township [Illinois] District Library. 2015. Determination of Money to Be Raised by Taxation—2015 Tax Levy. In Ordinance No. 2015/2016-4.

Schudel, Matt. 2004. "D.C. Public Library Director Hardy R. Franklin, 75." *Washington Post*, August 27, B06. www.washingtonpost.com/wp-dyn/articles/A37279-2004Aug26.html.

SirsiDynix. 2017. "BLUEcloud Analytics." www.sirsidynix.com/products/bluecloud-analytics.

Snyder, Herbert, and Julia Hersberger. 1997. "Public libraries and Embezzlement: An Examination of Internal Control and Financial Misconduct." *Library Quarterly* 67 (1): 23.

Wygant, Larry J. 1988. "Employee No-Shows: Managing Library Absenteeism." *Bulletin of the Medical Library Association* 76, no. 3 (July 1988): 213–15.

Sacramento Public Library Authority

September 24, 2015   Agenda Item 15.0: Final Budget -- FY 2015-16

TO: Sacramento Public Library Authority Board

FROM: Denise M. Davis, Deputy Library Director

RE: Final Budget -- FY 2015-16

RECOMMENDED ACTION:
Adopt Resolution 15-31, approving the FY 2015-16 Sacramento Public Library Authority Final Budget.

FY 2015-16 FINAL BUDGET
This budget document highlights budget changes identified since the Proposed Budget was adopted in May 2015.

Sacramento Public Library Budget Summary – FY 2015-16
The Authority's proposed final budget for FY 2015-16 for all services, support and operations is $38,144,635. The following charts provide an illustration of the FY 2015-16 proposed Final Budget.

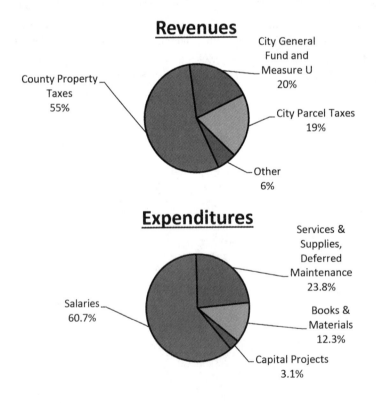

Attached to this report are Summary Schedules (Exhibits A-1 through A-5) that provide an overview of the Authority's Final Budget for FY 2015-16, including detailed summaries that outline anticipated revenues and expenditures for FY 2015-16 (Exhibits A-3 and A-4) in the County/Cities Fund, and the City of Sacramento General and Parcel Tax Funds.

The Authority's budget is a tale of two budgets. The County/Cities Unit is robust, with a fund balance of approximately $24 million. Therefore, staff is recommending using fund balance in the amount of $1,022,020 to increase services and for one-time improvements to the Arden-Dimick and Southgate Libraries. The City of Sacramento Unit, on the other hand, with a fund balance of approximately $7.9 million, faces uncertainty with the expiration of the Measure X parcel tax in June 2017. Staff is maintaining services in FY 2015-16, while slightly increasing fund balance in the amount of $21,485. Total revenues in all funds are $37,335,600, reflecting no change from the prior May approved budget. Total expenditures in all funds are $38,144,635, reflecting an increase of $656,000 from the May budget. Using $809,035 in overall fund balance allows the Library to increase its commitment to serving the public and improve services.

Revenues
The vast majority of Library funding comes from three primary sources:

- Property Tax revenues in the County/Cities   55%
- General Fund and Measure U contributions, City of Sacramento 20%
- Parcel Taxes on parcels in the City of Sacramento   19%

The remaining 6% of funding comes from fines and fees, investment earnings, the Galleria and donations. Exhibit A-3 provides FY 2015-16 revenue details by fund source. There are no changes from the FY 2015-16 May Budget.

Other revenues include grants and miscellaneous funds received by the Library Authority. The Authority's practice is to recognize the grants and donations as they are received during the year, since they are not predictable from a budgetary perspective. Staff will present gifts, donations and grants to the Authority Board for inclusion in the FY 2015-16 Budget as they are received/awarded.

County/Cities Budget Unit
The County/Cities budget unit utilizes property taxes collected in the unincorporated areas of the county and within the cities of Citrus Heights, Elk Grove, Galt, Isleton and Rancho Cordova. These funds finance the operation of 16 branch libraries. Additional revenue is realized from fines and fees, interest income and the Sylvan Cell Tower.

Expenditures in the County/Cities fund reflect an overall net increase of $182,000 or .8% from the May approved budget, with decreases in services and supplies offset by increases in salaries, capital projects and shared cost allocation expenditures. Staff was very frugal during the past six years, preserving as much fund balance as possible and enabling staff to responsibly use $1,022,020 (Exhibit A-2) in fund balance in the County/Cities budget in FY 2015-16.

No Supplemental Funds will be available for distribution to member jurisdictions in FY 2015-16. Continued restoration of services and the possibility of Supplemental Funds distribution in FY 2016-17 will be evaluated based on actual funding.

City of Sacramento Budget Unit

The City of Sacramento budget unit utilizes revenue from two sources: the City General Fund supplemented with Measure U funding, and funding received from taxes levied on parcels within the city limits. These revenues support the operation of 11 library branches located in the City of Sacramento, plus the Central Library. Additional revenue is realized from fines and fees, interest income and the Library Galleria.

Expenditures in the City of Sacramento Fund reflect an overall net increase of $448,400, or 5.0%, from the May approved budget. Of that amount, $230,000 is for one-time improvements at the Martin Luther King, Central, South Natomas and North Sacramento Libraries. The deferred maintenance increase of $121,000 represents the "Assigned Fund Balance" carryover of unspent FY 2015 funds for the City of Sacramento branches ($84,000), plus an amount earmarked for Galleria chair replacement ($37,000).

Shared Cost Budget Unit

The Shared Cost Fund functions as an internal service fund, and is determined through a comprehensive cost allocation plan that is updated annually. The fund collects the common costs for operating and administering the Library organization that are then distributed to the operating funds through the cost allocation plan. The FY 2015-16 expenditures, minus miscellaneous revenue within the fund, are $13,197,200 an increase of $190,000, or 1.5%, from the May Approved Budget. As shown in Exhibit A-4, the total Shared Cost budget is allocated as follows:

- County/Cities Fund $7,918,320 or 60%
- Sacramento City General Fund, Measure U $3,431,270 or 26%
- Sac. City Parcel Tax Fund (X) $1,187,750 or   9%
- Sac. City Parcel Tax Fund (B) $659,860   or   5%

Revenues of $177,000 are directly attributed to the fund from cost recovery in the amount of $117,000 for IT support to partner libraries using SPL's Sierra catalog; and $60,000 for passport services.

An increase in services and supplies results in a net increase in expenditures of $190,000 from the FY 2015-16 May Approved Budget.

Capital Projects and Deferred Maintenance

The library has begun evaluating branch refresh needs, including paint, carpet, furnishings and workroom improvements. Six libraries were evaluated in FY 2014-15 (Arcade, Arden-Dimick, Martin Luther King, North Highlands-Antelope, Southgate and Sylvan Oaks) and three others had some improvements completed in the past fiscal year based on branch assessments completed in spring 2014 (Franklin, McKinley and Walnut Grove). Estimated capital improvement costs for 2015-16 for improvements to Arden-Dimick, Martin Luther King, North Highlands-Antelope and Southgate, along with scheduled deferred maintenance costs for furniture reupholstering and replacement at North Sacramento, South Natomas, Galleria and Courtland locations, total $1,295,000. The bulk of the expenses are not capitalizable improvements and therefore appear as increases to the services and supplies portions of the budget.

Budgeted Positions/Position Control

The net change to position control from May 2015 is an increase of one (1) FTE for a total of 283.5 FTEs system-wide. All other changes in position control are due to position reclassifications.

Sylvan Oaks
Addition of 1.0 FTE Circulation Supervisor
Reduction of a 1.0 FTE Library Supervisor 1
An employee previously grandfathered in as a Library Supervisor I was transferred to Sylvan Oaks as Circulation Supervisor a number of years ago. This employee has transferred to another branch as the branch supervisor, leaving the current position, Circulation Supervisor, to be filled at Sylvan Oaks. Library Supervisor I is a grade 7 and Circulation Supervisor is a grade 5, resulting in a small salary savings.

Valley-Hi North Laguna
Addition of 1.0 FTE Circulation Supervisor
Reduction of a 1.0 FTE Library Supervisor I
At Valley Hi, an employee was grandfathered in as a Library Supervisor I, but worked as Circulation Supervisor. The Library Supervisor I incumbent has retired, and the position will be filled as a Circulation Supervisor. Library Supervisor I is a grade 7 and Circulation Supervisor is a grade 5, resulting in a small salary savings.

Walnut Grove/Courtland
With the promotion and move of one Delta supervisor and the resignation of another, there is an opportunity to review community needs. It was determined that a Library Supervisor I and a Youth Services Librarian will broaden the skills available to users in the Delta branches.

Reduction of 1.0 FTE Library Supervisor I/Addition of a 1.0 FTE Librarian
A 1.0 FTE Librarian position is being added to support both the Walnut Grove and Courtland branches to provide consistent cross-coverage in the Delta and allow for more growth and flexibility in both branches and to better serve the schools. The Librarian position is being funded with the budget of the Library Supervisor I position lost through attrition at the Courtland branch. Previous to this change, neither Walnut Grove nor Courtland had a Librarian on staff. Librarian and Library Supervisor I are the same grade. The positions will be budgeted at 50% for each location.

Communications and Virtual Services
Addition of 1.0 Creative Project Coordinator
Reduction of a 1.0 FTE Library Supervisor II
No fiscal impact in FY15-16
The Creative Project Coordinator is a new position for Sacramento Public Library. As part of the library's commitment to meeting the community's needs, this position will develop creative messaging and campaigns that connect community members with relevant library services. The Creative Coordinator is also needed to ensure that messaging is consistent across the library's 28 locations. Primary functions of the position will be leading creative communications projects and utilizing analytics and market research to track and improve messaging efforts.

Addition of 1.0 Communications Assistant
No fiscal impact in FY15-16; $63,000 projected fiscal impact for FY16-17

The Communications Assistant is a new position for Sacramento Public Library. This position will assist in meeting the ever-increasing demand of the public to interact with the library online. Primary functions of the position will be designing promotional materials both in-print and online.

The change in Position Control of a reduction in the .5 FTE Library Services Assistant and the increase of a .5 FTE Technology Assistant reflect a change made at the Belle Cooledge Library in July. As authorized by Resolution 13-35, this information is being reported in this narrative.

Fine and Fee Schedule
Staff are recommending no changes to the Fine and Fee schedule at this time.

Future Challenges
The major challenge facing the Authority is City of Sacramento funding. General Fund and Measure U contributions ($7,128,500 and $507,000 respectively) remain at maintenance of effort levels, and use of fund balance for core services exceeds new revenue by approximately $1 million. As a result, fund balance will be depleted at the end of FY16-17.

City parcel tax Measure X, which provides 35% of City contributions, is set to expire in June 2017. A ballot to extend this measure will go before voters next year and, if approved, extend for 10 years. If the measure is not approved, the City's General Fund contribution would need to increase commensurate with the Measure X parcel tax amount and the ongoing shortfall in General Fund and Measure U contributions in order to maintain the 12 City branches and current service levels.

Staff will present recommended Mid-Year Budget adjustments for FY 2015-16 in early 2016. This Mid-Year Budget will include updates on funding from the County and the City of Sacramento, as well as refinements to expenditure amounts.

ATTACHMENTS:
Resolution 15-31, adopting the FY 2015-16 Final Budget for the Sacramento Public Library Authority

Sacramento Public Library Authority

RESOLUTION NO. 15-31

Adopted by the Governing Board of the Sacramento Public Library Authority on the date of:

September 24, 2015

APPROVING THE FY 2015-16 FINAL BUDGET, POSITION CONTROL LISTING, AND FINE AND FEE SCHEDULE FOR THE SACRAMENTO PUBLIC LIBRARY AUTHORITY

NOW THEREFORE BE IT RESOLVED BY THE GOVERNING BOARD OF THE SACRAMENTO PUBLIC LIBRARY AUTHORITY AS FOLLOWS:

1. The Sacramento Public Library Authority's FY 2015-16 Final Budget totaling $38,144,635 as presented in Exhibits A-1 through A-5 is approved.

2. The Sacramento Public Library Authority's revised FY 2015-16 Position Control Listing as presented in Exhibit B is approved.

3. The Sacramento Public Library Authority's revised FY 2015-16 Fine and Fee Structure as presented in Exhibit C is approved.

4. All increases or decreases to operating appropriations in excess of $50,000 shall be approved by the Library Authority Board.

5. Authority Reserves are appropriated as follows:

	County/Cities Fund	Sac City Fund	Sac City Parcel Tax X Fund	Sac City Parcel Tax B Fund	Total
Reserves for Economic Uncertainty	$2,098,000	$833,260	$526,000	$196,100	$3,653,360

This designated reserve will be maintained at the level of 10% of budgeted revenues for the purpose of absorbing unforeseen contingencies and allowing continuation of Approved Budget program levels.

_____
Jeff Slowey, Chair
Rick Jennings II, Vice Chair

Sacramento Public Library Authority

ATTEST:

Rivkah K. Sass, Secretary

By:_____
        Linda J. Beymer, Assistant Secretary

ATTACHMENT(S):

Exhibit A-1:	Budget Summary by Fund FY 2015-16
Exhibit A-2:	Proposed Budget Summary FY 2015-16
Exhibit A-3:	Revenue Details by Fund Source FY 2015-16
Exhibit A-4:	Expense Details by Fund Source FY 2015-16
Exhibit A-5:	Books and Materials Fund FY 2015-16
Exhibit B:	Sacramento Public Library Authority Position Control Listing for FY 2015-16
Exhibit C:	Fine and Fee Structure for FY 2015-16

Item 15.0, EXHIBITS A-1 TO A-5

FY 2015-16
FINAL BUDGET
EXHIBITS

Sacramento Public Library Authority

Final Budget FY 2015-16

Item 15.0, EXHIBIT A-1

Sacramento Public Library Authority
Budget Summary by Fund
Fiscal Year 2015-16

Fund	Beginning Fund Balance 06/30/14	Estimated Activity FY 2014-15		Estimated Fund Balance 06/30/15	Proposed Budget FY 2015-16		Economic Uncertainty Reserve	Unreserved Fund Balance 06/30/16
		Revenues	Expenses		Revenues	Expenses		
County/Cities	$23,369,560	$ 20,318,000	$ 18,930,000	$24,757,560	$ 20,980,000	$ 22,002,020	$ 2,098,000	$21,637,540
Sacramento City	2,269,881	8,330,000	8,288,000	2,311,881	8,332,600	9,405,270	833,260	405,951
Sac City Parcel Tax X	4,178,961	5,155,000	3,993,000	5,340,961	5,260,000	4,171,945	526,000	5,903,016
Sac City Parcel Tax B	-	1,900,000	1,710,000	190,000	1,961,000	1,954,900	196,100	-
Tech/Equip Replace	668,033	1,049,000	250,000	1,467,033	625,000	433,500	-	1,658,533
Shared Cost *	-	184,000	184,000	-	177,000	177,000	-	-
Total	**$30,486,435**	**$ 36,936,000**	**$33,355,000**	**$34,067,435**	**$ 37,335,600**	**$ 38,144,635**	**$ 3,653,360**	**$29,605,040**

Note: * Direct revenues and expenses

164

Item 15.0, EXHIBIT A-2

SACRAMENTO PUBLIC LIBRARY AUTHORITY
BUDGET SUMMARY
FISCAL YEAR 2015-16

	FY 15-16 APPROVED BUDGET (MAY)	FY 15-16 FINAL BUDGET	CHANGE Increase/(Decrease)	
Total Sources of Funds	**$ 37,335,600**	**$ 37,335,600**	**$ -**	**0.0%**
Salaries and Benefits	23,112,000	23,162,000	50,000	0.2%
Services and Supplies	8,608,135	8,882,135	274,000	3.2%
Materials/Books	4,700,000	4,700,000	-	0.0%
Equipment/Capital Projects	975,500	1,186,500	211,000	21.6%
Deferred Maintenance	93,000	214,000	121,000	130.1%
Total Expenses	**$ 37,488,635**	**$ 38,144,635**	**$ 656,000**	**1.7%**
Surplus/(Deficit)				
County/Cities Fund	(840,020)	(1,022,020)	(182,000)	21.7%
Sac City Fund	(624,270)	(1,072,670)	(448,400)	71.8%
Sac City Parcel Tax Measure X	1,113,655	1,088,055	(25,600)	-2.3%
Sac City Parcel Tax Measure B	6,100	6,100	-	0.0%
400s Fund	191,500	191,500	-	0.0%
Net Surplus/(Deficit)	**$ (153,035)**	**$ (809,035)**	**$ (656,000)**	**428.7%**

Note: FY 15-16 Final Budget includes use of $809,035 from Fund Balance reserves, primarily for one-time expenditures.

Item 15.0, EXHIBIT A-3

SACRAMENTO PUBLIC LIBRARY SOURCES OF FUNDS FISCAL YEAR 2015-16				
SOURCES OF FUNDS	**FY 15-16 APPROVED BUDGET (MAY)**	**FY 15-16 FINAL BUDGET**	**CHANGE Increase/(Decrease)**	
COUNTY/CITIES FUND				
County Contributions	$ 20,400,000	$ 20,400,000	$ -	0.0%
State Appropriations	-	-	-	0.0%
Interest Income	200,000	200,000	-	0.0%
Fines and Fees	350,000	350,000	-	0.0%
Other Revenue	30,000	30,000	-	0.0%
TOTAL	**$ 20,980,000**	**$ 20,980,000**	**$ -**	**0.0%**
SAC CITY FUND				
City Contributions	$ 7,635,600	$ 7,635,600	$ -	0.0%
State Appropriations	-	-	-	0.0%
Galleria	450,000	450,000	-	0.0%
Interest Income	17,000	17,000	-	0.0%
Fines and Fees	230,000	230,000	-	0.0%
Other Revenue	-	-	-	0.0%
TOTAL	**$ 8,332,600**	**$ 8,332,600**	**$ -**	**0.0%**
SAC CITY PARCEL TAX X				
Parcel Tax	$ 5,125,000	$ 5,125,000	$ -	0.0%
Interest Income	33,000	33,000	-	0.0%
Fines and Fees	91,000	91,000	-	0.0%
Other Revenue	11,000	11,000	-	0.0%
TOTAL	**$ 5,260,000**	**$ 5,260,000**	**$ -**	**0.0%**
SAC CITY PARCEL TAX B				
Parcel Tax	$ 1,960,000	$ 1,960,000	$ -	0%
Interest Income	1,000	1,000	-	0%
TOTAL	**$ 1,961,000**	**$ 1,961,000**	**$ -**	**0.0%**
SHARED FUND				
State Foundation/Grants	$ -	$ -	$ -	0.0%
Other Revenue	177,000	177,000	-	0.0%
TOTAL	**$ 177,000**	**$ 177,000**	**$ -**	**0.0%**
400s FUND				
E-rate Rebate	625,000	625,000	-	0.0%
TOTAL	**$ 625,000**	**$ 625,000**	**$ -**	**0.0%**
GRAND TOTAL	**$ 37,335,600**	**$ 37,335,600**	**$ -**	**0.0%**

SACRAMENTO PUBLIC LIBRARY
EXPENSE DETAILS BY FUND
FISCAL YEAR 2015-16

EXPENSE	FY 15-16 APPROVED BUDGET (MAY)	FY 15-16 FINAL BUDGET	CHANGE Increase/(Decrease)	
COUNTY/CITIES FUND				
Salaries and Benefits	7,740,000	7,743,000	3,000	0.0%
Services and Supplies	2,535,700	2,410,700	(125,000)	-4.9%
Materials/Books	2,820,000	2,820,000	-	0.0%
Capital Projects	870,000	1,060,000	190,000	21.8%
Deferred Maintenance	50,000	50,000	-	0.0%
Cost Allocation (60%)	7,804,320	7,918,320	114,000	1.5%
TOTAL	**$21,820,020**	**$22,002,020**	**$ 182,000**	**0.8%**
SAC CITY FUND				
Salaries and Benefits	4,257,000	4,295,500	38,500	0.9%
Services and Supplies	1,062,000	1,280,500	218,500	20.6%
Materials/Books	213,000	213,000	-	0.0%
Capital Projects	-	21,000	21,000	100.0%
Deferred Maintenance	43,000	164,000	121,000	281.4%
Cost Allocation (26%)	3,381,870	3,431,270	49,400	1.5%
TOTAL	**$ 8,956,870**	**$ 9,405,270**	**$ 448,400**	**5.0%**
SAC CITY PARCEL TAX X				
Salaries and Benefits	1,204,745	1,213,245	8,500	0.7%
Services and Supplies	103,950	103,950	-	0.0%
Materials/Books	1,667,000	1,667,000	-	0.0%
Capital Projects	-	-	-	0.0%
Deferred Maintenance	-	-	-	0.0%
Cost Allocation (9%)	1,170,650	1,187,750	17,100	1.5%
TOTAL	**$ 4,146,345**	**$ 4,171,945**	**$ 25,600**	**0.6%**
SAC CITY PARCEL TAX B				
Salaries and Benefits	1,160,255	1,160,255	-	0%
Services and Supplies	144,285	134,785	(9,500)	-7%
Materials/Books	-	-	-	0%
Cost Allocation (5%)	650,360	659,860	9,500	1%
TOTAL	**$ 1,954,900**	**$ 1,954,900**	**$ -**	**0%**
SHARED FUND				
Direct Expenses	177,000	177,000	-	0.0%
TOTAL	**$ 177,000**	**$ 177,000**	**$ -**	**0.0%**
400s FUND				
Equipment	$ 433,500	$ 433,500	-	0.0%
TOTAL	**$ 433,500**	**$ 433,500**	**$ -**	**0.0%**
TOTAL	**$37,488,635**	**$38,144,635**	**$ 656,000**	**1.7%**

Item 15.0, EXHIBIT A-5

SACRAMENTO PUBLIC LIBRARY BOOKS AND MATERIALS FUND FISCAL YEAR 2015-16				
	FY 15-16 APPROVED BUDGET (MAY)	FY 15-16 FINAL BUDGET	CHANGE Increase/(Decrease)	
REVENUES				
Transfers in from:				
County/Cities Fund	2,820,000	2,820,000	-	0.0%
Sac City Fund	213,000	213,000	-	0.0%
Sac City Measure X	1,667,000	1,667,000	-	0.0%
Sac City Measure B	-	-	-	0.0%
TOTAL	**$ 4,700,000**	**$ 4,700,000**	**$ -**	**0.0%**
EXPENDITURES				
Books/Materials	4,700,000	4,700,000	-	0.0%
TOTAL	**$ 4,700,000**	**$ 4,700,000**	**-**	**0.0%**

SACRAMENTO PUBLIC LIBRARY AUTHORITY
POSITION CONTROL REPORT
September 24, 2015

FINAL FY 2015-16 POSITION CONTROL

	FY 2015-16 Adopted May 28, 2015	FY 2015-16 Proposed September 24, 2015	Change
Accountant/Budget Analyst	1	1	
Accounting Specialist	2	2	
Administrative Analyst	1	1	
Administrative Assistant	3	3	
Administrative Technician	1	1	
Assistant Director - Infrastrucure	1	1	
Assistant Director - Public Services	1	1	
Building Maintenance Worker	2	2	
Capital Projects Manager	1	1	
Circulation Supervisor	17	19	2
Collection Management Services Manager	1	1	
Communications Assistant	0	1	1
Communications and Virtual Services Manager	1	1	
Community Services Manager	1	1	
Creative Project Coordinator	0	1	1
Custodial and Logistics Supervisor	1	1	
Custodian	11.5	11.5	
Deputy Library Director	1	1	
Early Literacy Specialist	1	1	
Events Coordinator	0.5	0.5	
Facilities Operations Manager	1	1	
Field Custodial Supervisor	1	1	
Finance Manager	1	1	
General Services Worker	5.5	5.5	
Human Resources Analyst	2	2	
Human Resources Manager	1	1	
Human Resources Technician	1	1	
Information Technology Supervisor	1	1	
Information Technology Technician	2	2	
Intergrated Library Services Supervisor	1	1	
K-12 Specialist	1	1	
Librarian	44.5	45.5	1
Library Associate*	5	5*	
Library Communications Analyst	1	1	
Library Director	1	1	
Library Program Specialist	1	1	
Library Services Assistant*	90.5	90*	-0.5
Library Services Specialist	1	1	
Library Supervisor I	14	11	-3
Library Supervisor II	10	9	-1
Library Supervisor III	13	13	
Library Technician	0	0	
Literacy and Homework Center Supervisor	1	1	
Materials Handler	1	1	
Procurement-Contract Coordinator	1	1	
Public Information Coordinator	1	1	
Public Services Manager	3	3	
Safety/Security Coordinator	1	1	
Senior Accounts Payable Technician	1	1	
Senior Information Technology Analyst	2	2	
Senior Information Technology Technician	2	2	
Senior Payroll Technician	1	1	
Special Projects and Remodeling Coordinator	1	1	
Technology Assistant	19	19.5	0.5
Visual Communications Specialist	1	1	
Youth and Literacy Services Manager	1	1	
Total FTEs	**282.5**	**283.5**	**1.0**

FTEs are full-time equivalent positions, equating part time positions into fraction of a full time position.

*There are three grant funded positions included one FTE Library Associate and two 0.5 FTEs Library Services Assistant - starting July 1, 2015 and ending June 30, 2018.

Item 15.0, Exhibit C

SACRAMENTO PUBLIC LIBRARY
FINE/FEE STRUCTURE
Approved: September 26, 2013

Categories	Current Fees
FINES	
Periodicals	$0.05/day to $1.00 maximum
All Juvenile and Young Adult (YA) materials	$0.05/day to $1.00 maximum
All Adult materials	$0.25/day to $5.00 maximum
Engravers	$0.25/day to $5.00 maximum
All visual media	$0.25/day to $5.00 maximum
Link + books	$1.00/day to $15.00 maximum
Interlibrary Loan (ILL) materials	$2.00/day up to the cost of the material
GENERAL FEES	
Self-service black & white photocopying	$0.15/page
OPAC printouts	The first five (5) pages of an individual print job are free to the patron, with subsequent pages costing $0.15 /page
Printouts (Computer, coin-operated microform, fax)	Updated Fee: $0.15/page
Self-service color photocopying	$0.50/page
Sacramento Room – archival photocopies	$0.50/page
Sacramento Room – Digital scans of materials Prints of digital scans CD with images Shipping charge per CD if mailed	$10/per scan $15/per print $5.00/CD $3.00 each
Replacement of Library Card	$2.00
Damaged material (repairable)	$2.50 Juvenile and Young Adult materials $5.00 Adult materials
Damaged media boxes and cases	$5.00 for all materials
Material processing Fee	$5.00 per cataloged item
Collection agency processing fee	$10.00
Returned check service fee	$30.00
Damaged material (unusable)	Unit cost of item + material processing fee
Programs, classes, publishing fees	$5.00 - $500.00* *Fee to be determined per program/class activity
Passport fees	$15 - $25
Reshelving fee	$1 per item

SACRAMENTO PUBLIC LIBRARY
FINE/FEE STRUCTURE
Approved: September 26, 2013

INTERLIBRARY LOAN FEES	
ILL request (SPL customers)	$5.00
ILL fee to send a book to out-of-state library	$20.00
LOST LIBRARY MATERIALS	
Lost periodical	$5.00
Lost item (ILL) Fee charged to SPL customer	$60.00 minimum to cost of item (fine goes to owning library, not SPL)
Link+ Lost Materials	$115.00 per item (fine goes to owning Library, not SPL)
All lost Juvenile, Young Adult and Adult items (cataloged)	Unit cost of item or "default cost"* plus material processing fee
Lost item (cataloged paperback)	Unit cost of item or "default cost"* plus material processing fee
*Default cost	$5.00 for a magazine $30.00 for a book
MEETING ROOMS	
After-hours fee (when staff/security must open or secure a meeting room when the library is not open)	$50.00
Excessive cleanup costs: Charge for post-event cleaning beyond normal custodial duty assignments	Actual costs, including labor, materials and outside services
PUBLIC RECORDS DISCLOSURE	
Duplication of Authority Board meeting DVD (with DVD provided)	Actual cost, excluding staff time
Photocopies	First ten (10) pages free; at cost thereafter
Copies of Campaign Statements and Conflict of Interest Statements (FPPC)	$0.10 per page
FPPC document retrieval fee (statements older than five years)	$5.00 per request
Authority Board agenda packets (Copy and send by mail)	$20.00 per packet
Authority Board agenda packets (Copy/send by Federal Express)	$30.00 per packet

Item 15.0, Exhibit C

SACRAMENTO PUBLIC LIBRARY
FINE/FEE STRUCTURE
Approved: September 26, 2013

LIBRARY GALLERIA MEETING ROOMS:

	Mon-Thurs	Friday	Saturday	Sunday
Main Floor (5 hrs.)	$950	$1,150	$1,950	$1,150
Main Floor (9 hrs.)	$1,175	$1,500	$2,500	$1,500
2nd Floor Balcony (5 hrs.)	$300	$450	$500	$450
2nd Floor Balcony (9 hrs.)	$450	$650	$800	$650
Meeting Room (1/2 Day)	$300	$300	$300	$300
Meeting Room (Full Day)	$400	$400	$400	$400
Meeting Room (Evening 6 PM+)	$400	$400	$400	$400
New Year's Eve (see Sat. rates)				

LIBRARY GALLERIA COMMUNITY USE POLICY AND FEES:

Community use policy states that the following groups may qualify for meeting room use at no charge:

- Neighborhood groups from the downtown district and other groups outside the downtown district that have been formed to improve conditions in their respective neighborhoods

- Public forums that have been called by elected city officials

- Interested groups must see Library Galleria staff for room use guidelines and availability.

Events may be subject to associated fees as described below.

Community Use Associated Fees				
Type of service/fee	Minimum hours required	Staff required	Rate per hour	Total
Library event duty	2 hrs.	1 coordinator	$30	$60
Security officer	4 hrs.	1 officer	$30	$120
Room Setup				
Up to 10 tables	4 hrs.	1 custodial	$20	$80
11+ tables	8 hrs./ea	2 custodial	$20	$320
Strike & clean	8 hrs.	1 custodial	$20	$160
Strike & clean	5 hrs./ea	2 custodial	$20	$200

Item 15.0, Exhibit C

SACRAMENTO PUBLIC LIBRARY
FINE/FEE STRUCTURE
Approved: September 26, 2013

Reception Space and Equipment Fees	
Space Rental	**Per Use**
Old Library Foyer entrance only	$ 100
Foyer entrance with food and beverage	$ 300
Equipment	
LCD Projector	$ 185
Conference phone	$ 50
Remote clicker	$ 25
Mac to VGA converter	$ 25
Projection screen, 8' portable	$ 45
Additional wireless microphones	$ 40
Additional wired microphones	$ 20
Additional lectern	$ 30
Whiteboard and pens	$ 15
Flip chart and pens	$ 15
Designer drape backdrop 25 - 40'	$ 120
Designer drape backdrop 17 - 24'	$ 100
Designer drape backdrop 16' or less	$ 60
Security guard, per hour	$ 30
Stage	$ 100

Wedding and Prom Packages	Sunday-Friday	Saturday
Wedding reception, main floor only	$ 1,150	$ 1,950
Wedding, main floor and balcony	$ 1,600	$ 2,450
Wedding and ceremony, main floor	$ 1,900	$ 2,900
Wedding and ceremony, main & balcony	$ 2,350	$ 3,400
Prom, main floor and foyer, 5 hours	$ 1,150	$ 1,950
Balcony, 5 hours	$ 450	$ 500
East meeting room and Old Foyer	$ 400	$ 400
Library Lobby as an entrance	$ 100	$ 100
New Year's Eve (see Saturday rates)		
Hourly rates after hours		
Galleria	$ 175	
Balcony	$ 50	

9

Budgetary Categories, Comparisons, Forms, and the Balanced Scorecard

Learning Objectives of This Chapter Are to:

☐ Identify the three main categories of library expenditures; salaries, materials, and operating expenses.

☐ Illustrate how to compare your library's budget to past budgets and the budgets of other libraries.

☐ Understand the role that forecasting and scenario analysis play in planning future budgets.

☐ Recognize how payroll and purchasing systems may be integrated into the library's budgetary system.

☐ Appreciate the role of the balanced scorecard in strategic planning.

☐ Know the use of several budgetary and financial forms.

Budgetary Categories

The overall library budget includes all the ongoing costs of maintaining a library: salary, materials, and operating expenditures. The percentage of budgeted funds for staff versus materials, versus other operating expenditures is a useful tool in creating a library's budget. The collective wisdom of how other libraries allocate their resources into the three categories provides guidelines for evaluating a library's budget.

Statistics documenting expenditures for academic libraries are found in *Academic Library Trends and Statistics*, published annually by the Association of College & Research Libraries. The report describes expenditures and statistics concerning collections, staffing, expenditures, and service activities of academic libraries.

> The 2015 data show that library expenditures for collection materials averaged $5,700,113 for doctoral degree-granting institutions, $725,826 for comprehensive degree-granting institutions, $524,184 for baccalaureate schools, and $ 146,542 for associate degree granting institutions. On average, doctoral degree-granting institutions spent 76.7% of their materials budgets on ongoing commitments to subscriptions in 2015, comprehensive schools spent an average of 76.8%, baccalaureate schools spent an average 72.4%, and associate degree-granting institutions spent an average of 55.5%. On average, academic libraries spent 70.4% of their materials budget on subscriptions. (ACRL 2017, 6)

> The 2015 data show that expenditures for salaries and wages accounted for 63.4% of the total library expenditures on average. Salaries and wages constituted 77.9% of total library expenditures for associate degree-granting institutions, 45.4% for baccalaureates, 87% for comprehensive schools, and 43.3% for doctoral/research institutions. (ACRL 2017)

The Publishers Communication Group issued a report on budget predictions for 2015. The overall predicted library budget includes the ongoing costs of maintaining a library, salary, materials, and operating expenditure.

> The Association of Research Libraries (ARL) gives an idea of how library budgets break down. The ARL statistics include details of collections, expenditures, staffing, and service activities for its member libraries and most of the libraries are large North American academic institutes. The latest data in the report from 115 ARL members is from 2013. Expenditures were broken down into three areas: salaries (44 percent, which has dropped 1 percent since 2011) materials (44 percent—up 1 percent), and other operating expenditures (12 percent) made up the remainder of the budget. (Publishers Communication Group 2015, 10)

Budget categories for public libraries are collected by the Public Library Data Service (PLDS) annual survey conducted by Counting Opinions (SQUIRE) Ltd. on behalf of the Public Library Association (PLA). According to the latest survey, "mean expenditures per capita on staff and 'other' rose past pre-recession levels, yet mean materials expenditure has yet to recover to those previous levels. Libraries are also adding more non-MLS than

MLS librarians to their staffs. Since 2011, mean staff expenditures per capita and mean other expenditures per capita increased an average of 1.5 percent per year, while mean materials expenditures grew by only 1.2 percent per year. Since FY 2008, the change in mean materials expenditures is, in fact, down versus staff and other expenditures and does appear to be a trend" (Reid 2016, 24–25).

What combination of library resource is best or most efficient? How much should be spent on staff versus materials, versus other operating expenses to create the best or most efficient library services?

> An economic definition of efficiency would state that a library will be 100 percent cost efficient if it is both technically efficient and allocatively efficient. A library is techni-cally efficient if no increase in outputs is possible for a given amount of physical inputs. Physical inputs would be staff, materials, and facilities. A library is allocatively efficient if these physical inputs are made in the correct proportions. The correct proportion is attained when one physical input is substituted for another to obtain the lowest cost without reducing the level of output. The unit price of each input determines the lowest cost. This economic definition is often referred to as "Pareto efficiency." This is of course an ideal model based on the assumption that a manager has perfect information about production and the prices of inputs. While this is never the case in the real world, mod-ern information technology is allowing managers to approach this goal. (Saunders 2003)

Selecting the correct proportions of staff, materials, and other costs is an art as well as a science and varies from library to library. After the optimal mix of the three resources is established, the next step is to determine the type of staff required. How many profes-sional librarians, paraprofessionals, and clerical staff will produce the best proportion? The same may be said of how to break down the materials budget into the varying num-ber of choices available now, that is, monographs versus serials, print versus electronic, and so on.

Budget Comparisons

One of the questions we often ask ourselves is "how are we doing?" Going back to high school and college reunions we sometimes compare who we were when we were in school and who we are now. We also tend to mentally evaluate our former classmates in the same way. Is the school jock now out of shape and does the homecoming queen still have the same magic that dazzled her classmates? We like to keep score because it is a natural tendency and we like to do the same thing with our libraries. How do we compare to where we were in the past and how do we compare to other libraries today?

In the case of library comparisons, we check to see if we are keeping up against internal standards. Has the ratio of librarians to students changed, or has spending on the public library's materials' collection kept up with inflation? Several techniques enable libraries to make these comparisons.

Historical Comparisons

Historical comparisons are primarily intended for internal comparisons rather than comparisons against a set of other libraries. For example, if a library wants to determine if its materials budget is keeping up with inflation and population changes, it would construct a table and insert historical materials about spending, population served, and cost inflation information.

TABLE 9.1

Library Materials Budget

YEAR	MATERIALS BUDGET ($)	POPULATION SERVED	SPENDING PER CAPITA	INCREASE IN INFLATION RATE/ COST OF MATERIALS	INFLATION COST	SPENDING PER CAPITA ADJUSTED FOR INFLATION
2016	$105,000	12,000	$8.75	4.00%	$0.35	$8.40
2015	$90,000	11,500	$7.83	4.00%	$0.31	$7.51
2014	$105,000	11,000	$9.55	4.00%	$0.38	$9.16
2013	$100,000	10,500	$9.52	4.00%	$0.38	$9.14
2012	$100,000	10,000	$10.00	Base Year	$0.00	$10.00

In this simple example (table 9.1), the historical comparison shows that the library faces several challenges. The population served increases over the five-year period by 20 percent, although even in the best years (2014 and 2015) the materials budget increases by only 5 percent. In 2015, due to budget cutbacks, the real materials budget declines by $15,000 from the previous year, causing a significant reduction in materials spending. In addition, inflation keeps occurring at a rate of 4 percent a year. The sad story is the real purchasing power of the library declines from $10 per capita in the 2012 base year to $8.40 in 2016, even though the actual budget is $5,000 more than it was in the base year.

When the library presents its budget to the parent institution, an administrator reviewing it might observe that the materials budget has not really declined, but was based on having to contend with inflation and a growth of population served by the library. And this analysis does not even consider new programs or obligations to which the library may be committed.

A library should keep track of historical data such as population served, inflation rates for library services, and new programs and activities to make an argument for a budget that at least meets increased costs.

Benchmarking, input and output measures, and guidelines and standards, which were reviewed in chapter 4, are good methods for determining how well your library measures up to other libraries.

Future Estimates

Budgeting is most often an annual activity, but good libraries anticipate not only what is happening in the next budget year but also in a time horizon that extends out for up to five years. A five-year forecast of revenues and expenses, as well as changes in the macro environment faced by the library, helps avoid surprises. Libraries should monitor their internal conditions and operations, changes that may be taking place with their parent institution, and shifts in the external environment.

FORECASTING

Forecasting is the development of plausible projections about the direction, scope, speed, and intensity of changes impacting a library. Libraries are most concerned with financial and environmental change and must forecast what their impact will be on the library.

A financial forecast identifies trends in external and internal historical data and projects those trends to provide library decision-makers with information about what the financial status of the library is likely to be at some point in the future. The purpose of the financial forecast is to evaluate current and future fiscal conditions to guide policy and programmatic decisions. A financial forecast is a fiscal management tool that presents estimated information based on past, current, and projected financial conditions and helps identify future revenue and expenditure trends that may have an immediate or long-term influence on the library's policies, strategic goals, or types of services offered.

The purpose of an environmental forecast is to envision change. Some of the areas where changes may impact the financial and operational decisions of a library may include those shown in table 9.2.

TABLE 9.2

Changes That May Impact Library Planning

ENVIRONMENTAL FACTOR:	QUESTIONS TO CONSIDER
Demographic	Aging population and aging workforce, differences in economic status, changes in ethnic composition of the workforce and customers, geographic distribution
Socio-Cultural	LGBTQ staff and customers, concern for the environment, health and wellness, work-life balance, the changes in the physical and built environment
Political Legal	Changes in political/legal system, Americans with Disabilities Act, minimum wage and overtime laws, taxation revisions, health care, immigration and guest workers
Technological	Three-dimensional printing, virtual reality, computer-aided design and manufacturing, artificial intelligence, growth of robot workers to replace humans, miniaturization of computer technologies, wireless communications, nanotechnology
Economic	Interest rates, unemployment rates, minimum wage, trends in the gross domestic product, consumer price index

An example of how a change in legislation might impact a budget is a 2016 California law (AB 1732) that requires all single stall public bathrooms to be gender neutral–open to everyone starting March 1, 2017. If a library wants to convert some of its existing bathrooms to comply with the law, it might have to switch budgeted funds from a funded library activity to pay for the conversion. It may need to reallocate funds from other funded activities to pay for the conversion. A five-year budget plan allows the library to plan expected changes to a future budget (Posnick-Goodwin 2017)

An organized planning effort as part of the budgeting process will allow the library to anticipate changes required to meet a shifting environment and anticipate the budgetary resources to meet the change.

SCENARIO ANALYSIS

Scenario analysis is a more in-depth approach to forecasting. A scenario is a view of what the future is likely to be. It draws on a range of disciplines and interests, among them economics, psychology, sociology, and demographics. It usually begins with a discussion of participants' thoughts on how societal trends, economics, politics, and technology may affect an issue. Scenario analysis involves the projection of future possible events. It does not rely on extrapolation of historical trends. Rather, it seeks to explore possible developments that may only be connected to the past (Dess, McNamara, and Eisner 2017, 42). Usually two to four different scenarios are developed to envision possible future outcomes. Participants in the scenario analysis meet to discuss the various scenarios and collaborate on their visions of the future.

A scenario planning exercise was conducted at the University of the West of England (UWE), a post 1992 university and the fifth largest in the United Kingdom, with approximately 3,000 academic staff and 30,000 students—a large proportion of whom are non-traditional students (i.e., part-time, distance learners). Several drivers for change, both internal and external to the organization, necessitated the decision to undertake a major restructuring of the Academic Services team (i.e., librarians) at the UWE Library beginning in March 2011. These drivers included:

- a need to do more for less because of a twenty-five percent budget cut over three years
- the need to simplify the existing overly complex patchwork of team roles and responsibilities that were inhibiting efficient staff deployment
- expanding service priorities—for example, to contribute far more to the research agenda of the university
- a changed teaching model that required delivery of information literacy skills to extremely large groups, while acknowledging that Academic Services team staff were already at breaking point

The Academic Services team comprises mainly qualified librarians who are focused on liaison activities with their respective faculties. They ensure that the collections meet the needs of the faculties' students and staff and that the students' information literacy skills are developed appropriately within the curriculum. Other roles within the team focus on support for research and for community engagement.

The decision to utilize scenario planning to address these challenges was influenced by prevailing conditions. The need to cope with high turbulence and increased levels of uncertainty within the team—a mechanism for providing a dynamic view of the future rather than simply a static one—was vital. A second condition was to develop an inclusive solution that Academic Services staff would shape and ultimately own themselves. This was especially important considering past difficulties regarding change management and some poor internal communication within the library service at UWE.

Scenario planning was chosen because attempts failed to compensate for both under- and over-prediction of change, two common errors in decision-making that had occurred in the past. Scenario planning allowed staff both to chart a middle course between these two potential extremes and expand the range of possibilities that could be envisaged, which also prevented staff from drifting into the realms of fantasy. In constructing initial scenarios, staff developed three scenarios; the hope was that a composite reality would emerge through discussion. It was crucial that the scenarios were consistent and plausible, and mapped trends and issues compatible with the specified time frame. Although none of the scenarios were attempts to prescribe specific futures, they represented a triangulation of thought that would enable academic services staff to discuss and highlight critical elements from within each that would enable the development of a summative, composite final version representing the best fit (or best guess) for thinking about a suitable future structure at that time.

The three scenarios were:

1. A gradual adjustment with few changes to the basic structure of Academic Services.
2. A "tough times" approach with an emphasis on rapidly increasing e-learning, with the team withdrawing from as much Y1/Y2 face-to-face teaching as possible.
3. A "high turbulence" scenario with Academic Service librarians changing their roles with more strategic engagement in course design and collection development and greater involvement with students and faculty.

Many meetings were held to refine the three scenarios, and the final selection was a combination of many ideas from the more change-oriented second and third choices (Maggs and Chelin 2013).

Budgetary Systems

Payroll and purchasing are the two largest budgetary expense categories for libraries, and should be integrated into the library's accounting system.

Payroll System

A payroll system is software designed to organize all the tasks of employee payment and the filing of employee taxes. This can include keeping track of hours, calculating wages, withholding taxes and deductions, printing and delivering checks, and paying employment taxes to the government.

According to the *CPA Journal*, an estimated eight to ten hours a month are required to process the payroll of an organization with fewer than twenty employees. Many organizations, including libraries, want to concentrate on their core business and outsource other aspects of their operations ("ADP, Staples Announce Payroll Service" 1999).

Contemporary payroll systems have many time- and cost-saving features including the capability to perform data sync with the library's accounting software, which allows data to appear in the accounting general ledger when the client activates the sync. Other payroll solutions are embedded and built inside of an accounting solution. With those types of solutions, payroll is deeply integrated in the accounting software from setup to paycheck and taxes, enabling the data to flow between the two products automatically without any client action. Many systems also include time-tracking software that can make running payroll much faster for clients because they don't have to enter employee hours manually.

As an aid to management, payroll systems can generate employer compliance products like workers' compensation insurance. Some payroll solutions offer convenient services such as pay-as-you-go workers' compensation, which helps clients manage cash flow by paying monthly on their actual labor force, instead of annually based on an estimated labor force ("Effortless Payroll Service Offerings" 2015).

Good payroll systems allow the uploading and storage of all employee documents to an electronic format, reducing errors by having one system of record. Systems can keep track of key events like birthdays, work anniversaries, and promotions. For on-boarding, systems can minimize the busy work associated with bringing on new hires by allowing employees to e-sign, organize, and store all the necessary hiring documents as electronic records. For ongoing time tracking, employees submit requests for administrative approval and the system automatically tracks balances and accruals for employees.

In most university and public libraries, the payroll system is managed by the parent institution. However, if the library must conduct payroll on its own as an independent agency, there are several procedures to follow to avoid legal and regulatory issues. The Small Business Association (SBA) has listed the following steps to make the payroll process as efficient as possible for those libraries handling their own payroll (SBA 2017).

1. *Obtain an Employer Identification Number (EIN).* Before hiring employees, you must obtain an EIN) from the Internal Revenue Service (IRS). The EIN is often referred to as an Employer Tax ID or as Form SS-4. It is necessary for reporting taxes and other documents to the IRS and when reporting information about your employees to state agencies. You can apply for an EIN online or contact the IRS directly.

2. *Check Whether You Need State or Local IDs.* Some state and local governments require businesses to obtain ID numbers to process taxes.

3. *Know the Difference between Independent Contractors and Employees.* Be clear on the distinction. In legal terms, the line between the two is not always clear, but it affects how you withhold income taxes, withhold and pay Social Security and Medicare taxes, and pay unemployment taxes. The federal government and most states try to define the differences between the two categories of workers in their tax publications.

4. *Take Care of Employee Paperwork.* New employees must fill out federal income tax withholding form W-4. They must complete the form and return it to you so that you can withhold the correct federal income tax from their paychecks.

5. *Decide on a Pay Period.* You may already have a manual process for this, but setting up a pay period (whether monthly or bimonthly) is sometimes determined by state law, with most favoring bimonthly payments. The IRS also requires that you withhold income tax for that time period even if your employee does not work the full period.

6. *Carefully Document Your Employee Compensation Terms.* As you set up payroll, you'll also want to consider how you handle paid time off (not a legal requirement, but offered by most businesses), how you track employee hours, if and how you pay overtime, and other variables. Don't forget that employee compensation and business deductibles such as health plan premiums and retirement contributions will also need to be deducted from employee paychecks and paid to the appropriate organizations.

7. *Choose a Payroll System.* Payroll administration requires acute attention to detail and accuracy, so it's worth doing some research to understand your options. Typically, your options for managing payroll include in-house or outsourced options. However, regardless of the option you choose, you, as the employer, are responsible for reporting and paying of all payroll taxes. There are many private companies, both large and small, that offer payroll services.

8. *Run Payroll.* Once you have all your forms and information collated, you can start running payroll. Depending on the payroll system you choose, you'll either enter it yourself or give the information to your accountant or an accounting service.

9. *Know What Records to Keep and How Long to Keep Them.* Federal and some state laws require that employers keep certain records for specified periods of time. For example, W-4 forms (on which employees indicate their tax withholding status) must be kept on file for all active employees and for three years after an employee is terminated. You also need to keep W-2s, copies of filed tax forms, and dates and amounts of all tax deposits.

10. *Report Payroll Taxes.* There are several payroll tax reports that you are required to submit to the appropriate authorities on either a quarterly or annual basis. If

you are in any way confused about your obligations, review the IRS's Employer's Tax Guide, which provides very clear guidance on all federal tax filing requirements. Visit your state tax agency for specific tax filing requirements for employers.

If your parent institution does not does not process your payroll, you should consider some type of payroll service. There are do-it-yourself payroll systems, where the payroll provider makes it easy for clients to set up, run payroll, and file taxes themselves. A second type is a full-service payroll service where the provider helps with setup, and files and pays quarterly taxes for the client. The client simply enters the hours and other information. There are many web-based services as well as brick-and-mortar service companies that make the time-consuming and sometimes tedious task of getting employees paid in an accurate and timely way ("Effortless Payroll Service Offerings" 2015).

Purchasing System

The second main system feeding records into the library's accounting system is the purchasing system. The purchasing process is an interacting structure of people, equipment, methods, and controls that is designed to handle the repetitive work routines of the purchasing department and the receiving department. Purchasing assists in the preparation of internal and external reports as required by the library's financial system. Although the purchasing process may vary from organization to organization, the major fundamental steps remain the same:

1. The first phase deals with identifying the need, what to buy, how much of it, and when it is needed for. There are two main ways of creating a requisition: manually (i.e., created on a form or other document) and created automatically via an ERP type system. The requisition will likely go through an approval process whereby authorization is given to purchase the item (or not).
2. Selecting a supplier is the next step. Buyers may already know which supplier to buy the item from that is being requested. If not a bid (or request for quote) process may be initiated to identify a supplier, price, and lead time.
3. A purchase order is created and sent to the supplier (either on paper or electronically) to inform the supplier of the intent to purchase. The purchase order will identify the item(s) being procured, the quantity required, and the price being paid. It will also identify delivery addresses and any terms and conditions that relate to the order.
4. The purchase order will be fulfilled when the supplier ships the goods to the library. Lead time might be required to allow the supplier to manufacture the item or obtain the item from its own suppliers.
5. Once the goods arrive at the library, they will typically go through some form of receiving process where the goods are checked to ensure that they match what was ordered and that they are of the correct quality.

6. At time of shipment the supplier will typically issue an invoice, which either accompanies the goods or is sent separately. This will be received by the library's finance department to process and pay (assuming the goods are received and are correct) ("How to Create" 2017).

These are the basic steps in the purchasing process, but companies use different procedures. Some may prefer to automate as much as possible (e.g., by replacing paper forms with electronic documents), and others may have complex approval rules, but despite these variations the fundamentals remain the same.

A library (and or its parent organization) should have a purchasing policy that answers the following questions:

- Who has the authority to purchase items for the library? What items can that person purchase? Are there any spending limitations?
- What are the business's requirements for adequate supplier competition and what criteria will be used to select possible vendors?
- What is the company's position on accepting gifts?
- Which types of contracts can the library enter into with successful bidders or vendors?
- What is the company's position on conflict of interest with suppliers?
- What kinds of information does the library consider confidential?
- What is the procedure for dealing with legal questions? ("How to Create" 2017)

In libraries, materials (books, periodicals, electronic media, etc.) are the largest dollar volume of purchases in the materials budget. Most library management systems have an interface between the library's parent accounting system and library management systems. This has clear advantages for both the library and the parent institution. Transferring payment information electronically from the library system to the parent accounting system eliminates rekeying data into the parent system by accounting staff at either the parent or library level. Staff no longer needed for that part of the payment process can be assigned other responsibilities, or, especially in a large institution, staffing may be reduced. In addition, electronic transfer of data reduces errors and speeds up the institutional payment process so vendors receive payments more quickly. Paying vendors more quickly, in turn, can lead to better working relationships between the library and its vendors (Lamborn and Smith 2001)

Balanced Scorecard

During the 1990s, Robert Kaplan and David Norton developed an approach called the *balanced scorecard,* which is a "carefully selected set of measures derived from an organization's strategy. The measures selected for the Scorecard represent a tool for leaders to use in communicating to employees and eternal stakeholders the outcomes and performance drivers by which the organization will achieve its objectives" (Finkler, Smith, Calabrese, and Purtell 2017, 277).

Using a balanced scorecard, the library develops a set of key performance indicators (KPIs) that management can use to monitor how well the library is achieving its goals with respect to four critical perspectives:

- financial
- customer
- internal business
- learning and growth

Because libraries are not profit-seeking organizations, instead of a financial perspective the library should evaluate its performance on the quality of library service to meet informational needs of its customers. Probably the best measure of the quality of library service would be the influence of the library's products and services on the information literacy of the population that it serves. For academic libraries, employ the library's impact on the educational process and the research results in the university (Poll 2001)

Libraries have many stakeholders who determine the customer perspective—not only the people who use the library, but also those who fund it, and those who may not use it but consider it an asset to their community or campus. The library must determine the products and services that are valued by its customers and parent organization, because in most cases those two groups are the most important stakeholders.

The goal of the internal process perspective is to understand the processes and activities critical to enabling the library to satisfy the needs of its customers and add value in their eyes. In developing its balanced scorecard, the library should be identifying and implementing strategies that allow it to offer distinctive and sustainable competitive advantages. Is the library innovative and does it deliver services efficiently and effectively? Costs, quality, throughput, productivity, and time measures are usually included in this perspective (Matthews 2006).

The learning and growth perspective considers factors such as whether the library is attracting and retaining competent employees and using continuing education to maintain staff and institutional expertise. This perspective comprises employee training and corporate cultural attitudes related to both individual and corporate self-improvement. In a knowledge-worker organization, people—the only repositories of knowledge—are the main resource. In the current climate of rapid technological change, it is becoming necessary for knowledge workers to be in a continuous learning mode. Metrics can be put into place to guide managers in focusing training funds where they can help the most. In any case, learning and growth constitute the essential foundation for success of any knowledge-worker organization. Kaplan and Norton emphasize that "learning" is more than "training." It also includes resources like mentors and tutors within the organization, as well as that ease of communication among workers that allows them to readily get help on a problem when it is needed, as well as technological tools, which the Baldrige criteria call "high performance work systems" ("Balanced Scorecard Basics" 2017).

In 2009, the ARL Library Scorecard Pilot was launched to test the use of the balanced scorecard (BSC) in research libraries. Four North American research libraries took part in the test: Johns Hopkins University, McMaster University, the University of Virginia, and the University of Washington. Each university sent a small group of librarians to develop their Scorecard initiatives and identified a lead member. The four teams met with a consultant and the ARL lead twice for face-to-face training in using the scorecard. Participants came together during monthly phone calls to review progress and discuss next steps. Additional face-to-face meetings were held throughout the year in conjunction with major library conferences.

The process of developing the scorecards included the following steps: defining a purpose statement, identifying strategic objectives, creating a strategy map, identifying measures, selecting appropriate measures, and setting targets. Many commonalities were evident in the four libraries' slates of strategic objectives. There were also many commonalities among measures, although the number chosen by each institution varied significantly, from twenty-six to forty-eight (Lewis, Hiller, Mengel, and Tolson 2013).

Many libraries continue to work with the balanced scorecard and many are integrating the process into their strategic planning and budgetary processes.

Financial and Budgetary Forms

There are several budgetary forms and sheets that are useful in working with budgets and financial statements, and some of the forms are listed below.

Uniform Chart of Accounts

A uniform chart of accounts is a uniform system of account numbers used to categorize revenues, expenditures, assets, liabilities, and fund equity. A chart of accounts provides the framework to capture original transactions, organize that data logically, and provide a robust basis for reporting on the results. (Refer to exhibit 2.3, which is a sample uniform chart of accounts.)

Balance Sheet

The balance sheet is a statement that summarizes the library's assets, liabilities, and equity at a specific point in time. It is a snapshot of the library on a certain date, and can be prepared on any day of the year, although it is most commonly prepared on the last day of a month, quarter, or year. At any point in time the balance sheet must be "in balance," that is, it must equal liabilities and owner's equity. (Refer to exhibit 2.1, the Schaumburg Township District Library balance sheet for January 31, 2016.)

Income Statement

An income statement summarizes the revenue and expenses of a library for a specific period. Unlike the balance sheet, an income statement is a "flow" statement. This means it summarizes the flow of revenues and expenses for the period. (Refer to exhibit 2.2, which reproduces the Schaumburg Township District Library 's income statement from July 1, 2015 through March 31, 2016.)

Statement of Cash Flows

The statement of cash flows summarizes the cash flow effects of a library's operating, investing, and financing activities for the period. It shows where the sources from which the library received cash during the year and how it used that cash. Cash flow illustrates how changes in balance sheet accounts and income affect cash and cash equivalents; for most libraries, cash flow is not significant because of the regular funding from the parent organization. However, if the library does not have the deep pockets of a parent organization, cash flow analysis is crucial to the library's financial survival. A simple cash flow spreadsheet can be found in **exhibit 9.1,** which shows the cash position of Library XYZ for six months.

Annual Operating Budget

The annual operating budget is a plan for expected revenues and expenses for the year. It may also be broken into monthly and quarterly budgets. The operating budget usually shows the past year or two for comparison, and percentage changes for each budget category are displayed. (Refer to exhibit 2.1, the Schaumburg Township District Library's 2015/2016 operating budget summary.)

Department Buildup Budget

A department *buildup budget* is an aid for creating the overall budget. (Refer to exhibit 5.4, a department budget for Schaumburg Township.) Compilation of departmental budgets are the basic information in creating the overall library budget. Another sub-budget is the branch budget for Hoffman Estates found in exhibit 5.5.

Program Budget

Sometimes a separate budget will be submitted for a program budget. For example, a library may sponsor a special exhibit. (Exhibit 5.3 lists some of the budgetary revenues and expenses required to host the exhibit.)

Capital Budget

A simple capital budget for a hypothetical branch library for the SDSU branch at a proposed Mission Valley branch is described in chapter 7.

Modifying Budgets for Windfalls and Downturns

A form for modifying budgets for windfalls and downturns is found in **exhibit 9.2.** This provides a formal approach to modifying budgets due to changes in revenues and/or expenses.

Summary

Library budgets fall into three main categories of staffing costs, materials, and other costs. The ratio of these three categories varies widely depending on the type of library and its financial condition.

It is important to periodically evaluate the library's financial condition by historical comparisons as well as comparing it to a peer selected group of libraries. Predicating the future is difficult but it is eased by forecasting and scenarios analysis.

Payroll and purchasing systems that seamlessly integrate into the library's accounting system ease the record keeping of the library.

The balanced scorecard is a concept that was popular about ten years ago and is still a viable tool that some libraries are starting to use in their strategic planning process.

To organize and capture the library's financial information, several financial forms may be used such as a balance sheet, annual budget form, and budget change form.

EXERCISES

1. Select five libraries that vary by type (e.g., public versus academic) and by size, and compare their budgets using the three main categories of salaries, materials, and other costs. What percentage variation do you determine and how do your account for the differences?

2. Select a library you know well, and consider what the five environmental factors (demographic, sociocultural, political/legal, technological, and economic) may mean to its services now and in the future. In your opinion, is the library responding well to its environment? Why or why not?

3. Select a library that you think has a problem that it must face and construct a scenario analysis using at least three decision options. Which one do you recommend, and why?

4. Choose a library and examine its payroll and purchasing systems. How well does it integrate into the library's accounting systems? Do you recommend any changes, and if so why?

5. Conduct a balanced scorecard analysis for a public and academic library using Joe Matthews's model (see Matthews 2006).

References

"ADP, Staples Announce Payroll Services." 1999. *CPA Journal* (July) http://archives.cpajournal.com/1999/0799/n_v/NV9.HTM.

Association of College & Research Libraries. 2017. "2015 Academic Library Trends and Statistics." *College and Research Library News* 78 (2): 63.

"Balanced Scorecard Basics." 2017. Balanced Scorecard Institute. www.balancedscorecard.org/Resources/About-the-Balanced-Scorecard.

Dess, Gregory G., Gerry McNamara, and Alan B. Eisner. 2017. *Strategic Management: Text and Cases*. 8th ed. New York: McGraw Hill Education.

"Effortless Payroll Service Offerings." 2015. *Journal of Accountancy*. (September). https://www.journalofaccountancy.com/issues/2015/sep/focus-report-payroll-services.html.

Finkler, Steven A., Daniel L. Smith, Thad D. Calabrese, and Roberty M. Purtell. 2017. *Financial Management for Public, Health, and Not-for-Profit Organizations*. Thousand Oaks, CA: Sage.

"How to Create a Formal Purchasing Program." 2017. *Entrepreneur*. https://www.entrepreneur.com/article/79798.

Lamborn, Joan G., and Patricia A Smith. 2001. "Institutional Ties: Developing an Interface between a Library Acquisitions System and a Parent Institution Accounting System." *Library Collections, Acquisitions and Technical Services*, 25 (3): 247–61.

Lewis, Vivian, Steve Hiller, Elizabeth Mengel, and Donna Tolson. 2013. "Building Scorecards in Academic Research Libraries: Performance Measurement and Organizational Issues." *Evidence Based Library and Information Practice* 8 (2).

Maggs, Pete, and Jackie Chelin. 2013. "Scenario Planning for an Uncertain Future?: Case Study of the Restructuring of the Academic Services Team at UWE Library." *Library Management* 34 (8/9): 664–76. doi: 10.1108/LM-02–2013–0017.

Matthews, Joe. 2006. "The Library Balanced Scorecard: Is It in Your Future?" *Public Libraries* 45 (6): 64–71. www.ala.org/pla/sites/ala.org.pla/files/content/publications/publiclibraries/pastissues/novdec2006pl.pdf.

Poll, Roswitha. 2001. "Performance, Processes and Costs: Managing Service Quality with the Balanced Scorecard." *Library Trends* 49 (4).

Posnick-Goodwin, Shirley. 2017. "Embracing the Gender Spectrum." *California Educator* 21 (6): 20–27.

Publishers Communication Group. 2015. Library Budget Predictions for 2015. www.pcgplus.com/wp-content/uploads/2016/05/Library-Budget-Prediction-2016-Final.pdf.

Reid, Ian. 2016. "The 2015 Public Library Data Service Statistical Report: Characteristics and Trends." *Public Libraries* 55 (3): 24–33.

Saunders, E. Stewart. 2003. "Cost Efficiency in ARL Academic Library." *Bottom Line* 16 (1): 5–14. doi: 10.1108/08880450310464009.

Small Business Association. 2017. "10 Steps to Setting Up a Payroll System." https://www.sba.gov/managing-business/running-business/managing-business-finances-accounting/10-steps-setting-payroll-system.

EXHIBIT 9.1: **Budgetary Revenues and Expenses Required to Host an Exhibit**

Budget Categories	Six Month Budget	MONTH					
		January	February	March	April	May	June
Tax Revenue	$442,000	$0	$0	$392,000	$0	$0	$50,000
Contributions	$12,000	$2,000	$2,000	$2,000	$2,000	$2,000	$2,000
Grants	$20,000	$0	$0	$0	$20,000	$0	$0
State Funding	$30,000	$0	$0	$30,000	$0	$0	$0
Total Cash Received	$504,000	$2,000	$2,000	$424,000	$22,000	$2,000	$52,000
Payroll	$420,000	$70,000	$70,000	$70,000	$70,000	$70,000	$70,000
Materials	$48,000	$8,000	$8,000	$8,000	$8,000	$8,000	$8,000
Space rental	$24,000	$4,000	$4,000	$4,000	$4,000	$4,000	$4,000
Equipment	$12,000	$2,000	$2,000	$2,000	$2,000	$2,000	$2,000
Total Cash Disbursed	$504,000	$84,000	$84,000	$84,000	$84,000	$84,000	$84,000
Cash surplus (deficit)		-$82,000	-$164,000	$176,000	$114,000	$32,000	$0
Cash balances at end of month							

EXHIBIT 9.2: **Budget Modification Form**

Department or Program: _____   Date Submitted: _____

By: _____   Date Reviewed: _____

Action Taken: _____   Date Acted On: _____

For Budget Year _____

REQUESTED MODIFICATION AND EXPLANATION	FUNDING SOURCE(S)	REQUESTED INCREASE (DECREASE)	APPROVED INCREASE (DECREASE)

Index